Fashion and Materialism

Technicities

Series Editors: John Armitage, Ryan Bishop and Joanne Roberts, Winchester School of Art, University of Southampton

The philosophy of technicities: exploring how technology mediates art, frames design and augments the mediated collective perception of everyday life.

Technicities will publish the latest philosophical thinking about our increasingly immaterial technocultural conditions, with a unique focus on the context of art, design and media.

Editorial Advisory Board
Benjamin Bratton, Cheryl Buckley, Sean Cubitt, Clive Dilnot, Jin Huimin, Arthur Kroker, Geert Lovink, Scott McQuire, Gunalan Nadarajan, Elin O'Hara Slavick, Li Shqiao, Geoffrey Winthrop-Young

Published
Lyotard and the Inhuman Condition: Reflections on Nihilism, Information and Art
    By Ashley Woodward

Critical Luxury Studies: Art, Design, Media
    Edited by John Armitage and Joanne Roberts

Cold War Legacies: Systems, Theory, Aesthetics
    Edited by John Beck and Ryan Bishop

Fashion and Materialism
    By Ulrich Lehmann

Queering Digital India: Activisms, Identities, Subjectivities
    Edited by Rohit K. Dasgupta and Debanuj DasGupta

Forthcoming Titles

Zero Degree Seeing: Barthes/Burgin and Political Aesthetics
    Edited by Ryan Bishop and Sunil Manghani

www.edinburghuniversitypress.com/series/tech

Fashion and Materialism

Ulrich Lehmann

EDINBURGH
University Press

Edinburgh University Press is one of the leading university presses in the UK. We publish academic books and journals in our selected subject areas across the humanities and social sciences, combining cutting-edge scholarship with high editorial and production values to produce academic works of lasting importance. For more information visit our website: www.edinburghuniversitypress.com

© Ulrich Lehmann, 2018

Edinburgh University Press Ltd
The Tun – Holyrood Road
12(2f) Jackson's Entry
Edinburgh EH8 8PJ

Typeset in Adode Sabon by
Servis Filmsetting Ltd, Stockport, Cheshire

A CIP record for this book is available from the British Library

ISBN 978 1 4744 0791 5 (hardback)
ISBN 978 1 4744 0792 2 (webready PDF)
ISBN 978 1 4744 0793 9 (epub)

The right of Ulrich Lehmann to be identified as the author of this work has been asserted in accordance with the Copyright, Designs and Patents Act 1988, and the Copyright and Related Rights Regulations 2003 (SI No. 2498).

Contents

Series Editors' Preface	vi
Introduction	1
1 Production into Consumption: Materialism in Fashion	14
2 Historical Materialism and Historicism: The Tiger's Leap	35
3 Sartorial Semantics: *Le Mot dans la mode*	69
4 Markets for Modernity: Salons, Galleries and Fashion	103
5 Structuralism and Materialism: The Language of a Pur(e)Suit	129
6 Dialectics in C.C.P.	160
7 Primary Material	197
Conclusion	230
Select Bibliography	234
Index	240

Series Editors' Preface

Technological transformation has profound and frequently unforeseen influences on art, design and media. At times technology emancipates art and enriches the quality of design. Occasionally it causes acute individual and collective problems of mediated perception. Time after time technological change accomplishes both simultaneously. This new book series explores and reflects philosophically on what new and emerging *technicities* do to our everyday lives and increasingly immaterial technocultural conditions. Moving beyond traditional conceptions of the philosophy of technology and of techne, the series presents new philosophical thinking on how technology constantly alters the essential conditions of beauty, invention and communication. From novel understandings of the world of technicity to new interpretations of aesthetic value, graphics and information, *Technicities* focuses on the relationships between critical theory and representation, the arts, broadcasting, print, technological genealogies/histories, material culture and digital technologies and our philosophical views of the world of art, design and media.

The series foregrounds contemporary work in art, design and media whilst remaining inclusive, both in terms of philosophical perspectives on technology and interdisciplinary contributions. For a philosophy of technicities is crucial to extant debates over the artistic, inventive, and informational aspects of technology. The books in the *Technicities* series concentrate on present-day and evolving technological advances but visual, design-led and mass-mediated questions are emphasised to further our knowledge of their often-combined means of digital transformation.

The editors of *Technicities* welcome proposals for monographs and well-considered edited collections that establish new paths of investigation.

John Armitage, Ryan Bishop and Joanne Roberts

Introduction

> Man's relations *with himself* have not been essentially transformed. These relations have changed much less than man's relation with the external world, which has fallen increasingly under the control of an ever powerful technicity ... Therefore, transformative action and radical critique have lagged behind the productive forces and the possibilities for transformation they harbour, and they are deflected from that goal.
>
> Henri Lefebvre, 1959–61[1]

This book posits fashion as a centre around which to explore positions of materialism. Fashion is understood first as a system that promotes the constant renewal of commodities and secondly, more specifically, as an industry that produces textiles and garments. Materialism is a focus on concrete, physical phenomena and on objects that are produced by subjects. It therefore incorporates a concentration on materiality, on the physical properties of things and how they are represented and perceived by the acting subject. The material world, that is, the world outside of consciousness, serves to found and determine thought. Materialism is understood further as a socio-economic philosophy that is concerned with social conditions of production and in particular with the relationship between labour and capital. These two understandings of materialism are epistemologically, in terms of the origin of knowledge, and historically contingent. In the initial rejection of any metaphysical entity (world spirit, God, etc.), *mechanistic materialism*, in particular during the eighteenth century in France, had determined human development through an interaction of physical forces, yet it had already applied this concept to social interaction and political emancipation, albeit in theory not in practice. An important feature of mechanistic materialism was change, exemplified by an understanding of the material world as particles of matter that are in constant interaction. This suggested already the usefulness of a *dialectical method* – reasoning by dynamically incorporating contradictions and negation – for understanding the distinction between static principles and movement, which would animate *dialectical* and subsequently *historical* materialism.

From this historical point of origin and potentised in the political impact of the French Revolution, the materialism of the start of the nineteenth century aimed at understanding things concretely in all their movements: social, political and economic, as well as in the changing conditions of production, with elements of change and interconnection determining the way in which people worked and lived. Accordingly, the development of *dialectical materialism* was not an abstract concept but a way to comprehend the concrete manifestations of reality, the material world as it presents itself in practice. Karl Marx famously wrote on this shift from the mechanistic to the dialectical: 'The chief defect of all hitherto existing materialism [...] is that the thing, reality, sensuousness, is conceived only in the form of the *object or of contemplation*, but not as *sensuous human activity, practice*, not subjectively.'[2] Marx's critique of subjectivity, determined by his adopting G. W. F. Hegel's integration of subject into object – which is a topic of my sixth chapter – is one of the bases for the discussion of ideas in this book.

Fashion has been seen as very subjective indeed, as expressed mainly through individual designers, select brands, the endorsement of certain celebrities or the (constantly changing) personal preference of the wearer. This is by no means a contemporary manoeuvre by the media; fashion's subjectivity has existed in the vast majority of historical accounts, theories of (decorative) art and even sociological studies. Fashion is said to inspire subjective individualism because the subject wants to distinguish her- or himself in relation to others, in particular through attire, hairstyle and make-up. Even when historians identify broad sweeps of sartorial movements or decorative trends they almost always return them to the individual: the member of a royal family, the dandy or style leader, the spouse or lover of an industrialist – all of whom represent a new style (of consumption) and are fêted for it. Collective movements or (politicised) class preferences in fashion are routinely underplayed or ignored. Such bias finds a parallel in the notion that the discourse of fashion, especially in so-called 'fashion studies', prefers consumption to production. In my view, this is due to the fact that the large majority of fashion historians and theorists (let alone materialist philosophers or political economists) display scant interest in the actual making of clothes or other fashion objects; they are not visiting manufacturers or studios but write their analyses based on the clothing that they see as a finished commodity represented in the media or on display in shops. Yet this bias is also due to the sway that *consumption theory* has held over material culture, cultural studies and their offspring such as fashion studies. Since the 1980s Anglo-American academia has touted the model of individual consumption – not production or its conditions – as the (fashionable) approach to assessing artefacts. Consumption theory and its variants in anthropology, sociology or economics are firmly placed in the set economic structure of capitalism and are retroactively applied to fashion history across periods and used to curate costumes in museums.[3] They affirm a structure that is already in place and thereby ignore the disruptive potential that the production of new things can entail. The understanding of history that is allied with the economic and discursive system of capitalism is essentially positivist: it assumes an idea of linear progress that leads, through trickle-down effects and participation through widening, conspicuous consumption, to a progressive 'democratising' of culture and fashion – which, in essence, is but a continuous economic expansion of the culture industry. Disruptions, interventions or repeat patterns of conflict and struggle are eschewed as guiding principles for the positivist, individualist perception (of the history) of fashion. Through alternative examples and the analysis of a historical materialist method, this book proposes a different understanding of the idea of fashion across a historical period in Europe – from circa 1830 to today – that runs parallel with the founding of the present fashion industry, modern textile production and the formation of the culture industry.

Dialectical materialism as practice (in thought, in political action) was extended in the nineteenth century to a wider epistemology, *historical materialism*. Its interest rests on the agents of social change and development and on concrete actions. Significantly, the method of historical materialism determines patterns and structures from these observations and emphasises their repetition over time. There is no linear, positivist progress in history, but the social conditions of production, for example the ownership of the means of production or the exploitation of workers, are constants in the renewal of trends and movements – as can be seen in history, from the rapid destitution of the Lyon silk weavers at the start of the nineteenth century to collapsed textile factories in today's Bangladesh. For Marx (and Friedrich Engels) both dialectical materialism as episteme and historical materialism as philosophy of history constituted *economy as the anatomy of society*, and this meant that rational and measurable facts must support speculation on emancipated social forms and also their cultural representation.[4]

As I argue at the beginning of the first chapter, misapprehending fashion as an emblem of consumption is not just a reflex on the part of fashion theorists but also on the part of social historians or political thinkers. Fashion – particularly in its reductive form as sartorial expression – continues to be regarded as a rather frivolous subject. To be sure, it is of sociological or psychological interest, but it is not deemed substantial enough to form the basis of and extended critical analysis of social or economic tenets. Equally, fashion as the nexus for a history of ideas continues to appear as a wilfully marginal choice. In the main, theorists are expected to use traditionally elevated expressions of our culture industry, such as literature, classical music or fine art, as examples with which to analyse patterns of thinking. Obviously, aberrant or marginal manifestations are to be acknowledged, yet in the main as mere counter-examples, not as equipollent (anti)theses in dialectical thought. For most social economists, the ephemeral character of fashion and the consumptive reflexes it generates negate any serious contemplation of its production, and fashion is seen therefore as having little cognitive impact proper on cultural development. In terms of its appearance and the methods associated with it, fashion is regarded as a superficial reflection of ideas that are much more substantially expressed elsewhere in our society and our culture; it is not a field in which general histories, modes of thinking or perception are formed. Looking at the paucity of critical thought on fashion, it seems to me that critical thinkers continue to assume that fashion, as a material expression, cannot contain philosophical or structural challenges; it is too affirmative and positivist in regard to existing power relations to instigate an actual, sustained critique of cultures, societies or economies.

In this context fashion appears in our present capitalist system only as an ephemeral placebo for the testing out of new cultural expressions and commodities within industrial and, in particular, post-industrial societies. Fashion is an insubstantial and decorative (sugar-coated) pill that has no real effect, but which, despite minor irritations – the taste of the pill might occasionally be challenging to get used to – sweetens the pervasive imposition of capitalist economic power structures on cultures and people. Notwithstanding where we perceive material changes to our lives being primarily made (in speculative finance, geopolitics, natural sciences, material engineering, etc.), the impact of culture as providing an aestheticised reflection of ideologies will remain a significant area of investigation. But this fact, for me, leads directly to the following question: if the globalised culture industry is seen as an increasingly significant reflection of capitalism in post-industrial and post-democratic structures, as the materialist analysis of the Frankfurt School or the Situationists had already begun to posit in the post-war period, should fashion not offer a very concrete means of critique, rather than, for instance, the forms of contemporary art production, which at present, although increasingly affected by the rhythm of the fashion system itself, profess still to be constitutive of an independent, critical medium? Market structures in the culture industry have been reflected upon and investigated in contemporary art, yet not in fashion. But the latter, through its double bind with materialism – political economy as well as objectifying the body of the subject – offers a very compelling case indeed for containing simultaneously the forms and the method of an innovative and composite materialist critique.

The above assessment has shaped, too, the selection of sources for this book. I aimed at bypassing the usual trajectory of fashion theories, save for a few traditional sources such as Georg Simmel, Walter Benjamin and Jean Baudrillard, which are subjected in this book to an expressly materialist critique. I return to the anti-idealism in G. W. F. Hegel and Karl Marx's political economy and cite renowned materialist works of the 1950s, 1960s and 1970s by Henri Lefebvre, Ernst Bloch, Lucien Sebag, Alfred Schmidt and Sebastiano Timpanaro. Yet my book is not meant to be esoteric or stoically *passé* in its approach; the ideas and manifestations of fashion – for example, nineteenth-century *Salon* paintings, Christian Dior's couture textiles or Alfred Hitchcock's films – are selected for their populist appeal. In order to emphasise *praxis* as the concrete evidence for social conditions of labour, I also use first-hand investigation into current textile and fashion production in northern Italy for the final couple of chapters, which are based on extensive interviews with makers. The selected sources combine to form a method that understands historic and contemporary ideas of producing culture, and especially fashion, in their proper contexts, not through retrospective applications but through research into the productive environment of the original cultural manifestation: linguistically, socio-politically, economically and materially, in terms of media, technique and tools.

A dialectic provides the foundation for this book. In the tradition of Plato and Hegel, it builds an argument that involves a contradictory process between apparently opposing sides. As mentioned above, conventional history and cultural critique posit materialism as contrary to fashion, yet materialism is also the very basis of fashion as both industry and temporal structure – in particular in its shared historical place within the simultaneous affirmation and critique of nineteenth-century capitalism. As Hegel details in the first part of his *Encyclopedia of Philosophical Science*, where he describes the final 'speculative moment' of the dialectic method, it must lead to the unity of the opposition between the two determinations, or become the positive result of the dissolution or transition of those determinations.[5] Recognising fashion as dependent on the double determination of materialism as 1) absolute commodification of the subject's social life in capitalism and 2) its concrete material basis in productive processes means that the two apparently opposing sides are integrated. Without materialism as a principle of political economy, fashion cannot be analysed in its origin and effect, but, equally, without a concrete understanding of how the production of fashion structures historical processes and patterns across modernity, materialism would not be able to set out its fundamental critique of the prevailing, exploitative economic system and its socio-political impact.

This book focuses on select themes that highlight the dialectic of fashion and materialism across cultural and social history, with attention to particular works of historical analysis and critique. It does not aim to provide a linear history of either materialism or fashion but rather focuses on instances that develop and display the repeated patterns of and in the dialectic itself. *Fashion and Materialism* opens with remarks that position my perspective on fashion, in order to help with situating my overall approach. It introduces the twofold relationship between fashion and materialism, and explores Marx's original approach to fashion as a structural and economic principle. Historical sources are paired with contemporary reflections to indicate how materialism continues to be significant for explaining the fashion system: not simply in the clothing industry but as a wider principle of constantly renewed consumption and its relation to production. To this end, the first chapter contains a brief critical analysis of Baudrillard's shifting interpretation of fashion, to point to one of the main origins of today's essentially anti-materialist approach to discussing the topic. I am arguing across the entire book that in order to write about fashion you do not have to side with fashion – neither by praising its manifestations or representations, nor by making it exemplary for a discursive trend, like the 'post'-modern turn or the synthetic methods in cultural and media studies.

In Chapter 2 the reprise of Benjamin's *Tigersprung* ('tiger's leap'), more than a dozen years after my first texts on him, is intended to balance my previous focus on cultural and historical detail with present materialist engagement. Although I have always struggled to accept fully one of Benjamin's assumed personae,

1 Leftover yarn wrapped around the lever of a mechanical loom at the Bonotto textile factory in Molvena, October 2016

the Marxist, proto-Frankfurt School theoretician, I feel that there is sufficient demonstrable reflection on Marxist positions in his texts (some acknowledged, others not) to merit a materialist re-reading of his opinions on fashion, in particular because Benjamin's assessment as a (historical) materialist has been underplayed in many of the cultural studies and art-historical writings that now use his texts as method. The second chapter therefore connects Benjamin's philosophical view of fashion and history to its production. It looks at the origins of couture and ready-to-wear clothing in early and mid-nineteenth-century France and concludes with an analysis of Christian Dior's historicist couture practice. The notion of *historicism* in relation to materialist critique thereby becomes a theme in this chapter. Historicism is analysed as an ambiguous method that can be allied to materialism while seemingly promoting linear narratives. As a dialectical method, I here propose a structural challenge to materialism through Benjamin's poetic evocations, which centred on fashion in its concrete expression in clothing and as a wider cultural principle.

The third chapter debates another structural challenge to materialism – this time through structuralism. I ask how structural inquiries into the very semantics of fashion, into the linguistic basis for the dialectic of fashion and materialism, can be retained for materialist critique. How can the writing of fashion be assessed as creating a material vocabulary? The chapter uses research into nineteenth-century literature as a basis for explaining how texts in modernity become subject to a pervasive fashion system within capitalist consumer culture, while at the same time entering into an original mode of aesthetic expression that is based on fashionable innovations: the birth of a veritable avant-garde that already embraces its later critical demise in and as culture industry.

The idea of fashion not as a mode of appearance but as a guiding principle for capitalist production and especially for the culture industry reaches across into the fourth chapter. Here, a structural parallel is drawn between the respective genesis of haute couture and the gallery system for avant-garde art in Paris in the second half of the nineteenth century. The connections are discussed as economic history and as cultural study. Like the previous chapters, the fourth chapter also contains a section on methods, where the particular problem of materialist art (but also costume) history is mobilised for the discussion.

The focus of the fifth chapter is placed on *fashion in representation*, exemplified through a reading of a well-known Hollywood film, which has also been subject to structuralist analysis. The move from structuralism to materialism draws distinctions between *costume*, *dress* and *fashion* to help the reader understand that covering the body and constructing appearances are subject to a variety of codes that result not simply from their semantic but from their concrete, material production as object and image.

The sixth chapter leaps forward in time to the present in providing a detailed study of contemporary fashion design and production, which, for political as well as aesthetic reasons, is positioned outside the commercial mainstream. The work of the renowned and coveted,[6] but reclusive and hermetic, designer C.C.P. (a 'Marcel Duchamp' or 'Thomas Bernhard' of fashion) is analysed in detail through first-hand research that draws on personal interviews and access to his personal archive. C.C.P.'s work shows a rare attempt to put social and political ideas concretely into fashion practice, through a process that is technically and materially as progressive as it is subversive within the economy of the fashion industry.

The final chapter provides a further case study on production, in addition to the discussion of studio manufacture in the previous chapter. The independent weaver and textile producer Bonotto in Molvena (in the Veneto region of northern Italy) serves as a case study for a mix of local production and global distribution, distinguished by particularly innovative forms of developing fibres, yarns and fabrics. The company is connected to the international Fluxus movement through its second generation of family owners. In the early 1970s Luigi Bonotto became an avid collector and invited artists such as Joseph Beuys, Yoko Ono and John Cage to work with the factory and its workers (e.g. to intervene in weaving processes or compose machine music); his sons Giovanni and Lorenzo continue this approach and have allowed me access to their archive and facilities and to conduct a number of interviews. What distinguishes Giovanni Bonotto's work in particular is the commitment to *la fabbrica lenta* (the slow factory), a deliberately decelerated form of producing on old machines by changing the social condition of labour: concretely, through the creative intervention of the worker at the loom in order to innovate fabrics through experimental, subversive processes of making. My analysis of Bonotto's company is contextualised by the research of material economists and social scientists such as Guiseppe Nardin and Antonio Negri, who have investigated the Italian textile industry since the 1970s, and is substantiated by contemporary economic reports.

Returning to the method of this book, its last two chapters exemplify the concreteness of material and political *praxis* and how it is based on an economic, social and cultural superstructure, which I analyse through historical and comparative methods in the earlier chapters. The interplay between theoretical foundation and practical application in production therefore animates the book in each of its chapters and across its overall structure. The historical method implies that I have chosen, in the main, sources and references that date to the time at which the ideas I am discussing originated. Again, this does not mean that I succumb to nostalgia or want to eschew reassessments or contemporary interpretations. I am, rather, interested in showing the reader that the contemporaneity of fashion has always fascinated writers and thinkers across European history – or at least over the past two hundred and fifty years or so. Fashion and materialism both have strong roots in the cultural and socio-political dynamics of the 'long nineteenth century', and I feel that there is a still a lot of work to be done with sources and references from that time, rather than retrospectively applying present methods or ideas – despite an appreciation for deconstructing historical timelines and for the 'tiger's leap' back into the past. Much of the source material was written originally in French, Italian or German, and the location for the material examples lies in Paris or Milan, while the language of communicating these sources and examples is English. This is due to the significance of materialist positions in central European thinking and their continuing debate, especially after the Second World War, whereas the majority of Anglo-American discourses have preferred pragmatic and positivist views and have filtered materialism through them – essentially as an empirical method. Valuable as this approach is, I would like to offer some alternatives and attempt to find (and resurrect) historical references that might have been neglected or have fallen out of favour in the present discursive regime.

My history of ideas about fashion uses materialism simultaneously as reference for and tool to critique these ideas. As mentioned above in relation to the dialectical method, materialism appears to be posited in contrast to fashion, in view of the latter's affirmation of the capitalist system, which historical materialism, in particular, has aimed to expose and change. Yet fashion is also the material embodiment of the capitalist system, in objectifying, even reifying, bodies and in illustrating commodity fetishism through its approximation of social relations through relations of material things that are designed to act in the closest proximity to the body – clothes and accessories. Furthermore, fashion generates its own brand of materialist perceptions through a sustained focus on the constant renewal of commodities under the auspices of visual, stylistic movements and trends. Materialism denotes here the aberrant interest in the acquisition and possession of things only. This interest gives rise to fashion's rhythm within an increasing speed of consumption within our culture industry. When fashion appears as the materialisation of the political economy of capitalism and simultaneously as exposé or critique of this economic system, its place, simultaneously in and vis-à-vis materialism, is dialectical: the affirmation of the system carries its own negation within it.

The meaning of fashion for materialism moves between positivist thesis and critical antithesis. For example, the term 'primary matter' is used repeatedly in the later chapters. It refers to the objective, tactile material itself, in this case fibres, yarns and weaves, and is discussed in relation to its physical and plastic properties and how they influence production processes and thus the organisation of labour. Yet, at the same time, it refers more abstractly to the primacy of matter as a principle to order thinking about the world, by focusing on concrete relationships in exchange processes and social conditions of production that explain connections and communication not as discourses but as material facts.

It is important to understand fashion essentially *as object*. Even fashion as economic structure, for instance in the making, distributing, selling and showing of garments or accessories, can be perceived as an independent object of inquiry and interpretation. Fashion exists in and through its own materiality, which includes organic as well as modified materials, techniques of making and finishing, as well as processes of exposure and ageing. These aspects are initially independent of the body with which sartorial fashion is often conflated, so that the discussion of garments and accessories assumes an *a priori* relationship to the wearer, which might not be intentional at all on the part of the maker. Granted, the materiality of fashion is influenced by the body inhabiting the clothes, changing the material through bodily excretions, stretching at the seams and bulging the fabric, exposing the garment to natural elements, so that the material consistency and shape is impacted upon. Yet this is a consequence of wearing clothes and accessories, not a process that is necessarily built into their design or manufacture. There are rare cases where traces of wearing are anticipated or integrated into the fabric or garment, but these are exceptional and appear as conceptual statements, not as part of the basic understanding of fashion as a new thing that is produced in its pure state in order to be sold as a novelty.

From comprehending (sartorial) fashion in materialism as an object independent of the wearer follow two basic notions: first, the reduction of the object to its materiality; and second, its antithetical, that is non-contingent, relation to the subject. This reduction is essential to first establishing the material independence of clothes and accessories, together with an implied focus on making, before they are understood as commodities that are bound up in the capitalist process of exchange. Secondly, the non-contingent relation to the subject, to the body of the wearer, positions fashion in a philosophical discourse of materialism in which subject and object become part of a discursive and, significantly, political history that debates dualities, dialectics, nature, the body and commodity fetishism. These two essential meanings of materialism that animate this book combine to play off each other in the confluence of fashion practice and theory.

Notes

1. Henri Lefebvre, *Introduction to Modernity: Twelve Preludes, September 1959–May 1961* [1962] (London: Verso, 1995), p. 229.
2. Karl Marx, 'Theses on Feuerbach' [1845], in Karl Marx and Friedrich Engels, *The German Ideology* (Moscow: Progress, 1976), p. 615.
3. Such approaches are collected, for instance, in Neil McKendrick, John Brewer and John Harold Plumb (eds), *The Birth of a Consumer Society: Commercialisation of Eighteenth-Century England* (Bloomington, IN: Indiana University Press, 1982), and John Brewer and Roy Porter (eds), *Consumption and the World of Goods* (London: Routledge, 1993). Brewer, in a talk given at the Royal Society (London) in 2003 entitled 'The Error of Our Ways: Historians and the Birth of Consumer Society', aims to provide a riposte to those who criticise the dominance of the concept of consumption by claiming the theoretical high ground of the historian vis-à-vis the necessarily involved practice of the policymaker or consumer himself, and by distinguishing consumption as methodological abstraction from consumption as critical, social issue. Significantly, he then proceeds to map out quite succinctly the political environment for consumption studies, particularly during the Cold War period and in Thatcherite Britain, and concludes with a demand for an ambiguous 'middle ground between individual consumer and society' – all of which points to the complicity of consumption studies in the promotion of free market structures for consumer cultures; www.consume.bbk.ac.uk/working_papers/Brewer%talk.doc (last accessed 23 March 2017).
4. Alfred Schmidt, 'Friedrich Albert Lange als Historiker und Kritiker des vormarxschen Materialismus' [July 1974], introduction in Friedrich Albert Lange, *Geschichte des Materialismus* [1866, 2nd enlarged edn, 1875], 2 vols (Frankfurt a.M.: Suhrkamp, 1974), vol. 1, p. xv.
5. G. W. F. Hegel, *Enzyklopädie der Philosophischen Wissenschaften im Grundrisse* [1830] (Hamburg: Meiner, 1992), §§79–82, pp. 118–20; Eng. trans. by W. Wallace, *Hegel's Logic [Encyclopedia of Philosophical Sciences I]* (Oxford: Clarendon Press, 1975), pp. 113–21.
6. I could cite here fashion luminaries from Karl Lagerfeld and Jean-Paul

Gaultier to Suzy Menkes and Valerie Steele or 'collectors' of C.C.P. such as Seal, Brad Pitt and Jude Law on their preference for the label, but this would be an odd, almost self-defeating way of corroborating C.C.P.'s significance.

Chapter 1

Production into Consumption: Materialism in Fashion

Fashion is suspicious of the past and in particular of past economic and political theories that appeared to oppose the foundation of a fashion culture or ran counter to its promotion. Western cultural history shows us how bourgeois economists and historians have embraced fashion when it (be)fitted their understanding of a culture of consumption. In these instances fashion manifested through silhouettes, fabrics and accessories aspects of class, gender and ethnicity. In contrast, historical materialists and progressive economists have very rarely engaged with clothing or other elements of fashion, considering this a lost cause and structurally irrelevant to an emancipated society in which class distinctions and economic inequalities must be overcome. For them, bourgeois fashion was of the past and a progressive future would have to provide a different structure to clothe and distinguish people.

Of course this is a polemical summation, but it is indicative of both the position of fashion within a critical hierarchy of culture, the arts and design, as well as of its history as being written almost exclusively from a bourgeois, affirmative and positivist standpoint. It appears that if you do not appreciate fashion per se, if you do not applaud its fundamental principles and its ever-changing manifestations, you do not have to concern yourself with analysing it. A fundamental critique seems out of place and even out of the question.

I am arguing here that materialism should engage with fashion, by documenting how materialist and progressive writers have done so in the past, and how materialist positions can reveal much about fashion's principles, in particular the significance of production – in its interplay with consumption and, moreover, in its choice of working practices, use of materials and techniques, as well as labour relations. As explained in the introduction to this book, I read materialism as a focus on materials and as a progressive theory to explain economic, social, historical and cultural events; a theory that is often labelled closely as *historical materialism*, but one that expanded from a specific historical, socialist tradition to a wider critique of economic hegemonies and power structures.

In order to develop an understanding of how the dual perception of materialism can work in an analysis of fashion, it is useful to go back to the beginning, to Marx. Not only was he the first to construct a non-mechanistic, left-Hegelian materialism that is as philosophically instrumental as it is politically persuasive, he also applies this concretely to the subject–object relation in modernity, thereby exposing societal interaction as analogous to the relations between commodities. This situates Marx's inquiry into the fundamental dialectic of production and consumption within social dynamics, and in turn gives fashion a starring role within such a non-binary structure: as objectified, social pattern and, simultaneously, as subjectified gesture.

In this chapter I move from Marx's book *Grundrisse: Foundations of the Critique of Political Economy* (1858) and its exposition of production and consumption to the volumes of *Capital* (1867) and their featuring of textiles and clothes (especially the famous coat) to show the interrelationships of terms such as 'value' and 'labour'. The progression from fundamental critique to a new theory displays a method and an intellectual journey in Marx, by using both the material aspects of fashion and the various roles it plays within an analysis of the socio-economic structures of capitalism.

Fashion as the Agent of Capitalism

Fashion is embodied materialism: it creates an outer shell, a second skin for the body that becomes marked by socio-cultural structures, in particular within the system of corporeal commodification that is prevalent in industrial and post-industrial societies. The concrete construction of a surface around the body (as physical entity) and subject (as cognitive being) through materials and technologies is fused with the subject's changing relationship to the object, and this determines fashion's ambiguous position towards concrete socio-cultural expression and its diffusion of temporal rhythm. Fashion is both material covering and materialist representation of the body/subject beneath it, which defines itself through the consumption of particular clothes at certain points in time.

Fashion in its codified state – that is, as commodity, social signifier, branded good – is very rarely discussed by scholars and critics as a material fact. Away from communication between people working in the actual fashion industry, its objects are mostly observed as representations in the media. Fashion is seen in photographs, as moving images that are digitised and streamed, or on catwalks that arrange the display of fashion into a history of ritualised performances. When fashion is considered 'live', for example on the street or in clubs, its critical assessment occurs mainly along anthropological or sociological lines but is not based on a concrete observation of fabrics, pattern cutting, manufacturing techniques or networks for distribution and retail.

Obviously, fashion is much more than clothes and accessories and it reaches deep into customs in verbal language, postures, visual expressions and so on. For the purpose of this discussion I would like to remain with sartorial fashion in order to point to the dialectic between the avowed materialism within fashion consumption, in which everything is reduced to the latest expression of surplus value, and the related absence of materialism as a critical discourse on fashion, which would expose its absolute complicity in the socio-economic structure of capitalism. The central role of fashion as agent of capitalism manifests itself through the repositioning of the subject–object relation, the reification of mobility and sociability into pre-determined consumer groups, the objectification and codification of interpersonal communication (from verbal exchange to sexuality) and the commodification of subjectivity.

The above is not intended as a nostalgic, 'Frankfurt School'-inspired rant; in my view such a polemic remains integral to exposing some of the late modernist manoeuvres that claim to have overcome binary oppositions and that eschew dialectics for politically much less concrete forms of 'deconstruction' and plurality – manoeuvres that also coin to a great degree the contemporary discourse on art and design.

I would like to cite briefly a well-known, now almost 'historical' example: the move by Jean Baudrillard from a materialist method, which in the late 1960s had mixed structuralist ideas with neo-Marxist sociology (à la Henri Lefebvre), towards a simultaneous critique of Marxism and structuralism in his late modernist, 'post'-structuralist texts from the late 1970s and 1980s. In their synthetic method these latter texts marked a clear departure from the analytical origins of Baudrillard's cultural critique and they became templates for the diffusion of ideas about fashion within media and cultural studies. I would like to exemplify Baudrillard's move for our present context through his references to fashion (in clothes), and attempt to be concise by focusing on the two books that frame this move. This is not intended as an exegesis of Baudrillard's work. He serves as an example because his writing on fashion over the decades shows him to be a rare union of the materialist ignoring of fashion's meaning for production-consumption as well as the 'post'-modernist mediating of fashion solely as a simulacrum for the subject, that is, as part of a superficial sign system.

In the chapter on 'Models and Series' from his first prominent book *The System of Objects*, Baudrillard in 1968 had argued still from a more traditional, materialist, perhaps neo-Marxist position. In his analogous pairing of the material model and the series (in production) with the exclusive and mass-produced object of consumption, as well as with the high and low socio-economic position of the respective consumers, Baudrillard pressed complex and fluid circular patterns in the making and wearing of clothing into a binary socio-cultural structure.

> The socially immanent tendency whereby the series hews ever more narrowly to the model, while the model is continually being diffused into the series, has set up a perpetual dynamic which is in fact the very ideology of our society . . . [The model/series scheme] works fine in the realm of clothing (for example a dress from [haute couturier Jacques] Fath versus a ready-to-wear dress) . . .[1]

Baudrillard shows in his reference – oddly to a couturier whose house had ceased to exist after his death back in 1957[2] – a reductive understanding of stylistic or formal innovation, especially in the context of modern fashion production. During the 1960s couture had stopped providing 'models', despite the best efforts of the exclusive fashion media, and innovation resided, materially as well as stylistically, with ready-to-wear and 'street styles'. By 1968 couturiers such as Pierre Cardin and Yves Saint Laurent had acknowledged openly the significance of dress codes in youth culture for their silhouettes and cuts, as well as the related diffusion of boundaries in gender and age, while designers such as Paco Rabanne and André Courrèges made mechanically produced series of industrial materials the hallmark of their innovative work.[3] Beyond sustaining an outmoded cliché of haute couture, Baudrillard also showed a misapprehension of fashion's role as cultural rhythm. His take on choice and quality in fashion was determined by American sociological populism regarding 'planned obsolescence' or 'hidden persuasion',[4] which had little to contribute to analysing the complex history of sartorial fashion in Europe. In 1968 Baudrillard singled out the role fashion plays in the dynamic between model and series as a counter-productive and destructively superficial one.

> The accelerated replacement of models itself affects the object's quality. Thus stockings may now come in all colours but their quality will have declined (or perhaps research and development will have been cut back to finance an advertising campaign). Should the manipulated fluctuations of fashion fail to restimulate demand recourse can be had to an artificial sub-functionality – to 'deliberately shoddy construction'.[5]

The disdain for fashion was not only born from bias towards the 'replacement of models' – implicitly by series consumed by the masses – but also by a misconstruing of fashion's contemporary function. Cheap and cheerful stockings under 1960s miniskirts were not analogous to Packard's planned obsolescence for a washing machine that breaks down after a few years; in contrast, the fashion item *must* be replaced to make way for another trend or style. As materially insubstantial as this process might appear, it provided a fundamental rhythm that had been analysed already by Marx's dialectic between production and consumption, as we will see below.

Baudrillard's rather crude materialism in regard to fashion (qualified by insightful object analyses across research structures in the social sciences and humanities for *The Order of Things*) was replaced by a very different, much more diffuse take on the subject a decade later. His *Symbolic Exchange and Death* (1976) included an extensive assessment of fashion's mediation,[6] which set out an argument against binary structures in language and against class conflicts in political practice by abandoning the dialectic between production and consumption in radically simplified terms:

> The end of labor. The end of production. The end of political economy. The end of the signifier/signified dialectic which facilitates the accumulation of knowledge and of meaning, the linear syntagma of cumulative discourse. And at the same time, the end simultaneously of the exchange value/use value dialectic which is the only thing that makes accumulation and social production possible. The end of linear dimension of discourse. The end of the linear dimension of the commodity. The end of the classical era of the sign. The end of the era of production.[7]

This historical rupture, as played out in contemporary media structures and experience economies, altered radically for Baudrillard the potential of a materialist epistemology:

> Capital no longer belongs to the order of political economy: it operates with political economy as its simulated model. [...] A revolutionary dialectic corresponds to the commodity law of value and its

equivalents; only the scrupulous reversion of death corresponds to the code's indeterminacy and the structural law of value.[8]

The process of 'simulation' led to the emergence of simulacra, copies without originals, in which labour and production were reproduced for the sake of the reproduction of the work itself. However, this did not raise the spectre of fashion's immanent materialism that conditioned its discourse, but merely regarded it as representation without material basis.

Such (idealist) negations of production for inter-subjective relations in favour of representation and simulation cannot allow for the dialectics of fashion, let alone for any concrete inquiry into labour or commodification beyond the symbolic exchange in which Baudrillard – following Marcel Mauss and George Bataille – situated them. He rendered fashion's disavowal of materialism a discursive virtue, and 'indeterminacy' becomes a key term to mark the structural law of value that in his view has replaced, within the hyperreality of the code and late/'post'-modernist culture, the commodity law of use- and exchange value as well as the dialectic of production and consumption that is tied to it. Furthermore, Baudrillard suggested an exclusive structural relationship between modernity and fashion that is not based on an inherent dialectic that Charles Baudelaire had established in the 1860s between the 'eternal' and the 'transitory',[9] but merely superimposed fashion cycles on to linear progress.

> Fashion exists only within the framework of modernity, that is to say, in a schema of rupture, progress and innovation. In any actual context at all, the ancient and the 'modern' alternate in terms of their signification. For us however, since the Enlightenment and the Industrial Revolution, there exists only an historical and polemical structure of change and crisis. It seems that modernity sets up a linear time of technical progress, production and history, and, simultaneously, a cyclical time of fashion. This only *seems* to be a contradiction, since in fact modernity is never the radical rupture. Tradition is no longer the pre-eminence of the old over the new: it is unaware of either – modernity itself invents them both at once, at a single stroke, it is always and at the same time 'neo-' and '*rétro-*', modern and anachronistic. The dialectic of rupture very quickly becomes the dynamics of the amalgam and recycling. In politics, in technics, in art and in culture it is defined by the exchange rate that the system can tolerate without alteration to its fundamental order.[10]

The 'post'-modernists' habit of obfuscating contradictions through the notion of simultaneity permits almost any structural congruence.

Yet this habit does not disguise a fundamental fallacy in their thinking, namely that the socio-economic framework for modernity is said no longer to accept anything from culture but simulated, symbolic exchange. For Baudrillard and others in the early 'post'-modern 'movement', alas, concrete evaluation of use-, exchange- and surplus values were systemic challenges that late modern capitalism with its 'logic of fashion' ignored, and thus it did not form part of their reflexive analyses.[11] But even from the viewpoint of methodological innovation, the centrality of fashion for a structural analysis of symbolic exchanges in culture cannot simply ignore the economic foundation on which it rests, nor the real social consequences that have arisen historically from the conditions and structure of the industries of textiles, clothing and fashion.

The sustained focus on fashion in Baudrillard's books across a decade moved him from a rather traditional materialism, which discerned only the malign influence of fashion as capricious and socially codifying, towards a post-materialist simulation of class structures and economic relations in a culture determined by fashion's sign system. But the latter does not offer structural alternatives or systemic innovation for Baudrillard but mere representation and reflection. Neither orthodox materialism nor late modernist anti-materialism felt that it had anything constructive to attribute to fashion. Fashion's agency for capitalism, although certainly arousing curiosity, is rarely employed as a lever for exposure or critique of the system.

Fashion in Select Economic Histories

Fashion's materialism lies at the basis of its historical evaluation; from the very start fashion has been debated through its productive structure and its material value. In 1690 Nicolas Barbon, a Calvinist proponent of the free market, who significantly distinguished between monetary and moral aspects within economics, declared:

> Those Expences that most Promote Trade, are in Cloaths and Lodging: In Adorning the Body and the House, There are a Thousand Traders Imploy'd in providing Food. Belonging to Cloaths, is Fashion; which is the shape or Form of Apparel. In some places, it is fixt and certain; as all over Asia, and in Spain; but in France, England, and other places, the Dress alters; Fashion or the alteration of Dress, is a great Promoter of Trade, because it occasions the Expence of Cloaths, before the Old ones are worn out: It is the Spirit and Life of Trade; It makes a Circulation, and gives a Value by Turns, to all sorts of

Commodities; keeps the great Body of Trade in Motion; it is an Invention to Dress a Man, as if he lived in a perpetual Spring; he never sees the Autum of his Cloaths: [. . .] The Promoting of New Fashions, ought to be Encouraged, because it provides a Livelihood for a great Part of Mankind.[12]

And John Bellers, the late seventeenth-century Quaker, whom the political historian Eduard Bernstein praised as a 'champion of the poor',[13] used fashion as an example of the changes in assessing goods (not just luxurious ones) when they are evaluated through labour rather than through money:

The uncertainty of fashions does increase necessitous poor. It has two great mischiefs in it. 1st, The journeymen are miserable in winter for want of work, the mercers and master-weavers not daring to lay out their stocks to keep the journeymen employed before the spring comes, and they know what the fashion will then be; 2ndly, In the spring the journeymen are not sufficient, but the master-weavers must draw in many prentices, that they may supply the trade of the kingdom in a quarter or half a year, which robs the plough of hands, drains the country of labourers, and in a great part stocks the city with beggars, and starves some in winter that are ashamed to beg.[14]

Bellers, like Barbon, railed against mercantilism, as the pre-eminent economic doctrine of their time, not simply to embrace a free trade of goods to benefit capitalists but to guarantee a distribution and remuneration of labour that was not generated by the simple amassing of capital (bullionism) but by a more considerate interplay of factors. For these two economists, working during the very early phase of European industrialisation, the vagaries of fashion presented the advantageous economic particularity of a repeated, seasonal pattern of consumption; but at the level of method this very transitoriness precluded the embedding of the fashion trade into a structured economic system for whose analysis labour assumed a central role.

Marx, who quotes from Bellers repeatedly in the first volume of *Capital*, joined him in decrying 'the murderous, meaningless caprices of fashion, caprices that consort so badly with the system of modern industry'.[15] What Marx here regarded still in terms of working conditions – the quote on fashion is contextualised through concrete concerns about the regulation of child labour – and assessed essentially in social terms would become in the political economy of his *Grundrisse* a structurally more complex view of fashion as the exponent of both materiality and materialism in which productive structure and socio-political factors stand in dialectical relation.

Dialectics in Fashion

In the *Grundrisse* (a rough draft of which was completed in 1858) Marx employed the example of the itinerant tailor who visits his client in his home, in order to initiate an analysis of the relation between 'objectified labour' and 'living labour' within an initial system of 'simple circulation'.

> Both [the client and the artisan] in fact exchange only use values with one another; one exchanges necessaries, the other labour, a service which the other wants to consume, either directly – personal service – or he furnishes him the material etc. from which, with his labour, with the objectification of his labour, he makes a use value, a use value designed for A's consumption. For example, when the peasant takes a wandering tailor, the kind that existed in times past, into his house, and gives him the material to make clothes with ... The man who takes the cloth I supplied to him and makes me an article of clothing out of it gives me a use value. But instead of giving it directly in objective form, he gives it in the form of activity.[16]

So far, so good, in terms of a straightforward materialist presentation of labour and consumption: the materiality of the clothing is infused with labour, not only as an economic fact but also as a social instance. But Marx proceeded further with this example of cloth and tailoring – and he would continue to draw on it later in *Capital* and in his discussions with Friedrich Engels, who at the time was working in his family's yarn and textile factory in Manchester. In his *Grundrisse* Marx continued:

> Now, the article of clothing not only contains a specific, form-giving labour – a specific form of usefulness imparted to the cloth by the movement of labour – but also contains a certain quantity of labour – hence not only use value, but *value* generally, *value* as such. But this value does not exist for A, since he consumes the article, and is not a clothes-dealer. He has therefore exchanged the labour not as *value-posting* labour [*wertsetzende Arbeit*], but as an activity which creates utility, use value ... The point for A is not the objectification in the cloth of labour as such, of a certain amount of labour time, hence value, but rather the satisfaction of a certain need.[17]

In the scenario above, the object (cloth, garment) is not only an objectification arising from material production but one that is borne within

2 Mechanical loom at the Bonotto textile factory in Molvena, October 2016

consumption. Value is expressed as use value but is not perceived by the consumer as equivalent value to labour. In clothing for fashion, such use value is subordinate to another form of value, namely surplus value. The 'process of utilizing or exploiting [*Verwertungsprozess*]' becomes one of 'appropriation', especially within the framework of contemporary consumption.[18] The modern (industrialised) making of clothing becomes a primary example of objectifying living labour through means and processes of production, and although Marx did not furnish this *de facto* cultural denotation of an economic transformation, this action provides the foundation for fashion itself, since fashion is the one genre, the one group of goods or commodities that objectifies simultaneously the labour within it and its consumer. Marx alerted his reader again to the dialectic of production: 'the person objectifies himself in production, the thing subjectifies itself in the person',[19] and this dialectic is expressed in fashion through the material value of the object (the price of the fabric, the wages needed to pay for the labour in creating a garment, facilities of production, etc.) which is negated by the surplus value of the finished product as consumed by the wearer (within a social context), without which the production could not exist, as its economic viability could not be guaranteed. 'When cotton becomes yarn', wrote Marx,

> yarn becomes fabric, fabric becomes printed etc. or dyed etc. fabric, and this becomes, say, a garment, then ... in each of these subsequent processes, the material has obtained a more useful form, a form more appropriate for consumption; until it has obtained at the end the form in which it can directly become an object of consumption, when, therefore, the consumption of the material and the suspension of its form satisfies a human need, and the transformation is the same as its use. The substance of cotton preserves itself in all of these processes; it becomes extinct in one form of use value in order *to make way for a higher one, until the object exists as an object of direct consumption.*[20]

The transformation of the object coincides necessarily with the transformation of use value into surplus value, and this process appears as transitory and ephemeral, despite its very real socio-economic consequences which can be observed in historical time. Objectification and the accumulation of capital through amassing surplus value exist side by side as part of modernity's dependence on the acceleration of its own tempo – the speeding up of production as dependent on the constant increase of consumption by curtailing the use value of objects (now read: commodities) through temporal cessions, arriving finally, half a century later, at Georg Simmel's sociological – and exceedingly anti-materialist – analysis of the impact of rapid consumption on the phenomenology of urban life.

> The psychological basis of the metropolitan type of individuality consists in the *intensification of nervous stimulation* which results from the swift and uninterrupted change of outer and inner stimuli. Man is a differentiating creature. His mind is stimulated by the difference between a momentary impression and the one which preceded it. Lasting impressions, impressions which differ only slightly from one another, impressions which take a regular and habitual course and show regular and habitual contrasts – all these use up, so to speak, less consciousness than does the rapid crowding of changing images, the sharp discontinuity in the grasp of a single glance, and the unexpectedness of onrushing impressions. These are the psychological conditions which the metropolis creates.[21]

Yet much earlier Marx had already returned such subjectivity back to its materialist base.

> The transformation of the material by living labour, by the realisation of living labour in the material – a transformation which, as purpose, determines labour and is its purposeful activation (a transformation which does not only posit the form as external to the inanimate object, as a mere vanishing image of its material consistency) – thus preserves the material in a definite form, and subjugates the transformation of the material to the purpose of labour. Labour is the living, form-giving fire; it is the transitoriness of things, their temporality, as their formation by living time.[22]

The temporality and transitoriness of fashion – in the mode of living, the changing style of objects as well as of words that writers such as Honoré de Balzac, Théophile Gautier and Charles Baudelaire would observe around the same time as Marx's analyses – are based profanely and materially in the transformation of the labour process, and on the activity of the worker.[23]

The economic analysis of the *Grundrisse* must be seen in correlation with the historical and material demands that Marx and Engels had set out during the previous decade in the *German Ideology*, and its political praxis as demanded by the *Manifesto of the Communist Party*. The emphasis on the concrete and the objective must lead directly to a perception and assessment of the material object within historical development and the praxis of its production. In historical materialism, labour, in a form fundamentally distinct from capital, determines the self-consciousness and liberty of the subject through the appropriation of the object (of nature). In its first instance production can be regarded as a historical factor, which through particular forms and through certain implementations within capitalism can turn, for example, into an alienating process when labour and its products become estranged from the worker/maker. Conversely, subjectivity can arise from within the objectified, positivist character of historical development when the process of production becomes self-generative for developing historical consciousness, which in turn changes society through political and social action.

If fashion had been seen as a relativistic phenomenon of modernity that was celebrated for its fluidity as the supreme expression of a subjective spirit, then it must be analysed simultaneously as the product of processes that posit the object against the subject. In consequence, the objectification of the subject within this transformation and the creation of surplus value as fundamental to the dialectic of production cause the conflict within capitalist modernity that can be framed as economic alienation, social/class antagonism, and cultural ambiguity – and thus as compelling to the artist who allies himself or herself with the modern. Although the consumer's changing appearance and his or her objectification through sartorial shells would become a boundless terrain for aestheticisation by modernist art movements (Impressionism, Futurism, Surrealism, etc.), his or her activity has to be set against the action of the worker who, despite – or precisely because of – the structural dynamics and complexity of the modern labour process, exists without the chance of material intervention or real political agency.

The concept of 'transitoriness' in fashion as a hallmark of modernity, which we will encounter in the next chapter as a focus adapted from Baudelaire by Walter Benjamin for his *Arcades Project*, means little to the labourer who is oppressed by assembly- or piece-work. The constant passage of objects (or, often, objects' isolated parts) in front of the worker during a ten-hour shift does not denote a rhythm that is a source of artistic contemplation but alienates the subject as mere objectified constituent in an abstract process. If such a statement sounds reductive, one has only to take the historical example of the Lyon silk weavers at the outset of the nineteenth century, who were reduced in the space of some three decades from skilled artisans with a high degree of creative autonomy to alienated wage earners through basic changes in the production process: 1) the accumulation of capital by a new class of *fabricants-negociants* (producers-distributors) that rendered the weavers dependent on the advance of money and materials, and 2) the industrialisation of the looms through factory structures that were pioneered in Britain and the German Bund.[24]

Fashion played a vital role in these transformations due to the confluence of a material given – a particular labour structure, which resulted from accelerated demand for fashionable goods – together with a sociological factor – the objectification of the subject through modern sartorial forms. The dialectic of such production expressed through its negation – that is, through consumption – animates the role of fashion within the modern. Marx postulated in his *Grundrisse*:

> Consumption produces production in a double way, 1) because a product becomes a real product only by being consumed. For example, a garment becomes a real garment only in the act of being worn ... Only by disintegrating the product does consumption give the product the finishing stroke;[25] for the product is production not as objectified activity, but rather only as object for the active subject; 2) because consumption creates the need for *new* production, that is it creates the ideal, internally impelling cause for production, which is its presupposition. Consumption creates the motive for the production; it also creates the object which is active in production as determinant aim.[26]

Here we find a double meaning explored for production. On the one hand Marx emphasises his distinction between equivalent value – the amount of labour being put into an object's production as matched by its 'value' (not necessarily its price) – and exchange value – the object as a commodity whose value/price is far advanced from the value of labour invested in it originally. On the other hand he looks at consumption to finalise production within its 'usage' – which can be symbolic as well[27] – and which generates the need for new production. Importantly, the connection between contingent forms of value and the recurring need to produce them for an advancing consumer society is also anchored in the changing materiality of the object of commodity: from 'finishing stroke', via base material and surface value, to its material disintegrating (becoming old-fashioned) before the spectre of constantly renewed consumption.

Disintegration as the 'finishing stroke' is the apotheosis of modern fashion: the instant objectification of the subject through sartorial commodities in set socio-economic systems is raised to an artistic gesture, a social signifier, even an aesthetic concept (style), which must be cut short as its material base requires constant renewal, which, in turn, provides the tempo for the labour that produces the object for consumption. The ever-changing trends in modern culture provide an abstract rationale that conceals the market behind repeatedly actualised and formalised aesthetics.

Another Tailor

How much the changed circumstances of production allied themselves with an altered discourse that showed itself as subjectified, apolitical and anti-materialist can be seen by contrasting Marx's example of the tailor with one by Simmel, for whom the tailor, who comes into the house of the client to measure his suit, served for a very different argument. Simmel has been discussed repeatedly as the instigator of a sociology of fashion,[28] and his work can be said to combine set structures of social theory with an emphasis on consumption and the objectifying powers of modern culture,[29] which renders him a forebear of the Chicago School and also of many anthropologists of the twentieth century who used contemporary fashion as an area of inquiry. In *The Philosophy of Money* (published originally in 1900 and revised in 1907), Simmel employed fashion as a structural indicator for the subject–object relation that animated a philosophical discourse of modernity.

> The radical opposition between subject and object has been reconciled in theory by making the object part of the subject's perception. Similarly the opposition between subject and object does not evolve in practice as long as the object is produced by a single subject or for a single subject. Since the division of labour destroys custom production ... the subjective aura of the product also disappears in relation to the consumer because the commodity is now produced independently of him. It becomes an objective entity which the consumer approaches externally and whose specific existence and quality is autonomous of him. The difference, for instance, between the modern clothing store, geared towards the utmost specialisation, and the work of the tailor whom one used to invite into one's home, sharply emphasises the growing objectivity of the economic cosmos, its supra-individual independence in relation to the consuming subject with whom it was originally closely identified ... It is obvious how much this objectifies the whole character of transaction and how subjectivity is destroyed and transformed into cool reserve and anonymous objectivity once so many intermediate stages are introduced between the producer and the one who accepts his product that they lose sight of each other.[30]

In moving away from the Hegelian heritage that determined much of the nineteenth-century discussion on the subject through its movement between idealist and materialist interpretations, Simmel aligned himself with the older subjective idealism of Immanuel Kant, J. G. Fichte and F. W. J. Schelling.[31] Although this might have situated his work at the cusp of a contemporary philosophical trend,[32] it also rendered speculative his view of fashion. The production of clothing here alienates primarily the *bourgeois* consumer, as the erstwhile subjective input of the tailor's client into the creation of clothes cannot be maintained in purchasing a mass-produced suit in a modern department store. Although the significance of a haptic sensation for determining the wearer's relationship with clothing is still suggested, the consumer is adjudged to be no longer able to articulate his sociocultural status through an informed interaction with his tailor. Such an argument, though evocative in its ideological ambiguity, in the end affords subjectivism only to those who can pay for the sophisticated presentation ('cool reserve') of individuality through custom-made appearances. Obviously, such appearances are restricted by the market, and resistance to modernity's objectification thus seems to be granted only to those who have an appropriate amount of social education, cultural information and financial resources. Those who, for economic reasons, have to frequent department stores, thrift shops or flea markets to acquire pre-made (and often pre-worn) clothes are alienated from expressing subjectivity through fashion. The 'utmost specialisation' Simmel mentions is quickly exposed therefore as a market segmentation that functions along commodity prices, not changing cultural epistemologies.

Yet more significant in Simmel's citation is the restriction of the object's dominance over the subject to consumption and, implicitly, to the modernist disavowal of the craft base of the artisan/tailor. No mention is made of the objectification that is exercised by the modern means of production that we find in a clothing factory. It is obviously not the 'ladies paradise' of the department store (to paraphrase the English title of Émile Zola's novel from 1884) that objectifies and alienates, however much the neuroses of capitalism might show themselves there. It is rather the modern textile industry, with the introduction of particular productive structures across Europe throughout the nineteenth century, that furthered the alienation[33] of the subject and the reification of inter-social relations.

Conclusion: Hard Materialism

Conscious deference to fashion must expose the political consequences of celebrating an economy of the market which can be transposed back and forth between gendered, societal, cultural and ideological structures to mutually strengthen their cognitive potential. This is not to be confused with epistemological import, as cognition in fashion is very rarely governed by an assessment of the subject as carrier of meaning but rather by heightened subjectivity as absolute meaning in itself. In epistemological terms, fashion can provide a context for the subject in its opposition to the dominance of the object, but this historical position does not as such elucidate the meaning of how the relationships between objects become indicative for inter-subjective social relations. Here a materialist assessment is required, which fashion cannot condone as it would expose its own operational basis as facile subordination to economics in reifying socio-cultural appearances. Such a conclusion is not to be seen as a reductive critique of the way in which fashion is produced – although its labour structures have been criticised repeatedly for their alienating potential in binding the most exclusive material product into the most dire productive conditions (from Lyon silk weaving at the start of the nineteenth century to the outsourcing of contemporary luxury goods in Asia today); it is equally a critique of the anti-materialist stance that fashion and its discourse are wont to promote.

Materialism, as the principle of adherence to consuming material goods and evaluating oneself and others through this, must be recognised as supporting the socio-economic system in which fashion's impact is grounded, otherwise the objectification and even reification of inter-subjective relations could not manifest itself in clothes and accessories, and fashion's potential for modern cultures would not have been so dominant. Correspondingly, (critical/ historical) materialism must serve, too, as an epistemological tool to situate fashion within the culture industry at large, and its historical connection with modernity must be read in parallel with the way in which materialist ideas displaced idealist ones.

I would argue that any meaningful work on the fashion system now has to reassess fundamentally the relationship between capitalist 'empires' and their 'new clothes' on the streets, and in private and public buildings. By the same token writers on fashion have to remain aware of their complicity in an ideology of fashion that they prop up through costume histories, cultural studies and art criticism – each of which has its own distinct function and all of which serve to establish an interconnected primacy of fashion as a structuring principle of progress. For instance, costume history has traced the development of clothing forms and design discourses through a linear development of 'liberal' vis-à-vis 'conservative' efforts to renew what people wear; cultural studies has added a plethora of media references to expand the discourse of fashion towards its representation within a homogenised capitalist culture industry; and art criticism has used the late/'post'-modernist 'logic of fashion' as a means to present conceptual innovations as trends – often quite unaware of the inherent irony that resides in this analogous perception of the cultural meaning of modern fashion and modern art.

Fashion today pronounces a loss of locality and cultural specificity, despite its creation being concentrated in a number of traditional centres: first Paris, then Milan, much later New York and Tokyo, and today Mumbai, Seoul and Shanghai. I do not think that this is the appropriate place to debate original or late modernities as geopolitically 'globalised', but I would like to note that the formalising of aesthetic markers and the reification of contemporary social structures point concretely towards the universalising and abstracting quality of modern clothing styles. This abstraction stands in dialectical relation with a pronounced loss of sociability. In modern fashion the particularisation of the individual, rather than any synthetic or communal impulse, becomes a carrier of meaning. This appears at first counter-intuitive, as it seems that the very communal acceptance of a style, in particular a clothing style, moves fashion from the presentation of esoteric 'dress' towards its communal modification and acceptance as a prevalent style. I wear what you wear, so we're on the same side.

In modern cultures especially, this process of communal fashion is not to be confused with dress as a signifier of cultural allegiance: modern fashion was and is not the costume of a people, nor even the dress of a social stratum (although such codified expressions can stimulate creative impulses through their material contrasts); it is fashion for a heterogeneous group of consumers who are united through common adherence to an actualised stylistic principle in appearance (as well as gestures, speech, etc.).

In capitalism this shared stylistic principle is pronounced as a subjectified gesture: adherence to a common fashion is rephrased as a personal choice, as an individual style and as psychologically particular, rather than denoting its reality: the simultaneous commodification of select subjects within a distinct socio-economic structure under the auspices of consumption-as-reification. Here, again, the illusion of subjective agency (of 'choice') has to be maintained by an idealist conception of Being in order to conceal the materialist basis of the subject under the dominance of the object as part of social production.

The reification of change into consumption contradicts the dialectic of production as consumption that Marx had postulated. Fashion as it appears in today's capitalism cannot condone dialectical thought, despite the permanent negation of its basis through yet another actualised instalment. Fashion has to be unwavering in its idealist adherence to progress within the socio-economic system.

After fashion's rhythm in modernity was pronounced some one-and-a-half centuries ago, the pattern had to continue and become accelerated but could no longer contradict itself. Whenever an alternative social or economic system sought to dispense with constant changes in fashion and to establish a monolithic sartorial codex (Soviet work wear, 'Mao suit', etc.), sociological or psychological discourses in the industrialised West pointed towards decorative impulses or aspects of distinction that must render such codices inoperable. The need to establish a coherent and largely immovable basis for everyday fashion from which individual variations could afford the subject a mirage of choice and self-agency is not discussed as a structural principle, since the negation of fashion cannot be raised without calling the hegemony of our entire socio-economic system into question.

Notes

1. Jean Baudrillard, 'Models and Series', in *The System of Objects* [1968] (London: Verso, 1996), pp. 139–40.
2. Jacques Fath died of leukemia in 1954 and his couture house closed its doors three years later.
3. Cf. also Baudrillard's dated observation of the trickle-down effect in fashion, as borrowed from the economic modelling of laissez-faire capitalism ('trickle-down theory'): 'the office workers of today wear dresses derived from last season's haute couture models' (*The System of Objects*, p. 152), and his slightly more complex reiteration of the model/series dichotomy: 'The idea of the model has been obliged to seek refuge, concretely, in ever more subtle and definitive differences: such and such a skirt length, such and such a shade of red, such and such an advance in stereophony, or the few weeks that separate *haute couture* from Prisunic' (*The System of Objects*, p. 154).
4. Planned obsolescence was introduced as a term during the Great Depression in the US and resurrected by the journalist Vance Packard for his book *The Waste Makers* (New York: McKay, 1960), to show how commodities were designed to break down in order to stimulate repeat consumption. Packard also coined the term *The Hidden Persuaders* (New York: McKay, 1957) for malicious advertisers who tricked impressionable and hapless consumers into apparently following any fashion that they pre-determined. Even in Packard's day, sociological and economic research had demonstrated how the dynamic is much more bilateral and the role of consumers in determining production is much more active.
5. Baudrillard, *The System of Objects*, pp. 145–6.
6. Jean Baudrillard, 'Fashion, Or the Enchanting Spectacle of the Code',

in *Symbolic Exchange and Death* [1976], trans. I. H. Grant (London: SAGE, 1993), pp. 87–100.
7. Ibid., p. 8.
8. Ibid., pp. 2, 5.
9. For a critical reassessment of Baudelaire's take on fashion, see Chapter 2 below.
10. Baudrillard, *Symbolic Exchange and Death*, pp. 89–90.
11. Without wanting to sound facetious, Baudrillard's critique of Marx between 1973 (*The Mirror of Production*) and 1976 (*Symbolic Exchange and Death*) was also eminently fashionable in itself. In order to follow the trend away from the re-reading of Marx by Louis Althusser (with Étienne Balibar and others) in the 1960s, Baudrillard promoted in the early 1970s a nostalgic idealism of 'symbolic' exchanges, which since Durkheim, Mauss and Bataille had sought to replace economic analysis with cultural anthropology.
12. Nicolas Barbon, *Discourse on Trade* (London: Milbourn, 1690), p. 15.
13. Eduard Bernstein, *Kommunistische und demokratisch-sozialistische Strömungen während der englischen Revolution* (Stuttgart: Dietz, 1895); trans. as *Cromwell and Communism* (London: George Allen & Unwin, 1930), chapter XVII.
14. John Bellers, *Essays About the Poor, Manufactures, Trade, Plantations & Immorality . . .* (London: Sowle, 1699), p. 9.
15. Karl Marx, *Capital*, vol. 1 [1867], in Karl Marx and Friedrich Engels, *Collected Works*, vol. 35 (London: Lawrence & Wishart, 1996), p. 450.
16. Karl Marx, *Grundrisse der Kritik der politschen Ökonomie (Rohentwurf), 1857–1858* (Berlin: Dietz, 2nd edn, 1974 [1953]), p. 369; trans. by M. Nicolaus as *Grundrisse: Foundations of the Critique of Political Economy (Rough Draft)* (London: Allen Lane, 1973), p. 465.
17. Marx, *Grundrisse*, p. 370; trans., p. 466 [translation modified].
18. Ibid., p. 373; trans., p. 469.
19. Ibid., p. 11; trans., p. 89.
20. Ibid., p. 266; trans., p. 360.
21. Georg Simmel, 'Die Großstädte und das Geistesleben', in *Die Großstadt. Vorträge und Aufsätze zur Städteausstellung*, ed. Th. Petermann (Dresden: Jahrbuch der Gehe-Stiftung, vol. 9, 1903), p. 188; Eng. trans. 'The Metropolis and Mental Life', in Kurt Wolff (ed.), *The Sociology of Georg Simmel* (New York: Free Press, 1950), pp. 409–10.
22. Marx, *Grundrisse*, p. 266; trans., pp. 360–1.
23. As examples one could offer the dresses of 'La Duchesse de Langeais', written by Balzac in 1833 as part of his *Histoire de Treize*, in *La Comédie humaine*, vol. 5 (Paris: Gallimard, 1977); Théophile Gautier's essay *De la mode* (Paris: Poulet-Malassi & de Broise, 1858); and Baudelaire's feuilletons of 1861, collected as 'Le Peintre de la vie moderne'.
24. See, for example, Maurice Moissonnier, *Les Canuts: 'Vivre en*

travaillant ou mourir en combattant' [1958] (Paris: Messidor/Editions Sociales, 1988), pp. 74–5; or Fernand Rude, *L'Insurrection lyonnaise de novembre 1831: le mouvement ouvrier à Lyon de 1827–1832* (Paris: Anthropos, 1969), pp. 48ff.
25. In English in the original text.
26. Marx, *Grundrisse*, p. 13; trans., p. 91 [translation modified].
27. Thus making Baudrillard's tenet of the 'symbolic exchange' much less distanced from Marxism than he might have intended.
28. See, for instance, Deena and Michael Weinstein, 'Georg Simmel: Sociological Flâneur Bricoleur', *Theory, Culture and Society*, 8.3 (1991), pp. 151–68; Brigitta Nedelmann, 'Georg Simmel as an Analyst of Autonomous Dynamics: The Merry-Go-Round of Fashion', in Michael Kaern, Bernard S. Phillips and Robert S. Cohen (eds), *Georg Simmel and the Contemporary Sociology* (Dordrecht: Kluwer, 1990), pp. 243–57; Ulrich Lehmann, *Tigersprung: Fashion in Modernity* (Cambridge, MA: MIT Press, 2000), ch. 3; and Michael Carter, *Fashion Classics from Carlyle to Barthes* (Oxford: Berg, 2003), ch. 4.
29. Read, the market – although not acknowledged by Simmel as such.
30. Georg Simmel, *Die Philosophie des Geldes*, 2nd edn [1907], in Georg Simmel, *Gesamtausgabe*, vol. 6 (Frankfurt a.M.: Suhrkamp, 1989), pp. 633–4; trans. by T. Bottomore and D. Frisby, *The Philosophy of Money* (London: Routledge, 1990), p. 457 [translation modified].
31. See Chapter 6 below for more on the subject–object relation and Hegel.
32. See the 'fashionable' neo-Kantianism of the Marburg School in the works of Hermann Cohen, Heinrich Rickert et al. around 1890, which finds its reflection in the 'sociological' investigations by Simmel's contemporaries such as Max Weber or Werner Sombart. For a critical assessment, see, for example, Gillian Rose, *Hegel Contra Sociology* (London: Athlone, 1981).
33. In the context of industrial labour, alienation must be read as the materialist coinage of Simmel's 'utmost specialisation'.

Chapter 2

Historical Materialism and Historicism: The Tiger's Leap

> The tiger walks in a fairly human fashion on his hind legs; he is dressed like the most exquisite of dandies, and this suit is so perfectly cut that one can hardly make out the animal's body underneath the grey trousers with spats, the flowered waistcoat, the dazzling white jabot with its faultless pleats, and the expertly tailored frock coat.
> Jean Ferry, 'The Fashionable Tiger'[1]

In the opening chapter I looked at a theoretical basis for the use of materialism in analysing fashion; in this chapter I would like to proceed to an example in which this theoretical basis has been applied to the cultural discussion of fashion and its relation to history. As will become clear, I regard this example as being rather problematic. But despite, or, better, because of its ambiguous use of theory, the example remains apt, since it speaks in such an original and poetic manner about fashion's transient and diffuse nature, which can render rather reductive any exclusive analysis of its concrete function or material use. In this context, I consider the ambiguity inherent in fashion as the antithesis to its relation with materialism and materiality that I explored in the first chapter.

Often we find that promoting a particular critical method moves the field of inquiry away from the material basis that one might expect to be at the heart of such a critique.[2] This process might seem obvious in so far as abstract discourses regarding cultural phenomena are wont to ignore the actual, detailed circumstances of their production. But I intend to demonstrate in the following that abstraction has been crucial from the start to a historical discourse on fashion. At its most persuasive, abstraction shows the application of theory where universal patterns are traced and analysed across historical periods and cultural contexts, and it suggests the need to remove the object from its particular time and place and render it more generic (often approximating to a maxim) in order to explain, for example, wide-ranging anthropological or social processes.

In this chapter I would like to present the attempt by the cultural philosopher Walter Benjamin to trace, through oneiric and poetic evocations, a pre-history of modernity in the fashion of Paris after 1850. This allowed him to investigate through forward projection the concrete cultural, social and political foundations and manifestations within his own century and, more abstractly, to show the origin of a historical pattern of consumption to which he could apply a politicised, historical-materialist method.

Benjamin was an astute and sympathetic observer of fashion who nevertheless remained unfamiliar with its industry and practice, and therefore we have to debate with him the value of looking at fashion through representation and consumption, in contrast to analysing the effect of production on fashion discourses. My original inspiration for looking at Benjamin came more than a decade ago when I wrote a book entitled *Tigersprung: Fashion in Modernity*. In it the *Tigersprung* ('the tiger's leap') was used to inquire into an abstract principle behind fashion, in particular its function as providing rhythm to modern societies and cultures. The term *Tigersprung* came from Benjamin's scattered writings,[3] where it was used to denote a new model of history in which the past is activated in and through the present within a culture industry that demands constant renewal. Further on in this chapter I will discuss Benjamin's choice of this term in detail.

This tiger's leap can be found in Benjamin's notes from the 1930s, the context for which is provided by Parisian culture between 1850 and 1900. He chose these references out of a sense of nostalgia; not in the conservative manner of the traditionalist who bemoans the loss of the good old days but in the irreverent, at times even subversive manner of the Surrealists (with whom he associated and whose books he reviewed) who were tracing out strange undercurrents within the bourgeois, capitalist consumer culture of the previous century. Benjamin's relationship with history becomes a complex act of remembrance, and fashion for him is the visual – and materialist – tool to unravel such perception of things past. At first Benjamin indeed appeared to be influenced by Marcel Proust, whom he translated into German as early as 1925/26, but he proceeded to fuse Proust's poetic rendition of the Bergsonian concept of subjectified time (*la durée*) with a quasi-Marxist, materialist understanding of repetition and patterns across history. Although this produced a conflicting historical method, it highlighted the challenge that fashion offers to reading and understanding history through objects that are born from the dialectic of production and consumption (as mentioned in the previous chapter). Benjamin realised that fashion's double materialism can generate simultaneously a historical-materialist critique and an appreciation of the symbolic value of its objects – clothing and accessories, as well as gestures, postures, modes of transport or menus. And this simultaneity of affirmation and critique accounts for Benjamin's ambivalent fascination with the birth of a fashion culture in Paris in the latter half of the nineteenth century.

Confection and *Couture*

The structures that governed the production and, by extension, the consumption of clothes in Paris were subject to fundamental change in the latter half of the nineteenth century. This change was precipitated by economic and logistical factors such as the industrialisation of the clothing industry, including the invention of the sewing machine in 1830 by Barthélmy Thimissier, as well as being affected by the contemporary understanding of modernity as the transitory and fleeting principle for a culture governed by novelty and the promotion of ever-changing styles for consumers. The simple but dramatic interplay between the old and the new generated fashion's dynamic after 1850, by catering to the appetite of a growing petite bourgeoisie and, as a marked contrast, by promoting 'high' fashion as akin to original, subjective works of art. The development of *confection*, mass-produced clothing that could react to and even influence for the first time in costume history contemporary trends rather than simply copying traditional patterns or waiting for a trickle-down effect from fashion 'leaders', developed at the same time as the codification of material and technical expertise for exclusive fashion into *couture*.

These two types of producing fashion, *confection* and *couture*, established their trade association in the second half of the nineteenth century in Paris. In 1868 La Chambre syndicale de la confection et la couture pour dames et fillettes was inaugurated, which would elect simultaneously as its heads one *couturier* and one *confectionneur*, until 1910 when the two branches separated.[4] Their mutual origins reside in the shared use of materials and techniques, although their respective value and intricacy differed widely, from cheaply manufactured cotton work-shirts (*blouses bleues*), via simplified versions of high fashion dresses that were produced by local seamstresses, to the artistic pretensions of the self-styled 'father' of couture – and indeed one of the founders of the above association – Charles-Frederick

Worth. The emphasis on labour, artisanal or industrial, concerned with fabrics, pattern cutting and sewing techniques united the makers of clothing at either end of the social spectrum, and they shared a keen interest in reinforcing Paris as the world's capital of fashion trends. Yet the exclusive focus on subjective creation in Parisian *ateliers*, rather than, say, the incorporation of the industrial expertise in silk weaving in Lyon's factories or in lace making around Lille, reinforced the perception of new fashion as based around silhouettes and surface decoration instead of communicating the development of new textiles or specialised machinery.[5] This predicated the division between *confection* and *couture*, so that hybrid definitions were coined to distinguish intermediate branches of the fashion hierarchy in France. The term *couture en gros* was used in the second half of the nineteenth century to characterise work that used standardised patterns in larger workshops but still aspired to incorporate contemporary stylistic markers and which could be fitted to individual clients. Correspondingly, *couture* began to distinguish itself as *couture-création* and *haute couture* from the 1880s onwards in order to emphasise subjectivity and originality and the development of experimental garments that migrated from use- to symbolic value.[6]

Originally, in France from the 1830s onwards *confection* had denoted clothing for the working class. This was a standardised and serial production, which stood in stark contrast to the established manner of making clothes on demand, even those of the cheapest variety, and adapting them more or less skilfully to individual bodies. The progressive industrialisation of French clothing manufacture furthered this standardisation so that clothing types and styles would permeate class divides, and a pronounced contrast developed vis-à-vis the (more affluent) bourgeois who asked her seamstress or his tailor to make up individualised garments. The ubiquitous spectre of consumption had rendered clothes for working men and women, which were produced in standardised, reductive patterns, an analogy to their perception as a homogenised mass – where this homogeneity could be embodied either negatively as an undistinguished rabble or, more positively, as an activist crowd. Yet there was another connection between *confection* and the working class, one that encapsulates again the meaning of materialism as referring to material production as well as political economy.

Mass-manufactured clothing in France was pioneered in the making of uniforms by L'Atelier social (later L'Atelier national), the state-run workshop created by social reformer and historian Louis Blanc, who was charged with the reorganisation of labour in the wake of the February Revolution of 1848.[7] This work by some 2,000 workers producing an initial 100,000 uniforms for the National Guard was supervised by Blanc together with L'Association des tailleurs de Clichy, to investigate forms of creating and sponsoring labour in the clothing trade and to develop progressive forms of manufacture to economise on materials and ensure consistent quality and workable logistics in distribution. Subsequently, these progressive principles were applied to the making of civilian clothing, first extending the utilitarian function of army fatigues to the silhouette and cut of men's jackets and trousers, then projecting this principle further to the tailored aspects of womenswear. In this historical context mass manufacture was not indicative of low quality, that is, lacking in subjective formal innovation, but was a means of generating work for the unemployed and, in turn, providing affordable clothing for them. A progressive and emancipatory pattern of production thus generated its own form of responsive and responsible consumption.

The contrast between *confection* and *couture* appears as a material one between garments cut to standard patterns and produced by machines, and garments made to measure and produced by hand. Ostensibly, this distinction should lead to stylistic or qualitative – not necessarily quantitative – differences in the silhouette, cut and surface decoration of garments, in a way that is similar to the difference between mass-produced, processed food which is heated up at home and the menu conceived by a chef and his team in an exclusive restaurant, or the difference between the attraction of a mechanical piano at a fairground and the concert hall performance of a renowned pianist. Initially, this ostensible difference had manifested itself in nineteenth-century fashion through a time lag. Once a particular style was coined and accepted by a certain social set or sub-group it was transferred after a certain period to a different set or group and reformulated through modified production techniques and a different selection of materials. Such a process was prominent in developing designs for style 'leaders' (actresses, *demi-mondaines* (escorts), dandies, sportsmen, etc.), who were designated as carrying the subjective imprint of a *couturier* or made-to-measure tailor. The new style was then progressed through subsequent discourses of identifying it first as novel 'experiment', then as 'fashionable dress', then as 'popular' and finally as 'outmoded', before the garments were recycled within different segments of the market. Designs progressed from rich bourgeois clients via hand-me-downs for their valets or chambermaids to the second-hand clothing market for the working class in Paris, and then down to the *chiffonier* who would collect the used-up, frayed and torn sartorial detritus and sell it on to the poorest of the poor.

This trickle-down of styles from social high to low became an accepted theory to indicate the spread of fashion ideas and discourses across social strata. The German jurist and sociologist of law Rudolf von Jhering adjudged 'the character of contemporary fashion' in the first volume of his unfinished book *Der Zweck im Recht* (On Purpose in Law) to have emerged thus: 'First comes its origin in the higher echelon of society and its imitation in the middle one. Fashion moves from top to bottom, not from bottom to top.'[8] However, Jhering qualified his reductive statement about fashion being hierarchically dispersed by adding a structural and temporal explanation that was more in keeping with his own period, rather than being based on an outmoded dress history. 'Next the constant change in fashion ... Novelty is the indispensable condition for fashion, if it has to fulfil its purpose ... Fashion's lifespan stands in inverse relationship to the speed of its distribution.'[9] For the bourgeois lawmakers, philosophers and sociologists at the end of the nineteenth century, fashion continued to pose a moral question. The French sociologist Émile Durkheim, in reviewing Jhering's book, wrote that fashion evidenced 'class vanity' and, as being contagious to the lower (read, more susceptible) classes, it stood thus 'outside morality'.[10] Durkheim's compatriot and fervent critic, the pioneering sociologist Gabriel Tarde, in contrast recast imitation in fashion as part of a complex interaction of behavioural-deterministic and socio-economic factors in *The Laws of Imitation* in 1890. For Tarde, fashion is an 'influence extra-logique' on society, the result of a prevailing political economy as much as an epistemological factor that allows people to situate themselves.[11] As further social research demonstrated at the end of the nineteenth century, and as Jhering had acknowledged already with regard to the working class,[12] it was the very rich and the very poor who, for socio-economic reasons, tended most to resist fashion cycles and who extolled the sartorial status quo.[13] The growing middle classes in Paris (and other urban centres) took the lead in consuming and rejecting constantly renewed styles in dress. This bourgeoisie, catered for by a growing number of more or less distinguished local *couturiers* and *couturières* from the 1860s and 1870s onwards, was happy to take inspiration from 'high' as well as 'low' to emphasise their mobility. Trickle-down and trickle-up existed simultaneously as material reference for new fashions. The bonnets of milkmaids, the aprons of kitchen staff, the printed calicos of shop-girls or the shoes of farmers all served as inspiration for fashions in Paris during the nineteenth century in the same way that the extravagant costumes of actresses or ephemeral dandies inspired new shapes, textures and colours.

Sartorial innovation often had very concrete material roots, where the usage and use value of clothing determined its look. In a photograph from 1895, for instance, we see the female workforce at Louis and Auguste Lumière's photographic equipment factory in Monplaisir sporting loosely cut, coarsely woven cotton or linen trousers. We can detect significant customisation and styling across these mass-manufactured and standardised outfits, using accessories as well as re-tailoring. Here, the garments are being individually fashioned by the labourers in order to reflect current trends or fashions within the context of workwear. By contrast, costume history has habitually dated the advent of trousers for women some three decades later in the 1920s, constructed as a parallel between the couture designs of Jean Patou or Gabrielle Chanel and contemporary female emancipation. This is history from an exclusive, stylistic perspective, which ignores the material reality of working-class women sporting trousers for protection and ease of wear (while at the same time fashioning them according to personal preferences). A similar misdirection can be seen in the alternative history of the 'harem pants', publicised in 1910/11 by couturier Paul Poiret, which are said to refer to the costume designs of the Ballets Russes (by Léon Bakst and others), which suggests that loose, bifurcated nether garments for women were inspired not by the reality of mass-produced trousers for working women, or indeed by ethnographic models, but instead by esoteric costume fantasies, which had to remain exclusive to a haute bourgeois audience and progressive, artistic designers. Poiret himself famously in 1928 wore dungarees and a shirt-jacket made from raw denim, standing next to his photographer friend Boris Lipnitzky in his off-the-peg three-piece suit, underscoring the socio-cultural horizontality of stylistic inspiration and material production. We learn that fashion's relentless search for innovative formal and material solutions trickled up as well as down, and its motivation can be traced in social emancipation as much as in trying to seek out novel ideas.

The transposition of styles from one social context to another did indeed differentiate between *couture* and *confection*, but this was not a unilateral progression. Whereas a hand-made dress for a wealthy client used machine stitching only for lining or for underskirts (if at all) and ostensibly remained exclusive in promoting elaborate handcraft, popular versions of new fashion ideas were disseminated by new economic factors of production. In reproducing labour-intensive embroidery through printed calicos or replacing knitted silk by cotton jersey *tricotage*, modern manufacture progressively imposed novel stylistic tenets – even in the most subjective of fashion creations. For instance, Jeanne Lanvin used machine top-stitching in her haute couture of the 1910s and 1920s, often emphasised as parallel lines, to programmatically embrace mechanised production as a hallmark of the modern.

Historical Materialism and Historicism

The above-mentioned historical aspects within clothing manufacture in France are meant to show how much the historical evaluation of fashion, and of culture in general, depends on recognising a multilateral movement between commodity consumption and (innovative, mechanised) patterns of production. This movement provides a significant part of the historical and economic background for Benjamin's cultural philosophy of fashion. And within it the term materialism became instrumental through its own historicity.

From the second half of the eighteenth to the first half of the nineteenth century France and other European cultures saw the radicalisation of the term 'materialism'. It developed from a 'mechanical' definition, which had rejected religious explanations of the world as well as the idealist ontologies of the Enlightenment in favour of scientific observations and objectivity: from Joseph de la Mettrie's *L'Homme machine* (1748), via Denis Diderot's and Jean le Rond d'Alembert's *Encyclopédie ou Dictionnaire raisonné des sciences, des arts et des métiers* (first edition in 1752), to Baron d'Holbach's *Système de la nature ou des loix du monde physique & du monde moral* (1770). The second step came with the application of materialism as a critical term within political economy. In this context it was employed to consider particular structures such as labour conditions, and to discern historical patterns such as class conflicts.[14] This movement from mechanical to socio-politically 'applied' materialism culminated in Marx's and Engels's developing definition of historical materialism from 1845 onwards.[15] It was based on a number of fundamental premises. 1) Self-preservation and -realisation of the individual are founded in social configurations and working relationships; a view that is thus pitched against idealism and individualism. 2) The objectively observed social movement is propelled by social contradictions (class wars), not by the self-realisation of a 'universal spirit' – as Hegel had argued. 3) Historical development is subjugated to an objective law that is comparable to natural law. 4) This development can be dialectically reconstructed and becomes relevant for the present. 5) Any revelation of the historical development can and must inspire revolutionary practice, which will lead eventually towards a classless society.

For a discussion of historical methods, points 3 and 4 are of particular interest, because here historical materialism stands in opposition to a method that perceives history as a set of singular, individualised events. This view, which was a near contemporary to historical materialism, is termed historism – *Historismus* in German, which is used in English often indiscriminately with the term historicism (*Historizismus* in German).[16] The English historism and historicism, in their historiographical context, jointly relegate historical occurrences and objects firmly to the past and do not attempt to distinguish a socio-historical pattern or structure. Historical events become particularised, as do methods of historical inquiry; they cannot be compared to one another and are to be regarded as subjectified and driven by individual historical actors. Historism and historicism can be contextualised in the latter half of the nineteenth century through strong tendencies of individualism, political liberalism and the view that any action or movement must remain essentially open and unpredictable, thus making reform through future prediction impossible.[17] In France, at least since Alexis de Tocqueville's classical, historicist account of the United States of America,[18] such refutation of historical patterns or universalising histories shaped a positivist perspective that is essential to capitalism (technological progress, free movement of goods, trickle-down effect of wealth, etc.) and that is also germane to fashion as the unpredictable stimulator for consumption.

Like historical materialism, historicism (and its proxy historism) also claims to be 'objective' and aspires to a quasi-scientific rationale. But historicism does so not in a critical but in a positivist sense; while stressing evolutionary concepts it is anti-Hegelian in its refutation of a 'philosophy of history', of a systematic, structural explanation. Historicist historians are intent on dealing with the geographical and temporal particularity of facts and turning their back on present ideas in order to situate past progression. In contrast, historical materialists aim to establish laws so as to predict the recurrence of historical patterns and to foretell certain events, therefore promoting a method that claims a form of scientific validity for itself. Historicism's method regards historical events as untainted by present speculation, as being objectively truthful regarding the way in which they occurred in the past – thereby it approximates hermeneutics as a contextualising but essentially self-contained method of interpreting source material. Reductively speaking, historical materialism as a form of historical method is concerned with movement and socio-historical patterns, while historism and historicism are concerned with events and individuals.

The shared origin of these contrasting historical methods in the nineteenth century not only accounts for their (quasi-)scientific positivism, it also aligns them with the birth of modernity as a critical refutation of the past, shown in the artistic as well as stylistic celebration of modern society and culture by Théophile Gautier, Charles Baudelaire and other French writers after 1848. For these artists, modernity defined itself prominently through the constantly renewed fashion in clothing, especially through a changing, critical and often dramatic interplay between mass-produced garments, the *confection* one could observe in the streets, and the material extravagance of *couture*. This interplay, although rooted concretely in production processes, aided artists in the symbolic representation of characters and their interaction through the clothes and accessories they wore and the postures and gestures they assumed. This artistic lineage provided another reason for Benjamin's fascination with fashion. Read through Baudelaire's feuilletons (as well as through Proustian remembrance), clothes and objects assumed for him a mystique that, over time, became more and more obscured, ambiguous and transitory and thus allowed for retrospective and poetic speculation on history and culture. Such a view of fashion is grounded in the interplay of divergent historical perceptions that becomes concrete in the interaction between historical materialism and historism/historicism: broad evolutionary tendencies in clothing, which in themselves are conflicting (progressive bourgeoisation, functionality instead of representation, etc.), pitched against the particularity of individual choices (dandy or romantic artist as extreme stylists or singular 'inventions' like Paul Poiret's harem pants or Jean Patou's beach trousers).

Turning Up the Lapels

Discussing historical materialist methods within a late modernist context, the literary scholar Fredric Jameson has described historicism as a term 'which cannot today be pronounced without furtively turning up one's lapels and glancing over one's shoulder'.[19] This image is noticeable not just for the secrecy it evokes in favouring a marginalised approach but also for the fact that clothing is employed here as a metaphor. It seems hardly an indiscriminate image, as Jameson's turned-up lapels establish a semantic connection with the earlier, correspondent use of this metaphor by Benjamin.[20]

For the latter, the lapels – he used the French term *revers* – displayed the inside as a paradigmatic other of an outer sartorial shell. The silk lining that was turned over on the woollen lapels of the nineteenth-century jacket (for both men and women) constitutes for the historical materialist the dialectics of a thesis which is the sombre wool *drap* and its antithesis which is the flamboyant colours or patterns of the lining. As Benjamin subsequently criticised historicism (*Historizismus*) via his own interpretation of fashion, we find here a particular perception of clothing that leads directly to a historical method as distinct from historism and historicism – but, as we will see, from historical materialism as well.

Jameson, in attempting to consolidate the Marxist perception of history within the anti-materialism of late modernist discourses,[21] defined the problem of subscribing to a particular historical method thus:

> The dilemma of any 'historicism' can be dramatised by the peculiar, unavoidable, yet seemingly unresolvable alternation between Identity and Difference. This is indeed the first arbitrary decision we are called on to make with respect to any form or object from out of the past.[22]

It is this reference to oneself, to the subject, that renders problematic material objects from the past in serving as elements of a historical perception, in preference to the interpretation of textual sources. When we look upon a material artefact we assess first its proximity to our own experience.[23] If this experience moves beyond intellectual recognition and touches the realm of the senses, for instance creating a haptic experience of the cloth enveloping the body, the 'alternation between identity and difference' becomes materialised. However, this phenomenological approach to the object is necessarily qualified by applying a historical-materialist understanding of the object, in particular its use- and exchange value. We recognise the object from the past as a product of material and technical production and ascribe to it a certain commodity value, which is most likely to be monetised, as part of an extended culture industry that projects the historical relevance of objects backwards and forwards.

For example, if we look at a dress from the late nineteenth century, we have the option of identifying with it, realising that its cut has come back into fashion and that we could acquire one now in the form of a bustled skirt from the collection of a contemporary designer, for example Raf Simons for Christian Dior Haute Couture. Conversely, we could focus on its inherent difference, stating that this garment is purely of 'historical' interest – which remains distinct from a 'historical piece' of costume that might well capture our imagination – and that it is of no relevance to our present manner of dressing. In fashion, with its constant reference to its own stylistic source book, such allusions can become quite complex, such as when a dress by Simons for Dior Couture refers back in pattern cut and formal construction (as well as floral decoration)[24] to designs by Christian Dior from the late 1940s or early 1950s, with their material extravagance promoted by textile producer Marcel Boussac, for which the art-historically educated couturier in turn had referenced shapes from the second half of the nineteenth century, regarded as the salad days of haute couture. In such cases the historical alignment of gowns through a shared principle of material profusion and extravagance renders the interest in fashion history a cultural commodity that can be used to promote and sell a continuous vision of female high fashion.

The dilemma that Jameson remarked upon arrives when we use identity as a trope to make the past object accessible to our present. We then take away the character that identified it as a historical artefact in the first place. We fail to appreciate the genuine stylistic and social impact of the bustled design when we mediate it through our look on this or last season's catwalk. On the other hand, were we to concentrate on the radical difference and temporal particularity of the cultural object, as historicism is wont to do, we define our own culture as alien from the previous one which thus remains unconnected to our experience and does not allow us to discern repeat patterns or appreciate the object's potential for historical abstraction. Fashion, as indicated by the example from Dior, 'solves' this dilemma – albeit not paradigmatically, because its primary concern remains with the success of the commodity – by postulating stylistic *dicta* that provide a dialectical environment in which any past object, that is, a garment or accessory, is potentially seen as historicist, where it is rooted in the past and identifiable as such, but simultaneously as a basis for a contemporary rendition, a novel version of an old form revived for the latest trend which in turn signposts the fashion to come.

The Historical Narrative

History is very often described in terms of cause and effect. Traditional costume history follows this pattern in analysing one form of clothing as dependent on the previous iteration, as developing or opposing it according to changed social conventions or political ideas. Most historical models appear to favour the historical narrative, that is, linear storytelling: historical periods follow one another, according to conventional wisdom, and they react to the previous tendencies in a positivist manner.

Fashion has to be regarded as essentially working against such a historical narrative. It does not follow a linear path, progressing from one form to a more advanced iteration, a 'better' piece of clothing. Fashion, unlike costume or dress, exists first and foremost for eminently changeable stylistic reasons, and although industrial advances become manifest in developing new materials, textiles, fabrics, methods of fastening, even novel ways of cutting patterns, there is no teleological progress towards a goal or an aim or a material purpose – apart from, for a particular brand or company that is active in the marketplace, selling an increasing number of garments each season. Were one to design what would be universally accepted as the ultimate dress or the complete pair of trousers, akin to the now optimised design of disposable nappies or cotton aprons, the fashion cycle would come to a halt.

Fashion works erratically through its method of quotation. It wilfully cites any style from the past in a novel incarnation or present rendition. Clothing types may be retained, yet their appearance is renewed by using past elements. Fashion thus constitutes an aesthetic rewriting of history. Therefore it also provides a fitting support for a dialectical philosophy of history, in which ideas and concepts are pursued across different temporal, geographical and methodological zones, rather than a chronological following of events. Using a dialectical view, the historian can take the tiger's leap from one concept to a related one from another period without having to use intermediary stages. This non-narrative rewriting constitutes a basis for historical materialism. Yet in the mind of some critics this very leap aligns itself also with historicism as a result of the interpretation and rewriting of historical events or periods as constituents of the present. Jameson accounted for a critical attitude towards these views in a book of 1981 that followed on directly from his earlier essay on Marxism and historicism:

> It is ... increasingly clear that hermeneutics or interpretive activity has become one of the basic polemic targets of contemporary post-structuralism in France, which – powerfully buttressed by the authority of Nietzsche – has tended to identify such operations with historicism, and in particular with the dialectic and its valorisation of absence and the negative, its assertion of the necessity and priority of totalising thought.[25]

Jameson here had in mind late modernist and anti-materialist writers such as Jean Baudrillard. But while Jameson posited literary interpretation alongside materialism as being misunderstood by the relativism of late modernist thinkers, his lumping together of hermeneutics, historicism and dialectics divests them of their rather divergent interpretations of historical structures. Yet it does indicate how closely interwoven their origins appear and that they had existed previously as contemporary efforts to find a veritable historical method.

Ironically, fashion, with its anti-narrative that is an exemplary catalyst for social and political history as well as forming its changing aesthetics, is anything but supportive of historical materialism, due to the role it occupies in capitalist society. In its most progressive form, which has been traditionally occupied by the sartorial inventions in haute couture, fashion is regarded by materialist critics as the ultimate bourgeois symbol and indicator of status. It is a fugitive, and many Marxist historians would argue obsolete, element in a commodity culture that has gone well beyond its point of saturation. The pairing of dressing and addressing history may thus appear as superficial and futile in its final social consequence; yet I would argue that fashion's relation with history goes beyond its impact as cultural object. Fashion rewrites the historical structure in an imaginative manner; it helps to shape a novel perception of the past which, according to Benjamin, is no less helpful to our understanding than historical materialism.[26]

Throughout the nineteenth century and the first decades of the twentieth, fashion's constant rewriting, the hermeneutics of sartorial history and the interpretation of past clothing styles all greatly increased the pace of historical and cultural development. Yet it was not only fashion's own pace that was upped, but the speed of successive reconfigurations in modern society as well, since fashion is to be considered as a pacemaker for modernity, as a prime and, moreover, constant indicator for change. In his book on the semantics of historical time, Reinhart Koselleck has said that the period between 1500 and 1800, that is, early modern times, constitutes a 'temporalisation [*Verzeitlichung*] of history, at the end of which there is the peculiar form of acceleration which characterises modernity'.[27] For Koselleck, it is precisely the act of thinking about historical time, the philosophy of history that emerged as a discipline during the Enlightenment, that separates the early modern period from its own past and opens up modernity. A consciousness of time had emerged that existed as a 'daring combination of politics and prophecy'. Progress was linked to the way in which politics had failed to satisfy its prognostic declarations and the impetus thus had moved on to the subject. Because prognostics implicitly contains diagnostics of the past, history was experienced essentially through its containing of an element of what was to come. 'Progress opened up a future that transcended the hitherto predictable, natural space of time and experience and thence – propelled by its own dynamic – provoked new, transnatural, and long term prognoses.'[28] For such a fundamentally novel view on history a new historical method was required, and historicism, dialectics and historical materialism took up the methodological challenge.

Progress in modernity is distinguished by two elements: it was rapid and seemingly unpredictable. This connects it with its aforementioned pacemaker fashion, which became equally accelerated and similarly unforeseeable throughout the infancy of haute couture. Therefore in order to assess modern times, various forms of historicism, dialectics and materialist history were proclaimed as indispensable tools, and the fashion that dressed the surface of capitalist modernity became a principal element not merely in its rewriting but in its very analysis.

Fashion, being both the prime object of aesthetic modernity and its social indicator, functions as an example for breaking up any positivist linearity in history, yet its apparent characteristics are far removed from the historical and political consequences that such a 'blasting of the continuum' (as Benjamin described it)[29] will produce. Fashion constitutes one dialectical element, that is, it is a purveyor, although an ambiguous one, of the critical rewriting of history as patterns by historical materialism; yet at the same time fashion carries its opposite or perhaps even its negation within itself, since it is instrumental to capitalist markers of conspicuous consumption, exploitation of the masses (cf. working conditions in the textile industry) and the materialisation and codification of social differences.

The dialectics inherent in fashion should have rendered it an important object in historical materialist thought, yet its outwardly ephemeral demeanour disqualified it from sustained critical analysis. Because it carries its frivolous opposite on the outside, clothing could not feature prominently within a new historical method. When culture was discussed in a historical materialist context, literature, painting or music were deemed relevant topics, while new developments in dressing had to be regarded as essentially bourgeois in origin and negligible with regard to their social connotations.

In Karl Marx's famous explanation of the economic fundamentals of capitalism, surplus value was described by the story of twenty yards of linen and a coat.[30] Marx did not use this example because the coat was a prominent fashion object of the 1860s,[31] but was prompted by his discussions with Friedrich Engels, whose family firm owned textile businesses in Manchester. Yet the coat served also as a 'dialectical image', as an argument that centred on negating the concrete value (of the roll of fabric) through its abstraction, which is marked by the fashionable confines in which the cut of the coat had to originate. The relation is not simply between commodity A and commodity B or between 'relative value form' and 'equivalent form' but also between raw material and cultural product, as I discussed in Chapter 1.[32]

The fact that fashion has to be set in time yet implicitly subverts its chronology carries the example beyond the obvious relation between the cloth and the clothing, and transforms it into a relation between a temporally independent product, the linen fabric, and a product with historical and cultural connotations, the cut and style of the frock coat. Therefore Marx's example includes – unintentionally perhaps – an additional observation on the codification of the product (a plus-surplus value, if you will), distinct from its original meaning. In his critique of Benjamin's historical method, the German philosopher of history H. D. Kittsteiner looked at this very example in Marx:

> The true myth of modernity is the myth of a complete heteronomy; in it no gods appear, no heroes or humans, only things. It has been told by Karl Marx: it is the story of the birth of money from the mutual reflection of twenty yards of linen and one coat.[33]

Kittsteiner called the above 'a real substratum of history',[34] which he said Benjamin refuted, and he claimed that this refusal was shared with historicism. He argued that Benjamin's interest was captured by the individual who is wearing the braided linen coat and not by the objectified surplus value generated by the piece of clothing. Yet the very fashion mentioned in the example serves as a model aid to overcome the limits of historicism, by spotting the potential of a trans-historical leap that, through a contemporary stylistic quotation, could bring the embroidered coat into the present.

In an unsettling twist, progress, and with it the acceleration of changes marked by sartorial fashion, continued to revolve around itself, due to the lack of social impetus, once capitalist modernity had established a stranglehold over Western societies. No radical novelty appeared possible,

3 Carol Christian Poell, open seam, glue-on seam allowances jacket (detail), object-tanned perforated unlined gloves (detail), 2008, male Off-Scene Collection
Photo: Deepti Barth

as the roles of men and women and what they wore had become more or less reified. Granted, certain emancipatory movements (most notably, feminism) and the acknowledgement of non-Western culture did provide some new pathways that fashion, and culture in general, could follow. But essentially, 'novel' sartorial ideas would always refer back to concepts already in existence. This glancing back, as a form of stylistic rewriting, must appear alien to established historical methods that perceive past events as individualised, unrelated and completed. Therefore, it seems imperative to appreciate fashion's significance within modernity through its potential to structure a novel manner through which the pace of modern times is shown, as well as the way in which the present employs the past. Fashion's anti-narrative is best reflected by a non-linear historical method. Yet if one were to choose, in consequence, historicism as a method, one would encounter fault-lines yet unresolved. Benjamin for one claimed that historicism could not contain all the hermeneutic possibilities for rewriting cultural history. For a probing interpretation of and challenge to the historical continuum and historicism alike, an understanding of sartorial fashion was required. And in his attempt to rewrite history, especially that of Paris in the nineteenth century, Benjamin aimed therefore at establishing foundations for a philosophy of fashion proper.

Leaping into History

Benjamin wanted to explore new approaches to interpreting history and, implicitly, writing or rewriting it. His 'Theses on the Concept of History' (of 1939/40) debated, through the neo-Kantian teachings of Heinrich Rickert and Georg Simmel and his own reading of historical materialism, the way in which historicism had tainted the impact that the past has on the present and the responsibility it carries within it. These 'Theses' also constitute some of the fundamental tenets that Benjamin was to use for his unfinished *Passagen-Werk* (*The Arcades Project*). In this study of nineteenth-century Paris, history was to be written from a novel perspective, employing both the structure of historical materialism, the evocative poetics of the Surrealists as well as Proust's literary version of the *mémoire involontaire*. Benjamin attempted to create a synthesis of a philosophy of history with the artistic perception of details from the childhood of modernity, situated in the latter half of the nineteenth century. These details were transformed through the glance back from the present to become estranged elements of commodity history, that is, fetishes able to evoke memories of customs and modes past.

The principal fetish – in both its psychoanalytical and materialist sense – and, more significantly, the catalyst for Benjamin's philosophy, was fashion. It was to be a main element in the *Arcades Project* as well as a metaphor in the exploration of Proust's writing and Surrealist perception. In one of the last 'Theses' one finds the following entry – fundamental to his understanding of both history and fashion:

> History is the subject of a construction whose site is not homogeneous, empty time, but is filled by now-time [*Jetztzeit*]. Thus, to Robespierre, ancient Rome was a past charged with now-time and blasted from the continuum of history. The French Revolution regarded itself as Rome reincarnated. It quoted ancient Rome as fashion quotes a past attire. Fashion has the scent for the modern wherever it stirs in the thicket of what has been. It is the tiger's leap into the past. Yet this leap occurs in an arena commanded by the ruling class. The same leap under the open skies of history constitutes the dialectical one, which is how Marx understood the revolution.[35]

Benjamin took this notion, as so much of his conceptual apparatus, directly from Marx and read it through his own penchant for poetic evocation within cultural history. Marx had begun his epochal *Eighteenth Brumaire of Louis Bonaparte* (1851/52) thus:

> Consideration of this world-historical necromancy reveals at once a salient difference. Camille Desmoulins, Danton, Robespierre, Saint-Just, Napoleon, the heroes as well as the parties and the masses of the old French Revolution, performed the task of their time in Roman costume and with Roman phrases, the task of unchaining and setting up modern *bourgeois* society. The first ones knocked the feudal basis to pieces and mowed off the feudal heads which had grown on it. The other created inside France the conditions under which free competition could first be developed, parcelled landed property exploited, and the unchained industrial productive forces of the nation employed; and beyond the French borders he everywhere swept the feudal institutions away, so far as was necessary to furnish bourgeois society in France with a suitable up-to-date environment on the European Continent.[36]

The principal dialectic of materialising a revolutionary act through adopting a fashion while at the same time preparing, through this very adoption, the ground for the materialism that is inherent in capitalist societies demonstrated and animated for Marx and Benjamin the debate about recurring patterns in history. A radical rupture occurred during the thinking and dressing of the French

Revolution that, in fateful irony, prepared the ground for what was to become a continuity of bourgeois progress which, in turn, would allow for reprising endlessly the motifs of past fashions for present consumption. The fetish of the sartorial commodity was born from the revolutionary change in Europe that freed up new classes: socially, but equally in terms of future consumption.

While the demonstrative adoption of a dress style can be seen as a parody, 'caricature' or indeed 'farce', as Marx judged the *coup d'état* by Napoleon's nephew,[37] the recurring of fashion activates historical events in material terms and applies them directly and concretely to the body (politic). For Benjamin, the methodological challenge lay in the way in which evaluating history had to be concerned with activating the past by injecting the present into it. Periods can be extracted from the false and positivist historical continuum and charged with 'now-time', filled with meaning and revolutionary potential for contemporary (cultural) expression. As such, the claim does not deviate from the view of historical materialism that the past must be seen as relevant for the present and for revolutionary practice in particular. But the manner in which Benjamin links history and revolution to fashion indeed appeared novel and rather idiosyncratic at first. The analogy Benjamin constructed between the way in which one social revolution quotes a previous one and the stylistic citation of a clothing style from the past within contemporary fashion was more acutely aware of its underlying implication than Marx's economic relation between the linen and the coat. Benjamin deliberately employed the sartorial commodity for its challenge to history. Fashion senses out the modern in the past, it actualises ideas that become important for the present. In doing so it follows the historical materialist dictum of history repeating itself: every past action can, in the hands of the materialist, become exemplary for the present because it will re-occur – perhaps different in appearance but certainly similar in its socio-political configuration. Thus one must revolutionise the past in order to learn from it – exactly what fashion designers claim to do when they repeatedly extol the virtues of their latest collections.

Benjamin shared the Marxist proviso towards clothing. Initially, its revolutionary impetus only occurred within the realm of the bourgeois; once this potential was freed under the 'open skies of history', that is in post-revolutionary times when historical awareness has been sharpened by the historical materialist view, then fashion would become truly a paradigm for modernity and a veritable indicator of necessary change.

Beyond the immediate reading of the 'tiger's leap' as fashion's critical potential, we find four separate additional meanings. 1) In quoting from past clothing styles fashion is able to break the historical continuum and become both transitory and trans-historical. 2) Fashion is irreverent in its quotations. Its superficial appearance creates a strange independence from recognisable contents – from there its metaphysical character can ensue. 3) Fashion is its most evocative in an imagined, 'dated' condition. The 'clothes of five years past' (as Benjamin would postulate vis-à-vis Surrealism), that is, the expression of a past that has just ceased to be fashionable, are the ones fuelling the imagination and phantasmagoria necessary for Benjamin's individual historiography. 4) The 'tiger's leap' is regarded by Benjamin as dialectical. It follows the philosophical tradition of Hegel, Engels, Marx and György Lukács. Through the sartorial quotation, fashion fuses the thesis that is the eternal or 'classical' ideal with its antithesis that is the openly contemporary. The apparent opposition between the eternal and the ephemeral is rendered obsolete by the leap that needs the past for any continuation of the present. Correspondingly, the trans-historical describes the position of fashion as detached both from the eternal, that is, an aesthetic ideal, and the continuous progression of history. Through the *Tigersprung*, fashion is able to leap from the contemporary to the ancient and back again without coming to rest exclusively in one temporal or aesthetic configuration. This generates a novel view of historical development. When coupled with the 'dialectical image', the tiger's leap 'under the open skies of history' marks a convergence that is revolutionary in essence.

The idea that a revolution – the transitory in history per se – quotes from the past in a manner similar to fashion applies Marx's political thought to aesthetics. The politically charged reification and abstraction of society is intimately bound to its latest sartorial appearance, as fashion exemplifies the political-economic power structure of capitalism in such a potent manner. Suddenly a temporal entity from the past is, through a stylistic quote, isolated in its impact (a genuinely materialist virtue) and thrown into the now. The historian takes a great leap to find the instantaneous and immediate in what has long gone. In German a *Katzensprung* (cat's leap) is the expression for something very close, something that is just a stone's-throw away. In the figure of the *Tigersprung* where the much bigger and more ferocious feline takes one great leap to land motionless on a far-away spot, the historical materialist method had thus found its precise and poetic metaphor.

Sartorial Remembrance

For Benjamin, sartorial fashion did not simply accompany a positivist history of progress towards ever-greater prosperity, by pitching more intricate, sumptuous or luxurious clothes to a greater number of people through technical developments, facilitated manufacture or more inclusive shopping environments. The sewing machines, improved pattern cutting or new department stores did not render Western capitalism a more egalitarian place, but simply widened the consumer base for its commodities. When equality was achieved, it was not equality before the law, not in regard to accessing cultural expression, but first and foremost equality *qua* the commodified object.

Yet fashion had, for Benjamin at least, a paradigmatic quality up its embroidered sleeve. Combining his reading of Marx and Engels with an intimate knowledge of Baudelaire and Proust, Benjamin singled out the quotation, the *mémoire involontaire* contained in clothing as characteristic for modernity. In fashion, quotation is sartorial remembrance, able to create an intricate temporal relation as well as charting metaphysical experience. For Benjamin, at home in both German and French, it was obvious that *modernité/mode* and *Modernität/Mode* shared a close etymological relation, a structural family union in which one term contained the other. Fashion requires quotation to rewrite its own history, yet not to hide past imperfection or stylistic sins but to allow for change, in which the latest sartorial motif can have recourse to an earlier one and thus evaluate again its impact for the present. The past is activated for the present and, significantly, in fashion design the present very quickly aligns itself with its own past. The philosopher and critic of the Frankfurt School Alfred Schmidt described in his work *History and Structure* how critical theory, when founded in the historical materialist method and 'aiming at a "revolutionary practice" [*umwälzende Praxis*], breaks with the capitalist immediacy, which daily deludes individuals with a nature-like invariance of their life relationships'.[38] The systemic immediacy of capitalism, its fronting of an ephemeral present and the presence of fashion therein are emblematic of the 'unhistorical and antihistorical character of bourgeois thought', wrote Schmidt, citing from Lukács's epochal work *History and Class Consciousness*. This shortcoming 'manifests itself most strikingly "when we consider the problem of the present as a historical problem"'.[39] The capitalist system glosses over the contradiction between the present and historical process, the synchronic and diachronic perception of history, because the historicism of isolated past events can thus be combined with the commodification of the now. Continuously, the immediate present is required as the engine for consumption, while the history of past systemic contradictions and patterns of conflict should be ignored. Fashion appears ambiguous in this context, as its 'tiger's leap' into the past isolates diachronically a figure or idea from history, yet activates it for the present and thereby underscores the notion of repeated configurations and patterns in the historical process. Fashion's dialectic lies in its profound immediacy which operates simultaneously as revolutionary breaks with the historical continuum. It appears historicist in its isolating of the historical momentum, but because it always leaps back into the commodity fetishism of the now it renders apparent a structure-transforming *praxis*.

For the historian, this dialectic view of fashion as contemporary *phenomenon* as well as historical *pattern* or *structure* is rendered more complex by the sociological assessment of how the latest trend in clothing or accessories is regarded as *passé* the very moment it reaches a wider audience. The present vanguard of fashion perceives its own present almost immediately as history because constant changes in the clothing industry have been accelerated to such a degree that invention, quotation and outright copy can become distinctive only through the isolated image and commercial potential of the designer, rather than through the actual chronology of the fashionable novelty.

The sartorial quotation instigates for the materialist historian a dialectical relationship between the ultra-modern present, that is, the latest twenty-first-century trend in dressing, and its 'prehistoric' past, the capitalist modernity of the nineteenth century that established the parameters for fashion's social and historical significance. Schmidt described how Marx 'refuses merely to register the reified, pseudo-objective structures of capitalist everyday life, but seeks instead to bring the history congealed in them back to life, he comes up against the specifically human, if deformed, reality'.[40] Like capital, which is not a mere fact but a 'relation between two people',[41] historical developments are remembered and enlivened through human behaviour and appearances. The events that were evoked in Benjamin's *Tigersprung* were particularly exemplified through clothing, establishing an intimate, corporeal relation between historical protagonists. Once again, sartorial quotation was the key: the July and February revolutions of 1830 and 1848 in France were also attempts to have recourse to the morals and ethics of the 1789/91 'original'. They were cited 'like fashion quotes a past attire'. For many, the ideals of antique Rome were re-dressed (and potentially redressed) to remind the public of the virtues of the French Revolutions. For other historical actors, as can be observed in the vacuous Empire fashion after 1800, the socio-political revolution was transcribed as a sartorial one, filled with Napoleonic grandeur and contemporary chic.

The Fashionable Commodity

Benjamin ascribed to all former epochs a multitude of expectations that had been left unfulfilled. 'The past carries with it a secret index, which refers it to its redemption',[42] he wrote in the late 1930s. A present that eagerly awaits the future has the task of remembering its past and accomplishing what had been expected. No original *Querelle des anciens et modernes*,[43] no ideological opposition between favouring the ancient or the modern exists for Benjamin, but a synthesis of the archaic and modernity within the object – positively in fashion's potential to leap, and negatively in the 'hell of commodities' that characterised Paris in the nineteenth century. This is why in Benjamin's 'dialectical image', above all in his *Tigersprung*, one conflicting element folds into the other. In these images the archaic gels with modern (aesthetic) expression. It contains both the threat of a repetition of past errors as well as a generic force that counterbalances the destructive potential of modernity to reify society and alienate man. This generic force is the 'redemption' Benjamin describes. It is distinguished by a mythical quality found in the remnants of commodities from a past century. When fashion makes its own use of these remnants by quoting past attires for new styles, it visualises and materialises the demand that was raised by Benjamin's dialectical image on an epistemological level.

In a letter dating from 1935 the philosopher Theodor W. Adorno questioned this very notion of his friend Benjamin. He cast doubt on both the redemption and the mythical character that the commodity was to contain:

> To understand the commodity as a dialectical image simply means to understand it also as the motif of its own demise and its 'abolition' [*Aufhebung*], instead of regarding it as pure regression to the old. On the one hand, the commodity is the alienated object and thus its utility value has withered away, on the other hand it is a surviving object that, having become alien, outlives its immediacy.[44]

When discussing the perception of the dated dress either as a quote or as merely of 'historic' interest, one has to look at its respective role as a commodity. The bustled dress from the 1880s is the commodity whose utility value has died, since one could not wear such a dress and expect to appear as anything but in disguise or in costume. On the other hand, putting on a bustled dress that is a sartorial quotation (our example from Christian Dior Haute Couture) means sporting a commodity that, after Adorno, has 'outlived its immediacy' because it has been alienated from its origin and activated for the present. Obviously, a truly fashionable design can never hope to be anything but the present; it will not be capable of overcoming it, for, as we have seen, it then would cease to exist as fashion and enter another function as an object, perhaps that of the 'eternal' artwork.

What the fashion commodity can achieve, however, is to escape its demise by ironically advancing its death and perpetually renewing itself. When the design has been 'accepted' into the sartorial mainstream, the actual innovation dies and the process of inventing and promoting a new style or look begins anew. The rewriting of (costume) history thus continues in rapid instalments, and by constantly prompting its own 'abolition' fashion avoids any regressive tendency. Therefore, the one commodity that is tailor-made as a dialectical image must be clothing, and Benjamin accordingly exemplified it in his tiger's leap.

Adorno concurred with Benjamin when he saw the pressure of future problems demanding a present ready to act with responsibility towards the past and at the same time becoming aware of the implications that its actions carry for the future. In extending this awareness retrospectively to the past, Benjamin created an intricate pattern of a future open to alternatives, a 'mobilised' past (visualised by sartorial fashion) and, in its midst, a transient present. 'Fashion is the eternal recurrence of the new. – Nevertheless, are there motives for redemption to be found especially in fashion?'[45] he asked, formulating the question vital for his own historiography. For a present that has become transient – thus, for Baudelaire and Benjamin, synonymous with modernity – fashion represents its essence. Not its substance, as its ephemeral characteristics deny it that, but a concentrated extract, which in embodying the 'now-time', together with an open reference to the past, can claim to constitute a beckoning future. Benjamin's interpretation of fashion allowed him to combine both the metaphysical side of a messianic past and the materialist side of socio-historical critique. The latter, although influenced by Engels' and Marx's critical reading of Hegel, did not consist of orthodox dialectics, but rather the 'aestheticisation' of the dialectical method (as Benjamin put it), as well as his own application of historical materialism. Because Marxism only became influential at a late stage in the *Arcades Project*, from circa 1934 onwards, the numerous references to a new form of social, cultural and historical critique, although progressive in appearance, always had to remain in progress. But Benjamin's efforts to discard historicism were determined enough to lead to a wholehearted embrace of its historical materialist opposition. An intricate historical pattern woven from yarns that symbolised related yet chronologically unconnected occurrences in, for example, Parisian revolutions was more important than following through the positivist continuum of a superficially observed social fabric throughout the nineteenth century.

To conclude this chapter I would like to give a brief example of how the dialectical image of the tiger's leap can be visualised in the collection of a fashion designer. This will not be a simple stylistic leap, as for example in the *Directoire* dresses that cited between 1795 and 1810 the civic virtues of Hellenist/Roman democracies and were subsequently revived in the sartorially revolutionary dispensing of the corset by Poiret's high-waisted designs a hundred years later. My example is rather based on changing production methods and materials. It befits therefore the need to materialise in a discipline such as fashion (and fashion studies, too) production-as-consumption – and vice versa. At the same time, the varying ways of making the shapes and motifs on the dresses emphasise the Benjaminian 'eternal recurrence of the new' as a desire to maintain the identity of a design house or brand.

Diorama: Conserving Novelties

> It seems odd that in 1956 people would pin the label of 'avant-garde' on men and works that we admired between the ages of fifteen and twenty, and who had already been known for ten years to our more enlightened elders, led by Guillaume Apollinaire.[46]

So wrote Christian Dior in his second autobiography, *Christian Dior et moi*. The sense that the avant-garde in art is repeating itself years later under different circumstances and in a different setting is profoundly influenced by Dior's experience in fashion. The latest styles and trends are suffering from a time lapse with regard to their distribution: first to 'the most alert of our elders', then to the youngsters who, like Dior as co-owner of a gallery in his twenties, moved in and out of progressive art circles and, finally, to the wider public. Yet avant-garde tendencies in art and fashion are also bound to be remade and rechristened at a later date in order to explore new materials and techniques, to see how a novel production method can be applied to an existing motif. Dior's stylistic trademarks followed this dictum, not simply in the gowns and dresses he created but equally in the formal identity of his couture house. His aesthetics had been formed by the neoclassicism of friends such as Jean Cocteau (for example, in films such as *Le Sang d'un poète* (1930), with its classicist statues coming to life, or *Orphée* of 1950), illustrator Christian Bérard[47] or his gallery-partner Jacques Paul Bonjean, who collected eighteenth-century French art. In 1946, for the inauguration of his *maison de couture*, Dior called on the historicism of decorator Victor Grandpierre to remake a salon in the style of Louis XVI, surrounding the latest fashion with a material reminder of the past. This recreation of an eighteenth-century aesthetic marks a complex 'tiger's leap', as the Louis XVI style had been neoclassical itself, evoking antiquity in the 1770s in the guise of contemporary furniture and tableware as much as costume. The 1946 remaking of Louis XVI chairs with 'medallion' backrests for Dior – a signature design that is in use for the brand even today – was in tune with his more abstract approach to a classical tradition. The first collections that were shown in Dior's Louis XVI salon, 'Corolle' et 'En 8' (in the figure of eight), were characterised thus by the couturier in retrospect:

> The success of the New Look (if I may dare to commingle a moment of fashion with something as profound as an evolution) was due to its being in the spirit of the epoch, an epoch that sought to leave the mechanical and inhuman in order to rediscover its traditions and constants.[48]

The 'new' look is in fact a return to tradition, a stylistic conceit that enveloped women in silhouettes and fabrics that harked back to previous centuries, when the couture of the nobility had been regarded as the sole tastemaker. In dialectical fashion, the 'constants' Dior spoke of are not evoked by a linear, continuing timeline but by select leaps back into neoclassical, socially conservative periods of Western culture, when political power structures found particular formal expressions that were characterised by a profusion of exclusive, labour-intensive materials under the guise of pared-down aesthetics for consumption by a wealthy elite. Correspondingly, Dior's work of the late 1940s is defined by an extravagant use of fabrics – especially in the context of post-war deprivation in Europe – realised as formally constrained silhouettes that define the wearer in terms of numbers or letters: from 'En 8' (1947) to the 'lignes H, A and Y' of 1954.

Yet Dior's materiality is not only a historicising, aesthetic choice but is marked by a historically pertinent economic strategy. La Maison Dior was founded in 1946 with a capital of 60 million French francs by Marcel Boussac, one of the principal textile manufacturers in France, who had inherited his father's *enterprise de confection*, and enlarged it through specialising in printed cottons but also by exploring surplus *toile d'avion* (formerly used for covering the wings of First World War biplanes), acquiring a roster of fabric manufacturers in France and North Africa and supplying uniforms to the occupying German army in the 1940s. After the war Boussac focused on Dior as reviving the self-reflexive tradition of haute couture, initially tailoring elaborate designs from readily available and (partly) mass-produced fabrics and subsequently innovating exclusive new silks and wools, made in the factories of the parent company, le Groupe Boussac.[49] Dior's remit was to demonstrate the most extensive use of fabric within designs, and this was realised by dramatically increasing the circumference of the lower part of the dresses and gowns, set in stark contrast to the fitted top by a cinched-in waist. This went to extremes, as in the 80 metres of silk that made up the volume of the 'Chérie' (spring/summer collection 1947), for which Dior used fabrics that Boussac had left over from parachute silk production during the war and that were therefore not subject to post-war material rationing in France.

An impression of an eighteenth-century court scenario with a profusion of soft materials floating around the lower part of the female body, tight bustiers that emphasise the décolleté and rounded shoulders that soften the silhouette is transposed into post-war Paris to evoke a continuous history of exclusive consumption while concretely quoting from formal ideas of previous centuries – all under the auspices of a conservative market strategy.[50] Dior assessed his own approach: 'Temperamentally I am reactionary [*réactionnaire*], not to be confused with backward looking [*rétrograde*].'[51] In the context of fashion, the stepping back in time appears as an ultimate sin while the temperament of the reactionary is actually suited to couture, serving as it does the establishment with a mere mirage of new appearances.

What are the structural implications of such an approach? Dior paralleled his comment on the recurring avant-garde by pronouncing a historical pattern. '"Fashion dies young", wrote Cocteau, and it is therefore natural that its rhythm should be more hectic than that of history.'[52] He continued to discern a trickle-down effect in this breathless pursuit of sartorial novelties, but equally suggested, like Benjamin, the eternal recurrence of the new as the structural need in fashion to renew itself constantly in order to pursue its economic objectives. 'When fashion spreads itself and is disseminated in the street, in the moment before it becomes a general fashion, it is de-fashioned and overtaken by itself [*elle se démodé d'elle-même*].'⁵³ As Simmel had remarked more cyclically at the end of the nineteenth century, fashion always dies at the moment it becomes accepted in order to be reborn the next instant.⁵⁴ In order to maintain this rhythmical structure, past styles need to be revived and re-contextualised at defined intervals, which are marked by shifts in socio-political mores, through contemporary material production.

In Dior's designs we can see a constant effort to preserve the *mémoire involontaire* which Benjamin had taken from Baudelaire and Proust to advance formal experimentation in haute couture. Yet this memory is necessarily selective in material terms, in quoting historical designs as much as continuing a tradition of consumption. For Dior, the use of traditional models is a material necessity demanded by the fashion system and the economic system that supported his work. The conflation of these systems in constantly revising historical models accounts for Dior's success – especially in a period of political and social reconstruction after the Second World War. It is perhaps ironic that the term chosen by an American fashion journalist for Dior's designs of 1947 was 'the new look', since there was nothing structurally 'new' about it. On the contrary, it continued and revived existing models in representing women and consuming fashion – but within a new productive environment.

Notes

1. Jean Ferry, 'Le Tigre mondain' [1953], in *Le Mécanicien et autres contes* (Paris: Maren Sell/Calmann-Lévy, 1992), p. 105; Eng. trans. by J. Stewart, 'The Fashionable Tiger', in *French Short Stories/Nouvelles Françaises 1* (Harmondsworth: Penguin, 1966), p. 103.
2. We will encounter this methodological challenge again in the next chapter on semiotics, fashion and materialism.
3. The *Tigersprung* comes from a text entitled 'Theses on the Concept of History', written between 1939 and 1940. These theses were an integral part of Benjamin's unfinished, posthumously published collection of writings, *The Arcades Project*. In this project, fashion occupies the largest manuscript sheaf, and the references collected for this topic encompass a multitude of approaches, from anecdotes and travellers' journals to literary and philosophical texts.
4. Didier Grumbach, *Histoires de la Mode* (Paris: Seuil, 1993), p. 11.
5. For an overview of the early development of the couture industry, see

the first two parts of Olivier Saillard (ed.), *Paris Haute Couture* (Paris: Flammarion, 2012), pp. 18–61.
6. See the recollections on national high fashion and politics by the former president of the Chambre syndical de la haute couture, Jacques Mouclier, *Haute Couture* (Paris: Laffont, 2004), pp. 55–62 *et passim*.
7. See Louis Blanc, *Organisation du travail* (Paris: Administration de librairie, 1841), 'Éclaircissement sur les doctrines du Luxembourg' [1850], in: *Histoire de la Révolution de 1848*, vol. 2 (Paris: Marpon/Flammarion, 1880), pp. 273–305, as well as Jean-Michel Humilière, *Louis Blanc (1811–1882)* (Paris: Éditions ouvrières, 1982), pp. 148–9.
8. Rudolf von Jhering, 'Die Mode', in *Der Zweck im Recht* [1877/1883] (Leipzig: Breitkopf & Härtel, 1905), pp. 180–9, here p. 187 (my translation). All translations from foreign languages are my own unless otherwise indicated.
9. Ibid. In the first volume of his book, first published in 1877, Jhering had discussed (folkloristic) dress (*Tracht*) in terms that determined his subsequent views on fashion; see *Der Zweck im Recht*, pp. 243–57.
10. Émile Durkheim, 'La Science positive de la morale en Allemagne' [pt. 1], *Revue philosophique de la France et de l'étranger*, 12.24 (1887), pp. 33–58, here p. 57.
11. Gabriel Tarde, *Les Lois de l'imitation* [1890] (Paris: Alcan, 1895), pp. 265–394; Eng. trans. by E. C. Parsons, *The Laws of Imitation* (New York: Holt, 1903), pp. 255–365.
12. Jhering, *Der Zweck im Recht*, p. 186.
13. See Georg Simmel, 'Fashion' [1904], in *On Individuality and Social Forms* (Chicago: University of Chicago Press, 1971), pp. 317–18. Simmel was profoundly influenced by Tarde's book on imitation, which he had reviewed upon its publication in France.
14. For a comprehensive account of materialism as a philosophical approach, see Friedrich Albert Lange, *The History of Materialism and Criticism of Its Present Importance* [1866], trans. E. C. Thomas (Boston: Osgood, 1877). This book remains very relevant as a reference, I would argue, for its origins in the discussion of materialism in the latter half of the nineteenth century as well as for the author's shifting political position. Lange had been a member of the first Internationale, founded in London by Marx and others in 1864, and was a friend of the prominent German socialist August Bebel. Yet Lange's history of materialism is neo-Kantian and idealist in its method (rather than Hegelian) and thereby appears revisionist with regard to materialism's critical application to social and economic development. Lange's book provided the basis for much of the discussion of materialist positions in early twentieth-century philosophy (e.g. Edmund Husserl's 'idealist' conception of phenomenology or Martin Heidegger's views on technology), which was almost entirely divested from analyses in political economy or practice.
15. See the historiographical development in Karl Marx and Friedrich

Engels, *The German Ideology* [1845–46], in Marx and Engels, *Collected Works*, vol. 5 (London: Lawrence & Wishart, 1973); then its application to contemporary politics in Marx's *The Eighteenth Brumaire of Louis Napoleon* [1851–52], in Marx and Engels, *Collected Works*, vol. 11 (London: Lawrence & Wishart, 1979), chs 1, 3 and 7; and the division in Engels' *Anti-Dühring*, in Marx and Engels, *Collected Works*, vol. 25 (London: Lawrence & Wishart, 1987), between Part 1: Philosophy and Part 2: Political Economy; and finally his, rather reductive, account in *Socialism: Utopian and Scientific* [1880], in Marx and Engels, *Collected Works*, vol. 24 (London: Lawrence & Wishart, 1989), pp. 281–324.
16. This can lead to quite erroneous conclusions, since the term *Historizismus* has been deployed very prominently by the conservative, positivist thinker Karl Popper to critique the universalising patterns in Hegel's and Marx's philosophy of history and their value for social and political predictions.
17. See Leopold von Ranke, *Ursprung und Beginn der Revolutionskriege 1791 und 1792* (*Origin and Beginning of the Revolutionary Wars 1791 and 1792*) (Leipzig: Dunker & Humblot, 1875); or, in philosophy, Wilhelm Dilthey, *Hermeneutics and the Study of History, Selected Works, vol. IV* [selected historiographical essays from 1860 through to 1903] (Princeton: Princeton University Press, 2010). For a retrospective critical assessment, see Benedetto Croce, *Theory and History of Historiography* [essays from 1912/13] (London: Harrap, 1921).
18. Alexis de Tocqueville, *Democracy in America* [two volumes, 1835/40], trans. A. Goldhammer (New York: Library of America, 2004).
19. Fredric Jameson, 'Marxism and Historicism', *New Literary History*, IX.1 (1979), pp. 41–73, here p. 43.
20. 'Comedy – or more precisely: the pure joke – is the essential inner side of mourning which from time to time, like the lining of a dress or the hem or lapel, makes its presence felt.' Walter Benjamin, 'Der Ursprung des deutschen Trauerspiels' [1924/25], in *Gesammelte Schriften I.1* (Frankfurt a.M.: Suhrkamp, 1991), p. 304; see also 'Pariser Tagebuch' [1929/30], in *Gesammelte Schriften IV.1* (Frankfurt a.M.: Suhrkamp, 1991), p. 584; Eng. trans. by J. Osborne, *The Origin of German Tragic Drama* (London: NLB, 1977), pp. 126–7.
21. An approach that is not dissimilar to Benjamin's attempt in the 1930s to fuse his understanding of historical materialism, informed by the nascent Frankfurt School of critical theory, with the open discourses of cultural critique by writers such as Edward Fuchs, the sociologist Georg Simmel or the Parisian Surrealists.
22. Jameson, 'Marxism and Historicism', p. 43.
23. This is less a phenomenological reflex than a psychological mechanism that tends to establish initially our own particular object-relation before we begin to contextualise – to varying degrees – the artefact.
24. As digital prints rather than woven into the fabric or embroidered on

to it – see the above reference to production techniques as markers of innovation.
25. Fredric Jameson, *The Political Unconscious* [1981] (London: Routledge, 1996), p. 21. Jameson's terminology appears ambivalent with regard to opposing historicism to contemporary forms of historical materialism. Partly, this might be due to problems in translating German terms such as *Historizmus*, i.e. historicism as it was employed by historians like Leopold von Ranke, and Karl Popper's critique of the Marxist rewriting of history as *Historizismus*. However, in his effort to substantiate present historical materialist methods against a post-structuralist critique in France, Jameson too readily accepts the Popperian equation of the historicist method with dialectical or materialist ones without any attempt to highlight the resulting methodological confusion.
26. Sándor Radnóti has made a similar point in discussing the relationship between Hans-Georg Gadamer's hermeneutics and Benjamin; see Sándor Radnóti, 'Benjamin's Dialectic of Art and Society', in Gary Smith (ed.), *Benjamin: Philosophy, History, Aesthetics* (Chicago: University of Chicago Press, 1989), pp. 126–57.
27. Reinhart Koselleck, *Vergangene Zukunft: Zur Semantik geschichtlicher Zeiten* [1979] (Frankfurt a.M.: Surhkamp, 1985), p. 19; Eng. trans. by K. Tribe, *Futures Past: On the Semantics of Historical Time* (Cambridge, MA: MIT Press, 1985), p. 5.
28. Ibid., p. 34; Eng. trans., p. 17.
29. Walter Benjamin, 'On the Concept of History' [1939/40], in *Selected Writings*, vol. 4 (Cambridge, MA: Belknap Press of Harvard University Press, 2006), p. 396. The more complete, and oddly 'macho', quote in Thesis XVI runs: 'Historicism offers the "eternal" image with the past; historical materialism supplies a unique experience with the past. The historical materialist leaves it to others to be drained by the whore called "Once upon a time" in historicism's bordello. He remains in control of his powers, man enough to blast open the continuum of history.' See also the convolute entries N9a,6 to N10,3 in Walter Benjamin, *The Arcades Project* (Cambridge, MA: Belknap Press of Harvard University Press, 1999), pp. 474–5.
30. Karl Marx, *Capital*, vol. 1 [1867/90], in Marx and Engels, *Collected Works*, vol. 35 (London: Lawrence & Wishart, 1996), pp. 59 *et passim*. *Das Kapital* was first published in 1867; the fourth edition of 1890 (edited by Engels) is generally accepted as the most authoritative.
31. Neither did Marx use his *Gehrock* to solve the financial problems of his London household, as Peter Stallybrass has argued in his biographical-revisionist narrative on 'Marx's Coat', in Patricia Spyer (ed.), *Border Fetishisms: Material Objects in Unstable Spaces* (London: Routledge, 1998), pp. 183–208.
32. In the first volume of *Capital* (pp. 68–9) Marx makes a similar transposition, but here the distinction lay between the weaving of the linen as 'concrete work' and the tailoring of the coat as 'abstract work'.

33. H. D. Kittsteiner, 'Walter Benjamin's Historicism', *New German Critique*, 39 (1986), pp. 179–215. The English-language version of this article wrongly translates on p. 214 *Rock* ('coat' in nineteenth-century German usage) as 'skirt' (the contemporary meaning of the word). In order to avoid altering the meaning of the metaphor discussed, I have preferred to use my own translation from the German original: 'Walter Benjamins Historismus', in Nobert Bolz and Bern Witte (eds), *Passagen: Walter Benjamin's Urgeschichte des XIX. Jahrhunderts* (Munich: Fink, 1984), p. 196.
34. Kittsteiner, 'Walter Benjamin's Historicism', p. 214.
35. Benjamin, 'On the Concept of History', p. 395 [translation modified].
36. Marx, *The Eighteenth Brumaire*, p. 104.
37. See the famous opening lines of his *Eighteenth Brumaire* that render concrete and political G. W. F. Hegel's philosophy of history: 'Hegel remarks somewhere that all great world-historic facts and personages appear, so to speak, twice. He forgot to add: the first time as tragedy, the second time as farce.' Marx, *The Eighteenth Brumaire*, p. 103.
38. Alfred Schmidt, *Geschichte und Struktur: Fragen einer marxistischen Historik* [1971] (Berlin: Ullstein, 1978), p. 131; Eng. trans. by J. Herf, *History and Structure: An Essay on Hegelian-Marxist and Structuralist Theories of History* (Cambridge, MA: MIT Press, 1981), p. 104.
39. Ibid. The citation is from György Lukács, *History and Class Consciousness* (Cambridge, MA: MIT Press, 1971), p. 157.
40. Schmidt, *History and Structure*, p. 61.
41. See the opening of the second chapter of *Capital*, vol. 1, pp. 101–2.
42. Benjamin, 'On the Concept of History', p. 390 [translation modified].
43. Charles Perrault's famous debate (initiated in 1688) between antiquity and the modern, whereby contemporariness renders antique models obsolete – in literature and, by extension, also in social and political thought. This 'quarrel' marked the beginning of a discourse on modernity in Europe. Charles Perrault, *Parallèle des anciens et des modernes en ce qui regarde les arts et les sciences* [1693], ed. Hans-Robert Jauß (Munich: Eidos, 1964). See also Joseph M. Levine, *The Battle of the Books: History and Literature in the Augustan Age* (Ithaca, NY: Cornell University Press, 1991).
44. Theodor W. Adorno to Walter Benjamin, letter dated Hornberg i. Schwarzwald, 2 August 1935, in *The Correspondence of Walter Benjamin 1910–1940*, trans. M. R. and E. M. Jacobson (Chicago: University of Chicago Press, 1994), pp. 497–8 [translation modified]; Benjamin's letters were edited by his friends Gershom Scholem and Theodor W. Adorno in the early 1970s.
45. Walter Benjamin, 'Central Park' [1939/40], *New German Critique*, 34 (winter 1985), pp. 32–58, here p. 46. The text was published as the concluding part to Benjamin's study of Charles Baudelaire in 1939/40.
46. Christian Dior, *Dior by Dior: The Autobiography of Christian Dior* [1956] (New York: Dutton, 1957), p. 224.

47. Bérard would decorate Dior's first boutique with updated versions of the late eighteenth-century printed cottons, the *toiles de Jouy*.
48. Christian Dior, *Je suis couturier* (Paris: Éditions du Conquistador, 1951), p. 126.
49. An overview of the business relationship between Boussac and Dior can be gleaned from Celia Bertin, *Haute Couture: terre inconnue* (Paris: Hachette, 1956), pp. 190–5, and Tomoko Okawa, 'Licensing Practices at Maison Christina Dior', in Regina Lee Blaszczyk (ed.), *Producing Fashion: Commerce, Culture and Consumers* (Philadelphia, PA: University of Pennsylvania Press, 2008), pp. 82–107.
50. The term 'conservative' is here not used in the socio-political sense but as pertaining to cultural conservation. Tellingly, Dior remembered his travels of 1931 when he had sought out political and economic alternatives: 'The desperate search for a new solution to the problems raised by our capitalist crisis drove me, quite naively, to put together a few thousand francs and join a group of architects who were leaving for a study trip to the U.S.S.R.' Dior, *Dior by Dior*, p. 231.
51. Ibid., p. 39.
52. Ibid., p. 83.
53. Dior, *Je suis couturier*, p. 56.
54. Simmel, 'Fashion', p. 302.

Chapter 3

Sartorial Semantics:
Le Mot dans la mode

The first two chapters prepared the theoretical ground for the dialectic of fashion and materialism. The first looked at the way in which political economy has used fashion to explain and critique cyclical renewal as well as the relationship between production and consumption; the second explored how such a critique has been extended to structuring anew the understanding of history as written. In the present chapter I want to move on to *writing fashion* more particularly; to the representation of textiles as text under the auspices of an internalised and originally self-referential fashion system, in which the written word became forced by socio-economic and cultural demands to adhere to a rule of constantly changing novelties (ideas, commodities, mores). Here, materialism, as an approach to simultaneously assessing objects via their materiality and economic position, is used to explain a structure in which the artist is forced to confront the material value of her or his writing, and must consider how such a forced confrontation can be made creatively productive, either by a conspicuous following of trends, an ironic comment on the system, or by its subversion. I want to show how such acts of confrontation were self-reflexive, due to the already established parameters for artistic practice in modernity, as well as the subjective character of the chosen texts, which were carefully designed to emulate, satirise and play with visual as well as semantic styles and trends.

In this third chapter the reading becomes more literal but at the same time more abstract. On the one hand I am looking at texts, not at textiles. On the other hand, the genre and type of texts – on fashion, dress and clothing – were designed/written as objects/products that have to be understood for their cultural position and not simply for their semantic content. In this context the conceptual pairing of materialism and fashion becomes manifest in the attempts to form clothes into words, sentences and narratives, whereby the endeavours veer towards formal experiments in literature that approximate fashion as a concept: as an absolutely contemporary, constantly changing expression in close proximity to the body. Thereby the subject–object relation – the more abstract argument in this chapter – can be anchored concretely in manifestations that are current and more commonly understood. Although an obvious exclusivity and absolute elitism infuses the designs in early French haute couture, this exclusivity/elitism also pervades the literary examples cited here, across the contemporary modernist poetry and prose of the latter half of the nineteenth century that aimed to represent its own material meaning and value.

The latter aspect can be taken 'literally'. For the writers discussed in this chapter, the material value of fashion lay in the form of dresses, boots, veils, jackets, hats, etc. that were innovated by *couturiers* and *couturières*; and the changing forms of these sartorial innovations were to be brought into semantic structures that aimed to be as contemporary and fashionable as the objects they described. Fashion, as an idea and as a system, prompted modern writers to find new forms of expression and to embrace change rather than eternal aesthetic values as guiding principles for their cultural production.

I would like to focus on three writers: Honoré de Balzac, Jules Barbey d'Aurevilly and Stéphane Mallarmé. Such a selection obviously cannot be representative of the gamut of Parisian novelists or poets who wrote about fashion, let alone account for the many writers around France, Europe and the rest of the nineteenth-century world who used clothing, dress or costume as their subject matter. One reason for selecting these three men, in the context of their artistic reputation and their established position in the canon of Western literature, is the fact that they all chose a female pseudonym to author their texts. They thereby reversed and subverted the expectations of contemporary literary production – most prominently that which claimed that if you wanted to succeed as a progressive novelist or poet, you had better not be female, a viewpoint that George Sand in France and George Eliot in Britain exemplified at the time. By using men who wrote as women for my examples, I want to contextualise the gender and sexual politics that surrounded fashion and cultural production in the second half of the nineteenth century in Europe. But, since I continue to focus on the materialism of fashion and not on fashion's function within a cultural discourse, these aspects become complementary to the analysis of the literary *products* of Balzac, Barbey d'Aurevilly and Mallarmé.

The quantifiable material aspect of a literary product can be, but must not be, commensurate with its materiality. What are the material circumstances of its production, publication and distribution (the latter two are obviously interrelated); when, how and by whom can it be consumed (restriction of access); what is its value in the culture industry (aesthetic plus economic considerations)? A limited edition for an exclusive audience of cultural cognoscenti accrues a different material value than a populist text in a daily newspaper – simply based on an economic measure of acquisition and sale price. Which, obviously, says little or nothing about any intellectual or aesthetic value of the literary product. In the following we will see that the examples from written fashion approximate the ephemeral and disposable character of its subject matter. Fashions come and go, so the texts devoted to them must be of the moment and are perceived to lose currency and aesthetic credo when the style and trend they describe move on.

Because the exclusive materiality and material value of high fashion at the time of Balzac's, Barbey d'Aurevilly's and Mallarmé's writing stood in emphatic contrast with its limited temporality and its apparent negation of lasting cultural value, the authors found in fashion the dialectics that they were eager to explore as stylistic tropes. Because the costs of fabric, trimmings and accessories and the labour costs of the artisans making the haute couture are so extreme, the brevity of its fashionable lifespan appears counter-intuitive at first. The product seems an absurd one, in which materialism is exponentiated to an absolute: in high fashion, the most costly materials and the greatest amount of labour produce a cultural product that assumes value for the shortest period of time – immediately after which further material, labour and cost need to be expended to create another fashionable product. The materiality of couture negates itself. It is at the same time the most substantial – carefully woven and decorated fabrics draped and tailored by hand – and the most transitory – its value is voided after a season or two when a new style comes about. The writers cited in this chapter were fascinated and appalled in equal measure by the dialectics of contemporary couture. Yet they also found therein the contemporariness that they craved. They distinguished their texts on fashion from habitual journalism by rendering them literary products – for instance, inventing words and syntax, as I will mention below – while placing them in the context of the fashion journal. For example, in Mallarmé's editorship of *La Dernière Mode* an entire context was built from the ground up in order to suggest a contemporary and transitory meaning for his writing. The authors were exclusive, but only for a short time; the rarity of their literary product did not reside in wilfully modernist experimentation, esoteric subject matter or rare editions (like so much of the output of the Romantics, Parnassians and Symbolists who surrounded them); it was achieved by placing texts in short-lived, fashionable journals that were casually skimmed by readers who remained unaware of the literary aspirations and prowess of the modernist poets hidden behind the (female) pseudonyms. The news on the fashion industry hawked by these fictional journalists thus united aesthetic template, subject matter, cultural structure – and a potential critique of materialism – in their particular literary output.

I would like to stress again that Balzac, Barbey d'Aurevilly and Mallarmé took a real interest in the materiality of the gowns, dresses and accessories they described. They learned about textiles, trimmings and colours, and how to use and invent a specialised vocabulary for them. So their materialism was a concrete one, in knowing about material and techniques and in communicating such specific information in their writing. Yet it was also a metaphorical one, in being acutely aware of the significance and value of their chosen subject matter. Their shared technique of literary cross-dressing suggests that the three men knew much about the contested cultural legitimacy of fashion. Thus they simultaneously introduced fashion as a subject of literary contemplation, as a substantial field of investigation and as an indicator of a new sensibility that was to pervade the second half of the nineteenth century, namely the notion of modernity. Modernity, or, better, *modernité* as Théophile Gautier's neologism of 1852 would have it, denotes an idea of a modern culture, of a material production of objects that expressively deals with the representation of modern times and embraces their fleeting and changeable nature. Gone were the epochs when cultural producers had to follow the classical canon and emulate models from antiquity to communicate contemporary ideas. Gautier wrote in his review of the annual Parisian art exhibition of the *Salon*:

> Therefore it is wrong to affect a certain revulsion or at least a certain disdain towards purely contemporary expressions. On our part, we think that there are new effects and unexpected aspects in the intelligent and faithful representation of what we should call *la modernité*. Thus when it comes to portraits one has to shake off the slavery of the old masters ... More than anybody else the portraitist can provide an idea of his epoch and make his painting bear an exact date ... The three portraits exhibited by him [Édouard Dubufe] display fashion, but unlike any fashion merchant. They express with spiritual negligence the affectations of an idle dilettantism, his quick sketches of the *high life* are surprising in the nonchalance of the attitudes they portray. Above all, they are moderns, modern in their poses, in their

intentions, in their clothes and accessories. Never has one progressed further into the intimacy of the salon.[1]

The connection between *mode et modernité* was made recognisable in an instant, as the need to dress contemporary expressions in a contemporary fashion and to articulate through the materiality of clothing and accessories the relevance of the present, not only as an immediate environment in which to situate (artistic) production but as a presence of mind and an understanding of history in which the present is not a foil for the achievements of the past or a negative base from which the future must be shaped, but a temporal entity that is activated and thus becomes dominant for and as experience. I have already detailed this approach in the preceding chapter, where I described Walter Benjamin imbuing with materialism the writings on fashion by Gautier's contemporary, Charles Baudelaire, in order to develop a critical philosophy of cultural production. Gautier had asked himself whether such activation of the present, such insistence on the immediacy of experience, such single-minded pursuit of the now could be capable of substantial analysis or whether it got lost in its own fashionability – hence the ambiguous interjection of terms such as 'high life' and 'nonchalance' into his critique. Highlighting the importance of the present, and of fashion within it as indicator and visual primer, often led not to a discourse on fashion but simply to a fashionable discourse, where the use or observation of a contemporary style was seen as relevant enough, while the interpretation of its meaning within the wider cultural structure that contained it was largely ignored. The virtue of the texts by Balzac, Barbey d'Aurevilly and Mallarmé lies for me in their simultaneous adherence to fashion and the contemplation of what such a deliberate manoeuvre means for cultural production. This understanding of the materiality of fashion, as much as its avowed materialism, separates these texts on clothes and style from the commercial imperative that nevertheless anchored them critically in contemporary commodity culture.

Publications as Material Environment

I would now like to proceed by sketching out very briefly the origin of fashion journals, from the French Revolution to the second half of the nineteenth century, providing a material environment for the writing of Balzac, Barbey d'Aurevilly and Mallarmé between 1830 and 1880. In order to understand what distinguishes the fashion journal from other publications that deal with decorative trends or the latest occurrences in culture (either as original contributions or as reviews), it might be useful to provide a taxonomy for this species of commercial writing. The fashion journal has to appear regularly, feature present or latest fashions, provide a mixture of text and image, and profess to take fashion seriously, that is, refrain from sustained satire or moral critique. And although it can contain other subjects in separate review sections, fashion is to be defined as pertaining to dress and accessories.

The fashion journal came into being because a new medium was required to advertise innovative, that is, exclusive, developments in urban dress that would supersede the extravagant and costly custom of dispatching fashion dolls that were made-up and attired in contemporary trends from Paris to the provinces and European courts, as Marie Antoinette's dressmaker Rose Bertin had been wont to do until the 1780s. In addition, the development and wide application of printing techniques such as engraving, etching, and eventually lithography (in the nineteenth century) would aid in establishing parity between new forms of writing that listed, described and evoked dress with its equally contemporary visual representation.

The early fashion journal replaced the previous fashion almanac or the bound collection of fashion plates in the form of a publication that featured significantly a written discourse on fashion. It constituted a curious phenomenon: the description of fashion without its materiality. The fashion journal merely evoked the dress or mentioned it by name only; it did not provide a detailed description. This immateriality was bound up with the gradual emergence of fashion illustrations that changed the erstwhile function of fashion semantics by allowing for a pairing of text with select images. Yet this immateriality also gave rise to something that is crucial to the understanding of the manner in which literary writers employed female pseudonyms and formed a distinct style of writing for their fashion texts. Evoking the dress without describing its material aspects certainly provided a poetic challenge but, more importantly, it generated a self-referential discourse that assumed intimate knowledge and understanding on the part of the readership when it came to the materiality of cut, fabric, colour, etc. When members of the court or of the upper bourgeoisie in France had their clothes produced, a conversation with the tailor or seamstress on material details of the dress was required. Usually it was initiated by the client showing a fashion image to the seamstress or by a verbal description of a design she had glimpsed in the box at the opera or at a ball, followed by a more or less detailed discussion about adapting the design or style to personal requirements through select fabrics and trimmings, and continuing all the way through intimate exchanges during fittings, when the material values (and costs) of the dress were brought up, as well as its desired aesthetic and social effect. The material knowledge that the consumers-as-readers had acquired during the commissioning and making of their dresses, gowns or hats allowed for an intimacy between them and the authors of the fashion journals. It would determine much of the commercial writing about fashion in the nineteenth century, not only as a socially codified 'confessional' between female confidantes about dress styles and novelties, but also through the secrecy that singled out the consumers who aspired to setting a new trend or movement. Here, intimacy created a forum for exclusivity in temporal and material terms that could be best affected by a female writer for her female readership. A male writer would not be readily accepted into the fold of such an exchange – for reasons of sexual difference and thus overtones of another, much less sanctioned form of intimacy. Further aspects of the intimacy between the reader and writer of fashion can be traced back to sumptuary laws that had traditionally regulated the consumption of clothing. These laws, which were decreed regularly to sanction garments and accessories in relation to gender, class and cultural hegemony, had given rise to the concept of emulation and of socially transgressive consumption especially in new fashions. This had led in turn to innovative clothes and accessories being restricted to an intimate or exclusive environment before they became public over time. Fashion espouses materially the revolution, it proposes new styles, materials and techniques for the making of new objects, but its social challenge needed to be contained, confined to an exclusive set who could act out sexually and socially transgressive modes of dress within the environment of the ruling class and its political economy.

Novelty in the fashion journal was an economic necessity and, occasionally, provided the culturally sanctioned scandal or frisson when it exposed, for instance, a part of the body that had been covered in a previous clothing style. But it obviously was not intended as a real social challenge to the class system. This is partly why the sans-culottes of the French Revolution became so notorious: the combination of liberal, even revolutionary behaviour and new, loose trousers for men and women was seen as epochal.

The first fashion journal proper is said to have been the *Cabinet des Modes*, which appeared in 1785 in Paris, preceding the actual political Revolution – rather than repeated revolutions in dress – by four years and thus falling into a time of considerable social and economic instability. Although the journal was designed to be consumed initially by the existing aristocracy and developing haute bourgeoisie of the *ancien régime*, it pointed towards the change that would allow new 'middle-class' consumers to become part of its subscription base. The political, social and economic ambiguities of the years before 1789 generated a sense of immediacy and of movement that acted as the economic and cultural backdrop for an early commercial forum of transitory and ephemeral fashion.

The subscribers of the *Cabinet des Modes* had been addressed initially as male – 'chers abonnés' – not simply to harmonise one form of address but because men were in the sole economic position to commit in signature to financial contributions, even if the actual readership and the consumers of fashion were their wives and lovers. After 1788 this address changed and the magazine acknowledged its principally female readership, who were beginning to benefit from the increased status of wider education that allowed for greater cultural literacy and economic knowledge among bourgeois women.

Linked to the aforementioned aspect of intimacy is the performative character of fashion journals in the nineteenth century. They were not obtained for solitary consumption but were meant to be looked at and read in company during afternoon tea or evening *soirées*, as a communicative device that allowed for the public display of (insider) knowledge with regard to novel cultural expression. This constituted a feminine, domestic analogy to the *cabinets de lecture*, the semi-public reading rooms that had sprung up in France (as well as in Britain, Scandinavia, the German and Italian states) since the second half of the eighteenth century at printers and publishers or in bookstores. These intimate reading rooms allowed a habitually male readership, for a small fee, to peruse a selection of political newspapers or scientific journals. For the educated bourgeois, these were sites of attaining and communicating knowledge within a shared social setting.

Similarly, the reading of fashion journals in the early nineteenth century in France was a quasi-communal act to initiate female members of the family, their friends and acquaintances into the constantly expanding world of fashionable commodities and to solicit discussions about fashion. Since fashion journals were, because of their elevated price and the exclusivity of their bourgeois readership, not collected by the growing number of municipal libraries in France until the end of the 1880s, their consumption remained a private act and as such was governed by rules of social engagement, which on the whole were performative. For the *bourgeoise* it was important to be seen to read a select fashion journal, as an indication of her cultural awareness and as a shared – and thus pre-sanctioned – display of taste. Initially, this performance of reading fashion was limited in scope since few fashion journals existed, but as the consumption of fashion grew among the bourgeoisie, the display of reading a particular magazine began to equal a related preference for progressive or conservative styles, risqué or safe manners of comportment or a taste in modern versus traditional art, respectively. A pattern of matching the nature of a text with the style of a dress, and vice versa, thus developed as a market-orientated form of positioning material identity.

As part of this analogous development of sartorial and semantic styles in high fashion in early nineteenth-century France, a new vocabulary emerged, generated especially by the need to describe or evoke colours. Comparatively few fashion plates, save in the most exclusive publications, were in colour and certainly this coloration was not good enough to represent the precise tone and hue of the fabric and trimmings that the weavers and dressmakers had created. Therefore a language was needed to provide signifiers through adjectives or associative descriptions, often placed in italics, similar to novel terms for textiles or unheard of names for creations. This early distinction of a fashion-specific language was considerable, but the adjectives or names of specific colours, textiles or designs were extremely short-lived. The neologisms that appeared in fashion writing only lasted as long as the fashions themselves. The structure of language thereby approximated an economic structure of repeated novelty production and, at the same time, generated a new value system for language that separated itself deliberately, perhaps even ironically, from the classical canon and terminologies. Language, like fashion, had to become subject to constant change within a developing medium. The need for a real political change, or just for a stylishly simulated one, created not just shifting or flickering signifiers, as Roland Barthes and Jean Baudrillard would describe in their analyses of fashion discourses in the 1960s and 1970s, but such signifiers arose and disappeared in quick succession along with outmoded styles of dress or dated accessories.

At the start of 1813 the *Journal des Dames et des Modes*, the second significant fashion magazine in France, edited by Pierre Antoine Leboux de La Mésangère (1761–1831), stated: 'Novelty ... daughter of curiosity and boredom ... thus provides our goddess. She alone can direct you towards fame and fortune ... Without her, without the cachet of originality, you will appear as nothing but servile copiers.'[2] A new perception of originality, coined by temporality, arose. What was original had to be new, first and foremost. Narrative or formal invention were linked to the contemporary. The emulation of traditions and classical forms did not behove the progressive artist of the early nineteenth century. He had to court novelty and satisfy its incessant demand for quick representation. This perception ushered in a significant shift from the eternal to the ephemeral within the dominant system of cultural value, and so it was no coincidence that Charles Baudelaire, in his programmatic series of texts written for newspaper feuilletons during the winter of 1863 and then collected as 'Le Peintre de la vie moderne' (The Painter of Modern Life), began his discourse on the modern by evoking these very fashion plates from the *Journal des Dames et des Modes*.

> I have before me a series of fashion plates dating from the Revolution and finishing more or less with the Consulate. These costumes, which seem laughable to many thoughtless people – people who are grave without true gravity – have a double natured charm, one both artistic and historical. They are often very beautiful and drawn with wit; but what to me is every bit as important, and what I am happy to find in all, or almost all of them, is the moral and aesthetic feeling of their time. The idea of beauty which man creates for himself imprints itself on his whole attire, crumples or stiffens the dress, rounds off or squares his gesture, and in the long run even ends by subtly penetrating the very features of his face. Man ends by looking like his ideal self.[3]

La Mésangère's fashion journal, which Baudelaire cited here as aesthetically and metaphysically evocative – man 'looking like his ideal self' – had begun by appearing six times a month, establishing a rhythm that was to be followed by all the major fashion publications from 1815 onwards. At the same time literature, in the form of serialised novels, poetry, etc., had in turn begun to appear in fashion journals. The market had opened up and a fusion of the review elements of daily or weekly papers and the fashionable content of the journals was effected.

Rivalling the *Journal des Dames et des Modes* as the most important fashion journal to emerge from the Restoration period in France was *La Mode*, not only in terms of distribution but also for the quality of its contributors. After its first issue in October 1829 *La Mode* almost overnight reached a circulation of 2,625 copies, compared with editions of around 1,000 copies for rival contemporary fashion magazines. Among the writers who contributed to *La Mode* over the next decade were George Sand, Eugène Sue, Alexandre Dumas, Gérard de Nerval, Alphonse de Lamartine and Honoré de Balzac. Many of them were relatively unknown at the time of their first contribution to the magazine. This might indicate a high degree of literary sensibility on the part of the commissioning editor for

La Mode, but it also stemmed from the fact that contributions to literary journals and high-calibre newspapers were now monitored by ambitious publishers, attempting to secure the services of writers who were known for a particular style and could thus be associated with a particular consumption of fashion. In its first issues *La Mode* courted political scandals and deliberately managed to get its patronage from the court withdrawn, thus disassociating itself economically and socially from the existing *ancien régime* – only in terms of generating and consuming new ideas in fashion of course. This lent the magazine a progressive cachet, while its target audience remained in fact aristocratic and even royalist.

Balzac's Materialism

I would like to look now at the first of the chosen examples, the contributions by Balzac to *La Mode* and *La Silhouette*. His writing is not found on the review pages, that is, in the established feuilleton, but in the body proper of the fashion magazine. Balzac's texts are integrated into the wider discourse on fashion and no separation occurs between the rules of literary production, as signalled by the author's already established reputation, and the structure of the fashion industry with its commercial forum, the journal.

Balzac contributed in 1830 to twenty issues of *La Mode*, while also working for three other literary and cultural journals, *Le Voleur*, *La Silhouette* and the *Revue de Paris*. To describe his writing of the period as 'journalistic' is appropriate only in relation to the context of publication. As can be seen in countless references across his series of novels, *La Comédie humaine*, fashion, accessories, make-up, hairstyles and so on remained constant within Balzac's literary production. For him, fashion was not simply a novelty to be covered in reviews, nor was it reduced to a mere social marker as part of a naturalist or even psychological discourse in his fiction. Clothes did not just serve to describe the sensibility or character of the wearer, nor did they render him or her part of a social group. For Balzac, fashion guarded its autonomy as a discourse: its temporality, structure, societal rules and psychological effects. Clothes were seen as independent from the wearer and from the industry that produced and communicated them. Fashion, as the system for such sartorial objects, was granted influence over other, hitherto more rationalised cultural discourses, such as physical anthropology or linguistics. These two concepts especially were connected to fashion in Balzac's texts.

Language and vocabulary became the themes for two important early essays in *La Mode*: 'Des mots à la mode' (On Fashionable Words) of 22 May 1830 and 'De la mode en littérature' (On Fashion in Literature) a week later. Balzac took concepts from physiologists such as Johann Caspar Lavater and Franz Josef Gall that had been popularised as cultural paradigms in the early nineteenth century. These concepts stated that facial expressions as well as head shapes and sizes could be linked to the physiology of the brain and thus to intelligence and social interaction. Balzac applied these ideas to clothing and accessories in his essay 'Physiologie de la toilette' (Physiology of Attire), published in *La Silhouette* between June and July 1830. He stated that social equality, a result of the French Revolution, had rendered obsolete the sartorial signifiers that had determined man's status among his peers. Fashion no longer established a fixed social context; bourgeois newcomers could easily and precisely emulate in cut and style the appearance of their aristocratic neighbours. Therefore the accessory closest to the face and head, the tie or cravat, now assumed the utmost importance.

> Henceforth the cravat acquired a new destiny: on this day it emerged into public life, it assumed a social significance, for it was called upon to re-establish the distinctions in attire that had been utterly eradicated, it became the criterion by which the proper man on the one hand could be distinguished from the uneducated man on the other ... [4]

This advance in education was a material one for Balzac. It was based on class, certainly, but also on understanding the mechanism of fashion proper.

> Narrow-minded, sterile, unimaginative souls these, without an original idea in their heads, who study one day the knot they will reproduce the next. What to make of this *servum pecus* of the cravat? I would compare them to those frivolous individuals who scan the gazettes each morning for the ideas they will espouse throughout the day ... [5]

According to Balzac, tying a cravat was for the most part a wholly unoriginal performance that did not show any inside knowledge but was derived from the intellectual education of others, for example from the famous Parisian dandy who, for social as well as psycho-sexual reasons, ended up becoming a cardinal:

> His soul had passed into the light fabric and there manifested itself in full. Detected in his cravat was that ease, that freedom of thought

without which there can be no originality, and above all that ardent spirit, that burning fire that was later to develop into religious zeal ...[6]

Balzac further developed his notion of a modern form of distinction that was gained through material objects in the absence of pre-established and fixed social structures and codes for his essay 'On Fashionable Words'.

> Today, nuances have acquired a veritable importance. As our customs are levelling out, when a sales assistant at a dime a dozen can pass for a count thanks to his manners and the elegance of his suit, and perhaps even by his forceful demeanour, it is the nuance that allows fashionable beings to recognise each other in the midst of the crowd.[7]

Men who 'possess the secret of fashionable language', opined Balzac, distinguish themselves through a linguistic code that extends far beyond speech or writing. They affect through their discourse a whole raft of manners and mores. As his first example the novelist evoked the following scene (an ironic signpost for his subsequent novel-sequence *La Comédie humaine*), which referenced the very medium in which it appeared and described the ritual that has been established for consuming the writing in fashion magazines.

> You arrive at a manor house, where in the evening one reads an essay in a journal, a book, a novel, or whatever you desire . . . Once the reading has finished everybody voices an opinion. Your turn comes; you find, in agreement with the mistress of the house, that the book is badly written, you concur with the husband that is it well thought out, you side with some about the illustrations, with others about characters.
> Yet, you add, this is not it! . . . Today . . .
> Everybody looks at you.
> Today books, like everything else of which there is a surplus, need to have actuality . . .
> Then you take up your glasses and proceed to glance around. The next day, nearly everybody will be using the word actuality, but often wrongly and misunderstood. Thus you can easily discern a person with esprit and style, a fashionable man or woman.[8]

Apart from the setting, which as we have seen established the performative character of consuming fashionable writing as a collective social display divided by gender roles,[9] the chosen example of coining a fashionable word was very telling indeed. 'Actuality' is the key term that underscores the notion of material to be of its time and subject to rules of temporality and transience. Whether it was a cravat, dress or word, the object was governed by a capitalist culture of consumption – 'like everything else of which there is a surplus' – and it had to be consumed within the now. It had to be actualised within history. The next day it would serve already as an established signifier to mark intellectual ability and discursive efficiency – as well as connoting the most important sign: as being *à la mode*.

Balzac ran through a gamut of fashionable words, deployed in a variety of social settings, from political debate at a financier's table, via the Parisian *Salon* where one judged fashionable appearances, to the supper at the latest restaurant appraising the new members of the opera's *corps de ballet*. Each neologism was set in italics, echoing the aforementioned semantic display of new terms for colours and fabrics that had become prevalent for fashion journals. At the beginning of his essay Balzac established his credo for the dominance of fashion as structuring the perception not just of time but of knowledge itself, while providing a quick sideway sweep at the very forum in which his article appeared. Such self-reference, given that those who might have disagreed with Balzac's assessment of fashion would not have had read the magazine in the first place, was reflective of the circuitous discourse of intimacy between authors, readers and consumers in the know.

> Fashion has to face its prejudices like any other branch of the human sciences. Previously, most people believed that being fashionable meant dressing according to the prescriptions of those vulgar journals that we are fighting with all our might. From such an attitude emanates all the disappointments that mortify the self-esteem of people so indifferent that they do not think at all about the obligations imposed by good taste and *savoir vivre*. It does not suffice to have the latest fabric, to buy clothes from Blain, to have one's dresses made by Victorine, one's carriages by Thomas-Baptiste, to get one's trousers from England, one's gloves at Bodier. To be fashionable one needs moreover to greet, talk, sing, sit, debate, eat, drink, walk, dance according to the wish and order of fashion.[10]

Contrasting 'brand' names of Parisian manufacturers with phenomenological perception, Balzac expanded the realm of fashion beyond dressing. For him, the task was indeed a synthetic one that linked a structural principle found in the constant change of new clothes and accessories to other cultural manifestations, and beyond them to economic and political life. Here, Balzac appeared as a supreme materialist, in matching economic structures such as the surplus value of commodities, accrued through the cultural position of, for example, a fashionable coachbuilder, with an analysis on how the relation of material things reflects our social relations – an application of commodity fetishism, literally, *avant la lettre*.

In his second text for *La Mode*, 'On Fashion in Literature', Balzac dispensed advice to a female aristocrat and amateur author with regard to the lack of style and psychological insight that marred present literary production.

> In literature, as we have it today Madame, there is a certain etiquette to which the personality and the work of an author have to submit themselves. In one word, there is a fashion in dress to observe, and here, I feel, is what should appear most significant to you. We are not dealing with style, or ideas, the plan or title of your book. God forbid that I should intrude on the secret that envelops such an act of creation. But still, to learn the age of an author is at the moment of the highest interest. We love green fruits. A young man fresh out of one of our great universities, a young girl not yet approaching her first communion are quite sure to capture the public imagination.[11]

Even at his most ironical, Balzac's view of the material production of literature hit home. A constant desire for youth put additional pressures on the rapid turnover not only of novels but of novelties. Fashion in literature is analogous to fashion in dress. The latest creation was the *ne plus ultra*; any dated product vanished from public perception, and not even the canon of established classics could save an outdated literary object. Here, Balzac, writing under the pseudonyms 'B.' or 'E.B.', performed an ambiguous role indeed. He stepped back from his own discourse to underscore the ephemeral nature of language and literature, separating himself from the hard-won autonomy of his own work, as a writer of contemporary novels with complex narratives and intricate psychologies. The forum of the fashion magazine allowed him to embrace transitoriness and 'actuality' while, dialectically, it reinforced the negative effect of the short-lived and insubstantial within creative production. What is dialectic here is *modernité* – and indeed Balzac had used the term fleetingly back in 1822[12] – as it embraced the latest expression yet had to distance itself from the (material) fashion it created by proclaiming lasting aesthetic or ethical values. Like a progressive *couturier* or *couturière* who could not be seen to follow a trend, and had to remain ahead of the pack in terms of materials and forms, the author in modernity could not afford to rest on an aesthetic precept; his or her production had to show itself, in themes as well as style, as radically fashionable, without this appearing merely an outward manifestation. And the three writers chosen for this chapter negotiated such dialectics in their artistic production by choosing contemporary subjects and by selecting the medium that would frame their respective discourses in the most contemporary form.

Barbey d'Aurevilly

The work of writer and critic Jules Amadée Barbey d'Aurevilly is today less read than Balzac's novels or Mallarmé's poetry. In the second half of the nineteenth century, however, novels such as *Les Diaboliques* or his study *Du Dandysme et de George Brummell* made Barbey d'Aurevilly a notorious figure, a fact that was augmented by the outrageous behaviour of a social gadfly and the hyperbolic dress sense of an effeminate dandy. While Balzac had described a misadventure with a pair of black cashmere trousers, torn to shreds by all too vigorous brushing,[13] Barbey d'Aurevilly would have regarded the black trousers a misadventure in themselves when compared to the aesthetic potential of wearing skin-tight leopard print or zebra stripes on his nether regions.[14]

The change from Balzac's to Barbey d'Aurevilly's time in journalism was marked by significant alterations to the fabric of fashion publications. After the July Revolution of 1830, the speculative fervour within the economic structure of advanced capitalism generated a volatile but also highly profitable environment in which to launch a host of new fashion magazines. From 1834 onwards such publications began to approximate generic capitalist structures. The subscribers were invited to become investors by acquiring bonds in the journal they read and shared in their drawing rooms. The bourgeois reader became part of his own consumption, and the sum of 100 francs allowed ready participation in such schemes. Fashion magazines multiplied and were modified according to an increasing segmentation of the market. A widening consumer base for fashion products meant that publications now had to consider potential readers from outside its existing constituency of aristocrats and wealthy bourgeois. These readers did not consume couture, of course, but the magazines could nevertheless present designs to them that could be copied at home or made up by reasonably skilled dressmakers in the *banlieues* or provinces. Women became progressively more literate in cultural styles and tastes and they used fashion journals as a prop to aid the performance of such literary proficiency in public. Industrialisation and colonial exploitation created exponential economic growth in France in the 1840s and 1850s and the consumption of commodities increased, which in turn multiplied their representation in media and entertainment. Bourgeois women began to enjoy more leisure time, while their male kinfolk started to perform the conspicuous consumption of fashion as well, as a result of a prolonged period of peace and increased material comfort in urban and domestic life. At the same time, the price of the fashion publications replaced the quality of their material production as the principal motif for their consumption. A segregation of discourses developed further within the French market for fashion magazines, yet this segregation did not occur according to traditional social segmentation but increasingly along economic lines. Most significantly, the fashion journal was no longer purchased exclusively through subscription, but instead single issues could be picked up in cafés or at the *kiosque* on the side of the street. The consumer could exercise a spontaneous decision to acquire a copy and did not have to remain loyal to one specific magazine. Thus the opportunities for an intimate dialogue between fashion writer and reader lessened and such encounters had to be brought about in different form. By 1840 the reader of fashion journals in France could choose between some forty titles compared to just four back in 1820, and this rendered the form of publication itself as transitory as the product it featured.

Two of the most successful journals of this period were *Le Moniteur de la Mode* and *Le Constitutionnel*, to which Barbey d'Aurevilly contributed between 1843 and 1846 articles such as 'De l'élégance' and 'Revue critique de la mode'. He began by spelling out a concept of an, ostensibly classical, aesthetic standard in dialectical relation with ephemeral style:

> Therefore between real beauty and elegance lies a vast difference; thus again elegance is beauty on a small scale, beauty in miniature. But beware all! Beauty in miniature is like a realm gone to seed. Both have a short lifespan.[15]

Beauty was juxtaposed by its modern component, elegance – a 'kingdom ruled by the female sex'. To appear elegantly dressed was far from being fashionable, and elegance could be achieved without beauty, even despite it. Modernity increasingly required reaction, not composure or contemplation. It left less and less time to cultivate an original, metaphysically coined concept of the beautiful. Barbey d'Aurevilly composed the lines above in 1843 under the female pseudonym of Maximilienne de Syrène, in remembrance of the woman he had 'silently adored' in his youth. Her particular style and grace, which he once evoked in a fragment of prose, was the sensual basis for his almost complete empathy with a woman's judgement of her clothes. 'Elegance is the small sex of beauty',[16] he claimed. Elegance, the smaller and fairer sex, exposed itself in the contemporary and modern. For Barbey d'Aurevilly there was no longer the normative character of eternal beauty that forced (wo)man into restrained boredom. The speed of life was reflected in the twists and turns that fashion traced.

> Among our own kind, we wrap ourselves in the most ceremonious words like an extravagant costume or a black uniform that we have worn for too long; while we consider the so-called tolerance that refers to a costume as 'extravagant' as impertinent indeed. For, in the end, what could be more charming, more sacred, more triumphant in the field of fashion than extravagance when it rests in the light of truthfulness? Within a society like ours, on the verge of profound boredom, one has to take up arms for extravagance in all its forms![17]

This extravagance was displayed by a fictional female character whom Barbey d'Aurevilly performed on the pages of the fashion journal. The idealised remembrance of his youthful infatuation with an obscure woman was transposed on to his conception of an idealised reification and commodification in fashion: elegance. He addressed the female readership of *Le Moniteur de la Mode* and *Le Constitutionnel* with the intimacy of one who shared their quest for the ideal form, the perfect make-up and the most beautiful gown. Yet Barbey d'Aurevilly was far from a romantic who liked to profess ignorance towards contemporary material reality. His empathy with women let him forsake the company of his fellow critics and seek refuge among female consumers; yet his fetish was not the female body but the commodity. Like Balzac's neologisms that had been born from his direct attachment to the fashion system, Barbey d'Aurevilly fetishised clothing for its novelty value, too. In 1845 he wrote to his friend, the translator and editor Guillaume-Stanislas Trébutien, about the significance of literary cross-dressing:

> Wearing petticoats [*jupons*] when writing, in the same way that George Sand wore trousers with a button fly, is to mock the public and make them swallow the fact that this emerges from a new pen, entirely virginal (alas, this is her only claim to virginity!), wielded by a woman of the world....[18]

As a contemporary of Marx, although there is no evidence of his ever having read him, Barbey d'Aurevilly saw the abstraction and reification within society not in terms of political economy, but rather looked upon it as an aesthetic challenge. In April 1846, while Baudelaire busied himself at the Louvre with composing the second of his *Salon* reviews, in which reflections on modernity would first surface, Barbey d'Aurevilly left the museum behind to find among female shoppers a less than sublime, mundane modernity.

> While the exhibition at the Louvre brings together the amateurs of painting, attentively judging works that have been submitted for their scrutiny, an exhibition of a different kind has the happy privilege of reuniting a crowd which, although less numerous, is in its entirety no less composed of admirers – though we should say *admiresses*, since it addresses women only. We are speaking here of the exhibition of shawls offered by the beautiful stores along the Chaussée-d'Antin.[19]

In the conflict between cultural tradition and the transitory beauty of fashion, Maximilienne de Syrène was sure about the side (s)he chose. As a true materialist of fashion, (s)he recognised the reifying power of the sartorial shell as animating the dialectics of modernity, when progress was jolted into action by transitory revolutions, and the sublime and the eternal had to contain the ephemeral in order to constantly renew questions of value. This value, as we saw in Chapter 1, is not use or exchange value but surplus value, which is quantifiable as an expression of shifting economic progress and ideological formation. Within these, the commodity was credited with ostensibly improving social existence, providing the signified of a more elevated position in society and glossing over otherwise fraught social relations. Through fashion, Marx's postulate of commodity fetishism was materialised as a positivist goal. The relationship between things in industrialised capitalism could indeed become analogous to social relations between people, as the clothes worn during encounters and interactions displayed to one another their fetishistic potential and proclaimed openly their surplus value. Although they were reined in by the understanding that such displays were temporary performances, they, despite their shortened lifespan, became fully sanctioned in that very moment of existence.

The Parisian women of the nineteenth century claimed the *journaux de modes* as their own. Excluded from contributing to any of the political, that is, 'serious', press, they were forced to train their interests, hopes and passions on the pages of fashion magazines. Since the producers and the vast majority of the editors of these publications were men, the contributors to this secluded world were expected to be feminine – if not in actual gender, at least in approach, as a performed sensitivity or simply in pseudonym. Within the columns of these journals, a successful style of writing was expected to contain a certain *poncif*, a trademark to distinguish the artist in the commercial world,[20] but its overall tone should resemble intimate, polite chat. The female subscribers were expected to receive compliments from the authors, be they gratuitous, frivolous or patronising. Yet to hint at the frivolity of fashion or to actually analyse, even favourably, the materiality or materialism of fashion was still felt inappropriate. The futility of female bourgeois existence might be the subject of gentle ridicule, but a writer could never cut the ground from under the delicate feet of his/her *abonnées*. The female pseudonyms of Balzac, Barbey d'Aurevilly and, subsequently, Stéphane Mallarmé, with their mix of contemplation and compliments, could enjoy only a (suitably) brief existence while exposing fashion's materialism to substantiate its role in modernity.

Fiction and Materialism in Mallarmé

Balzac and Barbey d'Aurevilly had extended their contributions to fashion journals over the course of many years, compelled initially by material and financial reasons, later emancipating their discourse to develop a broader definition of fashion as a temporal, cultural rhythm, and eventually progressing to an integration proper into their prose of changing apparels and styles to denote social positions and psychologies. Mallarmé, in contrast, would manage only six months of writing fashion. Yet he did not insert his work into an existing structure of fashion journalism and cultural reviews but invented a new form: *La Dernière Mode*, 'the last/latest fashion' – a *Gesamtkunstwerk* in the nineteenth-century Wagnerian and Nietzschean realm of total art, where all components of a structure and medium were conceived and controlled by the artist. In Mallarmé's case this was expanded to an ironic subversion of the established material order, as communicated through the medium of a haute bourgeois fashion journal, for which each 'contributor', right down to the fictional subscribers, was invented by the poet and given a distinct pseudonym and character to simulate a communion of modernist voices. *La Dernière Mode* therefore was truly the *latest* as much as the *last* fashion, a self-reflexive completion of the manner in which fashion as materialism can be mediated. A fiction and simulation for sure, but as such a concrete reflection on the role that fashion was to assume for modern culture from the time it was established as haute couture.

When Mallarmé composed his journal in the autumn of 1874 he trailed, as his references in *La Dernière Mode* manifest, the first creations by Charles-Frederick Worth, and later by Émile Pingat, Jacques Doucet, Jeanne Paquin and others. Mallarmé reflected on a new material form for fashion, the artful design of female clothes as ostensibly subjective, independent works that, in reality, became a hypertrophic extension of previous iterations in dress. Instead of a client taking the fashion journal that depicted a particular design, which had been seen at court, in the theatre box or at a ball, to a seamstress and having her realise a version, the couturier now proposed for and composed on to the body of the client a seasonal iteration of his aesthetic credo. Haute couture simulated the artistic gesture for the female body. Like the Impressionist painter and his canvas (which often depicted bourgeois dress designs), the couturier draped and tailored on to the woman a new aesthetic expression. As we will see in the next chapter, this confluence between couture and painting relied on the formation of a new culture industry and an economic structure of display that had to be formed in the latter half of the nineteenth century in France. For now I would like to remain with Mallarmé's formal, literary innovation of the fashion journal as a new and direct reflection by an artist on a culture of materialism.

Mallarmé's friend, the art critic, collector and poet Philippe Burty, commented upon having read *La Dernière Mode*: 'I have just received your second issue. It is perfect. You have invented *the word*, cast in the netting of three lines.'[21] The netting or fabric (*tissu*) that Burty spoke of is not a concealing mesh that needs to be activated by the poetry inside it, but a real material structure into which the poet embedded a new style of writing: a fictional appropriation of the political economy of fashion that started to dominate contemporary France during the reign of Louis Napoléon III. The nephew of the first Napoleon had ascended to power through his bloody *coup d'état* in December 1851 and crowned himself emperor a year later. The integration of a dynastic revival into free-market capitalism was reinforced by establishing a series of public engagements at court, where bourgeois *nouveaux riches* could mix with the re-established nobility. In this context the emphasis in modernity on the new as eternal recurrence, which was postulated by Baudelaire in the early 1850s, takes on a decidedly political meaning, as old-fashioned imperialism was dressed up as contemporary constitutional monarchy. It is only logical that this very period saw the emergence of haute couture, when Worth designed his first dresses for Louis Napoléon's wife, the empress Eugénie, as a conduit of bourgeois aspiration to an aristocratic past. Worth's couture was traditional in its shapes, retaining at first crinolines and waistlines but, under the patronage of the empress, he proposed notable changes that ushered in simpler fabrics and decoration to emphasise and subsequently define the composition of pattern cut and silhouette. An approximation of bourgeois taste to the representational simulacra of nobility can be found in this instance, when the new and the old fuse in the historicist designs of Worth, which were billed as the latest artistic creations to designate individual objectification of the prominent wearer.

> Eugénie had taken a liking to the young and vivacious Princess Metternich, and on that night when the empress noticed her dress (so the princess recounts in her memoirs) the following conversation took place: 'May I ask you, Madam,' she enquired, 'who made you that dress, so marvellously elegant and simple?'
> 'An Englishman, Madam, a star who has arisen in the firmament of fashion,' the Princess replied.
> 'And what is his name?'
> 'Worth.'
> 'Well,' concluded the Empress, 'please ask him to come and see me at ten o'clock tomorrow morning.'
> 'He was made, and I was lost,' wrote Princess Metternich jokingly, 'for from that moment there were no more dresses at 300 francs each.'[22]

Mallarmé did not only invent 'the word', as a semantic, modernist innovation that was concurrent with new designs in clothes. He ventured into the materialism of fashion, as combining the materiality of the fabric or dress with its exchange and surplus values. The first aspect of Mallarmé's materialist approach to fashion was grounded in abstraction, in the objectification of subjectivity through formal stylistics. His work exemplifies an oscillation between *le mode*, as manner of thinking and creating, and *la mode*, as fleeting reification of cultural manners and mores in the body and its sartorial covering. This oscillation acts as a semiotic 'shifter', which moves modernity back and forth in structural terms from the codification of thought as evidencing historical progress to the codification of clothes and accessories on the body as commodifying temporary revolutions. I have pointed out elsewhere the etymology of *mode,* as deriving from the Latin *modus* and shifting in the nineteenth century from *le mode* to *la mode*,[23] but I consider it important to situate this again more firmly within a materialist discourse. The materialist and structuralist thinker Henri Lefebvre identified, somewhat derogatorily, *la mode* as feminising the structural regularity of change that had rendered cycles of modern cultural discourse repetitive, and thus calculable and predictable – also in economic terms. For Lefebvre, the feminisation of modes made this structural mechanism 'unpredictable, charming, unexpected and spontaneous'[24] and these attributes are as negative as they are positive (and patronising) in their positioning of cultural thought within modernity's dialectics of the eternal and ephemeral. For Lefebvre, the relationship between modernity and fashion remained, despite his exegesis on Marx and Baudelaire in his *Introduction to Modernity*, 'paradoxical'. He did not consider the structural analogy between meta- and micro-levels, between social abstraction that leads to the alienating tendencies in labour and the corporeal abstraction through contemporary clothing within the ('post'-structuralist) economy of the sign. It would take Lefebvre's pupils and heirs such as Barthes and Baudrillard to inquire into this dimension. By then, however, as suggested in Chapter 1, they had abandoned Marx's political economy as a methodological template and had moved on to a late modernist refutation of historical or dialectical materialism. Thereby they missed the connection between fashion's materiality, which is inherent in its abstraction of the body, and the materialism that had demonstrated the objectification and commodification of social relations between these bodies.

One of the aspects of structuralist linguistics that materialist thinkers (such as Timpanaro) were interested in was the analysis of the diachronic nature of language and, by implication, culture at large. In the first three decades of the twentieth century the diachronic had been put into a dialectical relation with the established synchronic study of language by Russian formalists such as Viktor Shklovsky and the Prague linguistic circle around Roman Jakobson. For them, language was a social-political structure that opposed linear historicism and focused on developmental patterns across time. Their theories, revived through the nascent structuralism in France in the 1950s and 1960s, were espoused in particular by the critical journal *Change*. For its editorial 'collective' around the literary theorist Jean-Pierre Faye, 'form' was a central concern that united materialist analyses by Marx – via contemporary interpretations by, for example, Louis Althusser and Jacques Rancière – with studies of language and literary style. *Change* had published its first three issues on 'montage', 'destruction' (as material change) and the 'Prague circle', before its fourth issue was devoted to 'La Mode, l'invention'. This title indicated the understanding of fashion as formal and material novelty, whose expression was language as much as clothes and accessories. The interest in fashion was not based on the investigation of the techniques and materials of the industry, but rather it was seen as a structural phenomenon, which is vetted by the political economy of capitalism.[25] Fashion is a manifestation that occurs in the invention of language, as much semantically in new styles of writing as materially in the seasonal collection of clothes. A focus on the diachronicity of language and of fashion,[26] its changes and developmental patterns in history, served in this context as a link to historical materialism, in opposing historicist linearity and emphasising instead structural relations of economic, cultural and linguistic phenomena across periods.

As editor of *Change*, Faye contributed an extended essay on 'Mallarmé: l'écriture, la mode' to its fourth issue, connecting programmatically the poet's search for new semantic forms to an interest in the political economy of the fashion industry, exemplified in his fashion prose for the commercial enterprise of *La Dernière Mode*.

Mallarmé's fashion writing linked an awareness of contemporary economic structures with a detached commitment to novelty. He distanced himself ironically from the latest literary fashion, when his famous poem 'L'Après-midi d'un faune' was rejected by the reigning literary movement of the Parnassiens, by programmatically turning to a fashion publication as an enterprise in the market, embracing the material side of describing clothes to stimulate consumer impulses. The dialectic of distance from fashion as a trend and proximity to fashion as a material fact was reflected in Mallarmé's use of language: material fashion is concrete in his writing, as he detailed in *La Dernière Mode* silhouettes, trimmings, fabrics and so on, but it also occurs symbolically in the elaborate semantics of his prose. The fashion industry is presented by Mallarmé through a variety of structures, which are denoted by varying female pseudonyms: reviews of the contemporary haute couture around Worth by 'Mme. Marguerite de Ponty', a society column with the English title 'Fashion' penned by 'Miss Satin', and enigmatic advice on style by 'Ix.', as well as columns on new culinary and educational tendencies.[27] All these structures are determined by an avowed materialism. Mme. de Ponty described the latest offerings in couture and speculated about future developments. Ix. contextualised such offerings within a wider context of cognition: how did the public perceive and evaluate the eternal recurrence of the new (following the models of Balzac and Gautier as well as Baudelaire), while Miss Satin arranged the fashion in its social structure of display and performance. Each of Mallarmé's female 'authors' reflected formal innovation in clothes and accessories through their respective style of language, from the earnest and languid prose of Mme. de Ponty, via the syncopated flippancy of Miss Satin, to the obscure artifice of Ix.

These formal experiments were not confined to literary collections of editions of poetry; they appeared as actualised manifestations of the second aspect of material fashion: the materiality of clothes and the economic system of production, distribution and consumption. Mallarmé's 'word', therefore, would best be conceived and displayed in a fashion publication. Like Balzac and Barbey d'Aurevilly,

Mallarmé was attentive to the format that would allow him to find an audience that was prepared to receive radical formal innovation of words and syntax within the mundane context of stylish novelties that they wanted to consume. But in contrast to previous poets who had *written fashion*, Mallarmé extended the occasional, commercial prose of the fashion review towards the total work of art that was *La Dernière Mode*. Each component of the journal, from cover illustration to the letters to the subscribers, was controlled by the author, selecting the material form of the journal in the same way that he composed its semantic contents; and further beyond, by producing neologism to signify innovations in the latest couture.[28]

Unlike Balzac and Barbey d'Aurevilly, for whom clothes and accessories moved across fashion journalism to symbolism and psychology in their subsequent literary output, Mallarmé would remain consistent in his formalism. As mentioned above, Balzac had mused in his contributions to fashion journals on the right way to present a necktie and had detailed his misadventure with cashmere trousers, but when it came to his literary prose, the materiality of clothes was supplanted by the roles they assumed in his narratives: as character metaphors, as symbols for social position or as indicative of the psychological state of the novel's heroine. Fashion, for Balzac, remained still a largely representational structure that provided a temporal and social context for his 'human comedy'. It did not become concrete in its role within a political economy, although Balzac had remained very conscious of the fact that his own literary output was an essential part of such an economic system, and he never ceased to thematise this fact in his novels through allusion to human exploitation and alienation.

Mallarmé, writing almost half a century after Balzac, was supremely materialist in understanding fashion as exclusive to political economy; not yet Barthes's and Baudrillard's political economy of the sign and simulacrum, but the political economy of late nineteenth-century capitalism under the reign of Louis Napoléon III and his successors, the liberal Adolphe Thiers and the monarchist Patrice de MacMahon, who had alternated between political repression and economic laissez-faire. The written fashion in *La Dernière Mode* was entirely bound up with this extended system: it existed concretely as a journal for the market, conceived as a fully designed product that aimed to match the exclusivity of high fashion by the formal quality of its prose. Mallarmé's materialism was defined by adhering to the developing commerce of haute couture and by the formal integrity of his journal-project. His writing, down to the menus by a fictitious mulatto housekeeper and the letters by noblewomen in the provinces, was controlled to mirror the political economy of his time. The value of the gowns and dresses in *La Dernière Mode* appeared through the material detail in their description, the richness of the fabric surface, the intricacy of the flounces, the volume of the bustles. But it also appeared as concrete economic value, as evidenced in the correspondence pages of the journal, where Mallarmé featured the fictitious shipment of dresses to St Petersburg, ostensibly as a service to his reader who, while in receipt of his journal and thus *au courant* with the latest trend, had been unable to travel to Paris and therefore needed the sourcing and dispatch of the dresses.

> Mme La Princesse K____, From Saint Petersburg:
> We have received the sum that you, Princess, dispatched to us; the boxes will be shipped on the 29th of this month, containing a day dress in *cheviotte gisèle* [Scottish lamb's wool with relief embroidery in muslin], another very simple one in Persian light wool with jet-black trimming, a *toilette de visite* in slate-grey velvet and satin with decorative waves of feathers, another in rose-coloured cashmere under strips of white gauze, trimmed with smooth silk; also a ball gown in blue *poult-de-soie* [thick but pliable taffeta, its selvage having perpendicular edges] with a tulle effect in brilliant white and garlands in rose-coloured flowers. The three outfits for girls are very simple, since at fifteen one is still a child: a wool dress in navy, a dress in black velvet with a belt in rose-tinted satin, and a white gown in Chambéry gauze, embroidered with blue knotting. We have supplied also matching hats and veils for these various dresses and ensembles.[29]

As a formal invention this was surely Mallarmé's masterstroke: the dresses were invented on the pages of his journal as reflecting the haute couture he saw around him, and they thus gave occasion to a transposition from the visual to the lexical. Yet he continued to reinvent their materiality, by pretending in a letter to a subscriber that the dress as written could indeed be materialised in the act of economic exchange. Mallarmé wrote about the dresses being bought or commissioned from the couturier or perhaps from a skilled seamstress who had been provided with illustrations from *La Dernière Mode* as guidelines. They were then made up according to the budget he had received from Russia, carefully wrapped in tissue paper and sent abroad. This appeared as supremely materialist fiction – the initial value of the dresses was an immaterial one that existed originally as 'use' value for a literary product only, but in the

4 Typeset version of a page from Stéphane Mallarmé, 'Le Livre', between 1866–97, originally written in crayon

et +
repris en _||_
```
A B C         +
C A B         en 3
B C A         reprises
─────────────
              et
A C B         modes
C B A         de publ
B A C         repart
              en le double
+ +      ⌐ et ⌐ + 5
              = 90
× 4 (5 × 4 = 20) 360
```

fictional correspondence it turned into an exchange value where the dress is integrated into the economic system. Finally, in the imagined consumption the dispatched gowns assumed surplus value as a product of Parisian couture, with its assorted monetary mark-up, presented in the drawing rooms of St Petersburg.

Conclusion: Back in the Fold of Language

Materialism in fashion is obviously not a simple adherence to the market, otherwise fashion's effect on culture would be essentially economic. It is the ostensible neologism in its expressions that activates production – new clothes for new consumers – while retaining an established vocabulary that continually allows fashion to exist in the socio-economic structure of its, and all, times. Fashion is affirmative of and in its novelty. It does not change the structure as such, but as a structuring device of the new within the old it remains supremely innovative. Herein lies its key for understanding what materialists wanted to draw from history: the activation of the past in the present in order to realise the patterns that become instrumental for critique, reformation, eventual change and revolution. And although fashion can only accompany such reforms or revolts, its very role in the formation of modernity gave materialists a lever to prise apart the historicism that had been complicit with existing power structures. When the simulacrum of the new, the myth of constant fashionable novelties, is meant to animate modernity, then Mallarmé's supreme *fiction* of the new, the latest fashion as born from the pen of the poet, was already the ultimate ratio and complete gesture for this construct.

Mallarmé's relationship with fashion had been coined by his association with literary movements of the late nineteenth century, most notably with the Parnassiens and Symbolists. Despite the aspirations for commercial success, which Mallarmé had professed to in his correspondence with friends, *La Dernière Mode* was first and foremost a carefully contrived formal experiment. Although it might have echoed in composition, illustrations and, of course, in its themes existing fashion magazines, Mallarmé's experiment in journalism distinguished itself through language. His work was characterised by a quest for pictorial composition and at the same time by a forceful rejection of subjectivism. In fashion he found both his visual stimulus, through the colourful sweeping fabric of French couture between the 1850s and 1890s, and a subject matter that was regarded as marginal within the contemporary cultural hierarchy. The topic of fashion allowed Mallarmé to work against narratives, to remain resolutely subjective within the non-linear, associative rhythms of his verses but, simultaneously, to divest himself from the sublime and weighty subjectivism that had been considered necessary for symbolist poetry. *La Dernière Mode* used its dialogue with imaginary correspondents to celebrate the 'profound nothingness' that pervaded the life and sartorial consumption especially of the bourgeois female. Unlike Gustave Flaubert, Mallarmé uses the seemingly empty existence and ennui of a female readership not for narrative drama (as in *Madame Bovary*) but for a focus on formal questions. Fashion, seen as insignificant and ephemeral by the cultural status quo, became a carte blanche for a poetically elaborate, yet curiously precise description of fabrics, ribbons, pleats and folds – since the journal earnestly aspired to fulfilling its commercial function as a source of intimate sartorial information.

In particular the *pli modal*, the simultaneously textual and textile fold, operated as a material analogy to syntactic or stylistic innovation, where an idea or concept was hidden within the surface of the word proper, where one semantic construct referred to another unknown one and had to be drawn from the depth of the linguistic fabric through combinative or connotative efforts. When Burty credited *La Dernière Mode* with the 'invention of the word' he was also referring to the vocabulary in the journal that surpassed the description of clothes or accessories and moved to constitute fashion in the abstract, as a verbal equivalent of sartorial innovations in contemporary haute couture.

An obvious level of ignorance vis-à-vis stylistic minutiae as well as the hermetic discourse of many of its contributions rendered *La Dernière Mode* a commercially unviable product among competitive fashion journals. Yet the formal radicalism of Mallarmé's fashion prose (for example the 'metaphysical' musings of Marguerite de Ponty in her column 'La Mode') and the irony contained in its repeated references by Miss Satin to Worth and Pingat created a unique and extended text that flowed unconstrained by a specific stylistic period, and spoke as eloquently of the innovative sartorial form as it did of the literary one. Ix., in the first instalment of her column 'Chronique de Paris', had addressed her female readership with a mixture of ironic empathy and critique: empathy for the constrained social and cultural position the bourgeois woman had to occupy in France in 1874, critique for her not being prepared to reflect on the acceptance of this position: 'Only the lady in her isolation from politics and morose concerns has the necessary leisure to free herself, once her apparel is completed, in order to cater to the requirement of adorning the soul as well.'[30] The *bourgeoise*'s first duty is to choose the dress, her second to dress the soul. Both evoke the ancient within the modern; one through sartorial quotation, the other through poetic impression(ism).

> A book is closed very quickly, so boring; one lets one's gaze wander in this cloud of impressions that one has conjured up readily to interpose, like ancient gods, modern woman in the mundane adventures of her Self . . . Has not the external world had a profound influence on our deepest instincts? It provokes and refines them.
>
> One learns everything on the spot, even beauty; how to hold one's head; one has to learn it from someone; that is to say, from everyone, like the manner of wearing a dress. Shall we escape this world? One travels through it full steam ahead, in its external reality, with its landscapes, its places, to get somewhere else: a modern image of its insufficiency for us! Well, what if the pleasures we know within our four walls were to relinquish their season's lead in favour of games in the open air: long outings in the woods or regattas on the river; keen to rest our eyes in an oblivion created by the vast and naked horizon; so that we find a novel perception which is able to appreciate the paradox of the intricate and complex outfits which the ocean has embroidered at the hem with its foam?[31]

In this passage Ix. displayed not only the fashionable ennui of a dandy, but showed the ironic fatality of the decadent poet as well. Every profound impression in life, everything beautiful, was but a repetition – embodied in the style of the repeated fashion novelty. But where could one escape to find a genuine expression? Even the vaporous speed of modern life which allows for the most rapidly consumed distraction cannot, and does not intend to, alter the perception coined by the proximity of *mode et modernité*. Every phenomenon was judged according to the rules of contemporary commodified society. The horizon at the seaside resort might have offered a brief repose, yet in the very next instant, it became transformed again into the sartorial: a fabric, sky-blue as the cover of Mallarmé's magazine and subjected to the same rule of fashion.

Mallarmé's vocabulary in *La Dernière Mode* was characterised by the indefinable, transitory and immaterial. Words such as 'vapour', 'cloud', 'perfume' or 'dream' recurred in conjunction both with the female and her clothing and interposed them into surrounding space. The instantaneous creation of a shape or form was all that the object required for poetic rendition; in passing from the present, the form was akin to the short lifespan of fashion and the changing shape of modernity. Yet the voids that these creations were soon destined to leave behind were not negatives; for Mallarmé, they constitute a necessary antithesis to the material. The still vastness of the ocean contrasted with the busy fashionable crowd, the white space on the printed pages of his avant-garde poetry permitted the associative reading of his words.

It was the intangible that had created the allure of the woman and her gown. She had remained distant, aestheticised and thus essentially asexual. Although her figure and maybe even her mind were observed, only the sartorial ideal capable of defining her remained. As the modernist writer observed, the impact of the garment always lay in the abolition of eternal values, of ideals. Ix. had singled out in her first 'Chronique' a 'gown of vaporous fabrics creased in impatience'. Correspondingly, Miss Satin poetically evoked an ideal gown, captured in its transitory state and realised in the fashion for autumn/winter 1874/75, not forgetting a little commercial injection. 'We have all dreamed this gown without knowing it. M. [Charles Frederick] Worth alone knew how to design an apparel as fugitive as our thoughts.' The dress is not dreamed up as a material novelty alone; its impact was derived from its being eagerly anticipated in the collective imagination. The couturier only had to realise the attire which was as fugitive as the thoughts of his female clientele, whom Ix. had isolated from reality and confined to the salon and its 'rêve intérieur'. The female bourgeois was denoted as pure recipient, her appearance and existence determined by the male – in the figure of her husband and provider as well as through her artistically inclined couturier who composed her figure. While the man's thinking was ostensibly concerned with modernity's rationale, that is, political and economic progress, the woman's head was – literally as the vocabulary of the fashion magazine suggests – 'in the clouds', concerned with representing her impotent dreams.

The ephemerality and impotence, not just of the female consumer but of the subject of fashion itself, allowed for the intimate and secretive invention of a radically new discourse. Fashion magazines and their writing only came into being in the late eighteenth century, and it took time for their linguistic codes to be formed across modernity. Although literary journalism had existed before, manifest in reviews and occasional prose, there had been no model for the description of dresses and accessories. Like *la mode*, the mode of expression that was connected to it had to be created in its autonomy. Writers such as Balzac, Barbey d'Aurevilly and Mallarmé recognised the novelty inherent in their chosen discourses between 1830 and 1880. Therefore it appeared obvious to them to write about material novelties; and none was more transitory than fashion. To further the potential of the new, these writers composed female alter egos for themselves, who had not been connected to journalism or literary production at large. The novelists became women in their writing. *Mode et modernité* were reflected through a new medium, a new language and new personae, making the discourse on fashion in Balzac, Barbey d'Aurevilly and Mallarmé the most contemporary, fleeting, ephemeral and insubstantial, and thus most modern. The clothes were not material, even if Mallarmé's recipient in St Petersburg had seemed to affirm otherwise, but the discourse definitely was. The materialism of the text, allied in its format and content to highly priced couture and affluent consumers, resided in the environment that was formed around it in nineteenth-century Paris. Exposing the direct reflection of capitalism through fashion rendered the most fleeting its most influential critique.

Notes

1. Théophile Gautier, 'Salon de 1852', *La Presse*, 16 (27 May 1852), p. 2.
2. *Journal des Dames et des Modes*, 17.4 (20 January 1813), p. 25. The journal appeared at intervals of some five days in a format of 6 to 7 pages. The subscription for three months was 9 francs, so some ¾ of a franc per issue (a worker in the textile industry in 1813 earned around 2½ francs per day and a small bourgeois merchant around 5 francs).
3. Charles Baudelaire, 'Le Peintre de la vie moderne I: Le Beau, la mode et le bonheur', in *Œuvres complètes*, vol. 2 (Paris: Gallimard, 1976), p. 684; Eng. trans. by J. Mayne, *The Painter of Modern Life and Other Essays* (London: Phaidon, 1993), pp. 1–2.
4. E.B. [Honoré de Balzac], 'Physiologie de la toilette', in *Œuvres complètes*, vol. 39 (Paris: Conard, 1938), pp. 47–8; Eng. trans. by R. G. Elliott, 'Physiology of Attire', *Art in Translation*, 7.2 (2015), p. 179.
5. Ibid., p. 180; *servum pecus* had been used by the Roman poet Horace to decry a slavish crowd; see 'Epistularum Liber Primus XIX', in Horace, *Epistles*, ed. R. Mayer (Cambridge: Cambridge University Press, 1994), p. 84.
6. Balzac, 'Physiology of Attire', pp. 181–2.
7. H. de B. [Honoré de Balzac], 'Des mots à la mode', in *Œuvres complètes*, vol. 39, p. 34 .
8. H. de B., 'Des mots à la mode', pp. 34–5.
9. As a fitting cliché, the hostess is concerned with style, her husband with rational thought.
10. H. de B., 'Des mots à la mode', pp. 33–4.
11. H. de B., 'De la mode en littérature', in *Œuvres complètes*, vol. 39, p. 41.

12. In the novel *Le Centenaire ou Les Deux Béringheld*, published by Balzac under the pseudonym Horace de Saint-Aubin; see Yves Vadé, *Ce que modernité veut dire*, vol. 1 (Bordeaux: Presses universitaires de Bordeaux, 1998), p. 52.
13. Honoré de Balzac, 'D'un pantalon de poil de chèvre et de l'*étoile de Sirius*', *La Caricature*, 30 (26 May 1831).
14. See Barbey d'Aurevilly's diary-style entries about his daily routine of dressing (and hairdressing) in 'Premier Memorandum [13 August 1836–6 April 1838]' and 'Deuxième Memorandum [13 June 1838–22 January 1839]', in Jules Barbey d'Aurevilly, *Œuvres romanesques complètes*, vol. 2 (Paris: Gallimard, 1966), pp. 737–899 and 901–1026.
15. Maximilienne de Syrène, 'De l'élégance', in Jules Barbey d'Aurevilly, *Premiers articles* (Paris: Les Belles lettres, 1973), p. 86.
16. Ibid.
17. Maximilienne de Syrène, 'Revue critique de la mode', in Barbey d'Aurevilly, *Premiers articles*, p. 93.
18. The novel was *L'Amour impossible*, which had appeared in instalments in the pages of *Le Constitutionnel* in 1841. Barbey d'Aurevilly's letter to Trébutien is cited in Eugène Grelé, *Jules Barbey d'Aurevilly: sa vie et son oeuvre* (Caen: Jouan, 1902), p. 175.
19. Maximilienne de Syrène, 'Modes', in Barbey d'Aurevilly, *Premiers articles*, p. 311.
20. A term used by Baudelaire in the late 1850s: 'To create a trademark, that's genius. I must create a trademark.' Charles Baudelaire, 'Journaux intimes XIII: Fusees no. 20', in *Oeuvres complètes*, vol. 1 (Paris: Gallimard, 1975), p. 662; there is more on the *poncif* in the next chapter.
21. Philippe Burty, undated letter [September 1874] in James Lloyd Austin and Henri Mondor (eds), *Stéphane Mallarmé, Correspondance IV* (Paris: Gallimard, 1973), p. 587.
22. Princesse de Metternich, *Souvenirs de la Princesse Pauline de Metternich (1859–1871)* (Paris: Plon, 1922), p. 136.
23. Lehmann, *Tigersprung: Fashion in Modernity*, pp. 18–28.
24. Lefebvre, *Introduction to Modernity*, p. 171.
25. The fourth issue of *Change* featured excerpts from the 1935/36 book *Aesthetic Function* by the Czech formalist Jan Mukařovský, edited under the title 'structure, fashion, demand'; short excerpts from the structuralist study by Roland Barthes on *The Fashion System*; and a new essay by Michel Butor on fashion's essentially diachronic nature.
26. Michel Butor, 'Mode et moderne', *Change 4* (Paris: Seuil, 1968), pp. 13–28; Eng. trans. by R. G. Elliott, 'Fashion and the Modern', *Art in Translation*, 7.2 (2015), pp. 266–81.
27. The only contributions that appeared not as simulations of discourses but as actual products were the literary contributions by Mallarmé's writer friends. Education featured in the fashion journal as a result of

Mallarmé's day-to-day profession as a teacher in a Parisian secondary school.
28. More on the genesis and detailed composition of the journal can be found in Chapter 2 of my book *Tigersprung: Fashion in Modernity*.
29. Stéphane Mallarmé, 'Correspondence avec les abonnées', *La Dernière Mode*, 4 (18 October 1874), [p. 9]; see Stéphane Mallarmé, *Œuvres complètes* (Paris: Gallimard, 1945), p. 776.
30. Ix. 'Chronique de Paris', in Mallarmé, *Œuvres complètes*, p. 716.
31. Ibid.

Chapter 4

Markets for Modernity: Salons, Galleries and Fashion

I propose to stay in nineteenth-century France for this chapter and move on from fashion as written to its role in the formation of a new market for contemporary art. Fashion is abstracted again as a concept that goes beyond clothes and accessories, while the materialist method I am employing throughout this book continues to anchor the argument within the economic and social aspects of cultural production. For the present chapter this means discussing the history of the nascent gallery scene in Paris after 1860 as structurally congruent with an emergent fashion system. The setting for this congruency is the laissez-faire capitalism in France in the latter half of the nineteenth century, after Louis Napoléon III had staged a *coup d'état* and installed the Second Empire, recasting the reign of his uncle in the context of advanced industrialisation and the free market.[1]

In terms of method this means applying fashion studies to the historical research on the economic and cultural setting of Paris in the latter part of the nineteenth century. What does this imply for situating the discussion within, or indeed in contrast to, existing discourses on art and fashion? Materialist art history has a long tradition that begins with Hegel's books on aesthetics, and was politicised in historical-materialist writing towards the end of the nineteenth century, for instance in the work of Georgi Plekhanov. Subsequently, it experienced structural investigation in Soviet Productivism and (linguistic) formalism at the beginning of the twentieth century – as touched upon in Chapter 3 – and then returned to a self-consciously 'Marxist' art and cultural history through writers such as Max Raphael, Walter Benjamin and György Lucasz. The select writings on aesthetics by the Frankfurt School, who debated classical music and modern painting but also touched on the popular culture of, for example, magazines and films, were related to these endeavours. Their materialist take on cultural production and the culture industry has to be seen in the context of a left-Hegelian tradition that regards artistic and wider cultural expressions across history as concretely manifesting socio-political power structures and economic systems. Since the greater part of materialist art history up to the mid-1950s dealt with elevated, bourgeois culture, this economic system was assumed to be capitalist and its critique therefore continued to see artistic production as either confirmation of or a social challenge to an existing, implicitly exploitative and alienating political system. Concrete investigations into ownership and modes of production were regarded as a means to critically analyse the political-industrial complex that determined and was reflected in culture through a system of economic and cultural capital. Yet this was not explored by materialist art history to the same degree as social conditions and environments. It was not simply a matter of determining for whom artists produced works but who owned the networks of production and distribution for art. As argued above, the aspect of production became articulated when different forms of production, most notably between elitist and populist culture, began to be explored in the post-war period in France especially. Henri Lefebvre, the Situationists around Guy Debord, and the early writings of Roland Barthes started to contrast traditional forms of art production, for example in Balzac, or the structuring of urban spaces by town planners such as Baron Haussmann with populist expressions in advertising, sport or comic books. At this point the forms and ownership of production came to the fore, as the analogous character of commodity and art production was exposed.

The method of positioning 'fine' art next to populist art has, at least in France, a tradition that began with the Revolution and extended across the nineteenth century. Expressions in classical culture, from monumental architecture to easel paintings, were critically and politically contextualised through public discourses on demonstrations, commemorative events and entertainment spaces as well as applied art forms such as wallpaper or textile production. Implicit here was the focus on structures of production and consumption, not on the aesthetic theories of representation that had been discussed by educational and social elites. When art demonstratively encompassed, for instance, wallpaper designs in public buildings or firework displays in public gardens, its meaning was grounded in materiality, not in metaphysical precepts or aesthetic theories – but this very materiality then served as a political theory proper that fitted into emerging materialist histories and philosophies.

I therefore regard the present pairing of art history and fashion studies, the analogous reading of a market for culture and for couture in the latter half of the nineteenth century, as part of this structural approach of pairing of the classical or orthodox with the populist. Following Baudelaire and Benjamin, this can be rephrased as pairing the eternal with the transitory in order to show how such manifestations in contemporary art and contemporary fashion stand in the closest proximity and are subject to the same structural demands and socio-economic power structures in a shared culture industry.

This chapter looks at the structural relationship between the formation of a fashion industry (the erstwhile *couture-création*, later haute couture) and the developing market for contemporary art in Paris around the middle of the nineteenth century. Both are seen as mirror images of the economic and social conditions of the time, and this raises the question as to where one locates the origin of such closely related structures. Does fashion provide a model for art, or rather for its promotion; or, as traditional art history has postulated, did the art market emerge autonomously due to the progressive formation of a bourgeois society after the Industrial and French revolutions, while fashion, in order to gain cultural currency and status, attached itself to the rising significance of art in modernity? Anticipating here a conclusion to these queries, this chapter will argue for fashion having been constituent in forming the market for art, not vice versa. To reiterate, the word 'fashion' must not be reduced here to clothing and accessories, whether in *couture-création* or in mass-manufactured garments. Fashion in this historical and conceptual context means first of all a constant renewing of consumption. The notion of commodity fetishism, which always has to establish itself anew in the consciousness of the bourgeois market in order to generate novel products, and thereby approximates new economic and social relations, is directly and closely tied to the origin of fashion – as a mercantile structure of production, distribution and retail. As discussed above, one of the most significant concepts of modernity is that culture is based on the latest, ephemeral manifestations rather than on eternal and implicitly metaphysical or at least humanist values. This is the obvious consequence of an economic system based on competition between owners of capital and on the retention of the means of production, which propagates consumption as the principal social and cultural occupation, notwithstanding the fact that one part of consumption is ostensibly directed towards material products, another towards societal roles and yet another towards cultural learning.

Comparative Methods

I want now to explore the comparative approach for this chapter through a pairing of two extended quotations. Drawn from the same writer, these quotes also stand together by virtue of their shared socio-cultural setting, the salon. The first comes from a novel of 1871:

> His greatest treat was to accompany Renée to the illustrious Worms, the couturier of genius to whom the great ladies of the Second Empire bowed down. Maxime entered the salon of the great man with religious emotion. This salon was huge, square and furnished with enormous divans; it had a distinct female scent [. . .]
>
> It was often necessary for Renée and Maxime to attend in the antechamber for hours; a queue of at least twenty women sat there, waiting their turn, dipping biscuits into glasses of Madeira, helping themselves from the great table in the middle laden with bottles and plates of petits fours. The ladies had made themselves at home, talking freely, and when they ensconced themselves around the room, it was as if a flight of white lesbian doves had alighted on the sofas of a Parisian salon. [. . .] When at last the great Worms received Renée, Maxime accompanied her into the consulting room. He had ventured to speak on two or three occasions while the master was absorbed in contemplation of his client, much as Leonardo da Vinci is said by the high priests of art to have been absorbed in the presence of La Gioconda. The master had deigned to smile at the accuracy of Maxime's observations. He had Renée stand in front of a mirror that rose from the floor to the ceiling, and pondered with knit brows while Renée, in the grip of emotion, held her breath, so as not to move. After a few minutes, the master, as if seized and shaken by inspiration, sketched in bold, rapid strokes the work of art he had just conceived, exclaiming in short phrases:
>
> 'A Montespan dress in pale-grey faille. . ., the skirt describing a rounded basque in front. . ., large grey satin bows catching it up on the hips. . ., and a puffed apron of pearl-grey tulle, the puffs separated by strips of grey satin.' He pondered once again, seeming to reach down into the depths of his genius, and, with the triumphant facial contortion of a Sibyl on her tripod, concluded: 'We shall adorn the hair, on this delightful head, with Psyche's dreamy butterfly and its iridescent wings of azure.'
>
> But on other occasions, the inspiration was slow to come. In vain did the illustrious Worms summon it forth, concentrating all his faculties to no avail. He knitted his brows, turned pale, took his head in his hands and shook it in despair, until, beaten at last, he threw himself into an armchair, and would mutter in a pitiful voice:
>
> 'No, no, not today . . . It's impossible . . . You ladies expect too

much. My inspiration has completely dried up.' And he would show Renée the door, repeating: 'It's impossible, impossible, dear lady, you must come back another day . . . You elude me this morning.'²

The second quote opens an essay entitled 'L'Ouverture' (The Opening), which had been published a couple of years earlier:

> In terms of art we enter here the realm of the true specialist; I know of certain gentlemen who have gained an enormous reputation for themselves by doing nothing but scratch into their paint the same good lady sitting on the same haystack.
> We can see small-scale high reliefs that could serve confectionery and assorted sweets to beautiful ladies. Such small reliefs are a smashing success. The figurines on them are sculpted in wood or ivory with a delicacy that renders the masses excited and awestruck. One wonders why a free man would amuse himself by imitating the work of prisoners who are made to carve coconuts?
> [. . .]
> But I am forgetting the portraits. The flood of portraits mounts every year and threatens to drown the entire Salon. The explanation for this is very simple: there are many people who want to have their portrait painted but then do not buy the painting.³

A few weeks later the author intensified his polemic in adjudging 'the Actualists':

> Our artists are like coquettish women. They flirt with the masses. As soon as they perceive that classical painting has become a bit of a bore for the audience, they quickly abandon classical painting. Some risk putting on the austere black suit;⁴ most, however, prefer to dress themselves in the rich dresses of bourgeois and aristocratic women. There is not the slightest wish to appear truthful, not the merest endeavour to renew art and to elevate it by studying our present times. One senses that these painters would all paint stoppers for carafes if it were a fashion to paint stoppers for carafes. They cut their canvases to the modern, that's all. They are tailors whose only concern is to satisfy their clientele.⁵

Granted, it is an ambiguous undertaking to employ literary quotations as source material for research into art-historical structures, especially when pairing fiction with feuilleton. Yet the novel from which the first quotation is drawn is a prime example of nineteenth-century realism and an attempt to integrate art through its theme and manner of publication into the concrete material circumstances of its production. Émile Zola's novels of the RougonMacquart cycle were thoroughly researched and embraced an objective, or at least an anti-subjective, approach through the use of journalistic research, reference to newspaper cuttings, police reports, governmental decrees and so on, in order to pioneer a political and documentary form of literature that was later espoused by writers such as Henri Barbusse, Alfred Döblin and Upton Sinclair.[6] Furthermore, Zola's novel from which the above passage is drawn first appeared in instalments in the radically democratic satirical weekly *La Cloche* – banned by the Attorney General of the Third Republic[7] – and thereby experienced a form of exposure and distribution that opened up the work to diverse and politically interested audiences through sales at *kiosques* and public access in working men's libraries. In more general terms, the use of the above quotations seems pertinent also as they originated in a form of literary realism that took temporality and the rhythm of contemporary time as a measuring device for both its form and content – thereby performing an approximation of fashion and literature in modernity. Although using quotes from a novel or an art review is not an empirical method by any means, the above section on Worms, that is, the couturier Charles Frederick Worth, does not constitute a simple satire but a well-researched genre painting of contemporary cultural phenomena. Like Zola's novel on the art and artists of Paris, *L'Œuvre*, the quote above is germane to the social and cultural reality that was present in news stories, parliamentary reports, the minutes of court injunctions (e.g. on censorship), as well as the author's direct studies of the milieu. And as with the contemporary painters whom Zola assessed in *Mon Salon*, 'the Actualists' whom art history would later come to re-label as Impressionists, the novelist was concerned with a material presentation of modernity. Here, the fashionable salon (of the arts) and indeed the couture salon offered its best setting.

When Worms – or rather, Worth – purported to be an artist, and when his clients engaged in a form of consumption that was similar to the one that drew visitors in Paris in the second half of the nineteenth century to the annual *Salon* in the Musée du Louvre, the parallel between fashion and art is raised from its spatial and factual environment to a structural level. In *La Curée* the reader learned of a technique that had been employed by the couturier to present himself as an independent 'artist', and thereby distance himself from the vagaries of the market. This was seen as imperative to lending his designs the subjective autonomy that fashion in clothing as a social phenomenon, even in its rarified form as *couture-création*, was thought not to possess (unless it were to exist as an eccentric, esoteric costume). In an age when the industrialised production of commodities began to proliferate, including mass-produced clothing made by mechanised weaving and industrial sewing machines, the notion of the creative maker who can imbue a sartorial novelty by hand with a new style and a decorative or material trend became central. The name of the *couturier* or *couturière* was not simply identifying a particular use of fabrics, pattern cut or embellishment, but authored a work of applied art as a material gesture. The skilled hand of the fashion designer ostensibly touched and guided each stage of the production process and thereby removed the prominent figure of labour from the cultural equation: the owner of production (capital) and the worker (labour) were synthesised in the figure of the *couturier/couturière*, and the capitalist process that divided labour (both artisanal and industrial) into productive fields could be safely ignored. For the consumers of couture who sustained themselves mostly by profits from capital investments, financial or real estate speculation – thus demonstrably not working themselves[8] – this synthetic manifestation of capital and labour was very attractive. The transitoriness of existence, especially for bourgeois females who were expressively removed from concrete economic structures, became fixed in the latest dress for a season, and the traces of making, even when performed arduously by a group of poorly paid *petits mains* in the couture studio, were erased in favour of the 'artistic' gestures of the couturier.

Aligning sartorial fashion with subjectivity in modern art became a historical trait that started with couturiers such as Worth and continued via Paul Poiret, Elsa Schiaparelli and Yves Saint Laurent to the early work of the Maison Martin Margiela in the late 1990s or today's endeavours by the various brands in the LMVH or Kering stables. We will see later on in this chapter how this trait has given rise to particular structures in today's market for contemporary art, but I would like to return now to the question of what art has taken from fashion – not in formal terms, but structurally.

Poncif: Marking Trade

The salon is the site for a particular form of cultural production and consumption. Baudelaire, who had researched the significance of the black suit as the epitome of the meaning proper of fashion for his contemporary culture, and who was the first writer to link etymologically and conceptually the words *mode* and *modernité*, exclaimed in the early 1860s: 'To create a *poncif* is genius. I must create a *poncif*.'[9] The *poncif*, logo or trademark creates the status of the artist, forms him as a creative subject, distinguishes him culturally, and renders him competitive in the marketplace. Baudelaire, like Zola after him, combined the epistemological design of the artist's subjectivity with the economic reality of the Second Empire. He would further determine this concept by placing it within the newly defined connection between fashion and modernity. As we have seen, it was fashion for clothing in particular that appeared to Baudelaire as programmatic, and partly also metaphorical, in its constant desire to renew the aesthetic and stylistic approaches to the production of objects in material culture.

Once again it is important to connect metaphorical meaning with the materialism of the object. The etymology of the *poncif* as an artistic cliché or commonplace that is repeated without any trace of originality and which dated back to the 1820s had originated in the perforated paper pattern that was used to transfer a drawing on to a canvas or dressmaker's *toile* – a meaning that went back to the mid-sixteenth century in France. The word *ponce*, from which *poncif* derives, had come to denote, from around 1725 onwards, a special ink made from oil and lampblack that was used to mark and trace outlines on fabric. This corresponded concretely with the idea of the trademark as a particular expression that rendered a product instantly recognisable. A *disegno*, the sketch for a design, was made and transferred to a paper pattern, which could be used to trace numerous copies on to a canvas or calico *toile*, or even directly on to fabric. This was done by using a tracing wheel to perforate the pattern paper and then employing a small, open-weave fabric pouch filled with the *ponce* to tap along the perforations so as to produce a dotted outline on the fabric which the dressmaker or tailor used to cut out the pieces for the garment.

In dialectical fashion, the *poncif* as indicator of reproducibility encompassed the material thesis, in being able to produce copies, with its immaterial antithesis, in reducing subjectivity in favour of an economically recognised trademark. The *poncif* allowed for the wider distribution of a creative idea through (mechanised) copies but thereby allocated the idea to the market, away from its cognitive origin in the mind of the writer at his desk, the painter at his easel or indeed the couturier at his dress stand.[10] At the beginning of haute couture, as can be seen in Zola's ironic account of Worth creating a new outfit for his client, a division had opened up between the designer sketching rapidly to achieve a 'composition' of fabrics, trimmings and accessories, and the making of flat patterns in the studio that incorporated the copy of a successful pattern-design to be kept and reused for different designs and in diverse textiles. This in turn led to the formation of two distinct couture studios as reflections of high fashion's distinct methods of production and of the *poncif*'s structure, which could signify simultaneously a subjective trademark and an objectified, serial reproduction. In one sense the *poncif* is the elusive commodification of a personal style, in the other a material technique. One studio realises the individualist, 'artistic' technique of modelling on the stand, where fabrics are draped around the female figure (the model or dress-form). This is the *atelier flou*, the studio in the couture house devoted to three-dimensional, creative pattern cutting in pliable, often flowing (*flou*) textiles. The other studio realises flat pattern cuts, often having recourse to 'blocks' or pre-designed paper patterns, where *ponce* has been employed to delineate the design. This is the *atelier tailleur* where tailoring techniques are used to assemble garments constructively from heavier and stiffer textiles.[11]

This structural distinction reflects on the dialectics of the original and the copy in fashion, the subjective and the objectified, the artwork and the commodity. The 'artistic composition' of draping and the structured pattern cut are both used by the *couturier* or *couturière* and can easily be synthesised in one and the same design or across one outfit. Yet the two distinct forms of making marked the coming together of new and individually composed forms and silhouettes, for example when the volume of a bustled skirt is paired with the established pattern cut for a jacket front with lapels. In the latter half of the nineteenth century the fusing of the immaterial and material in the double meaning of the word *poncif* came to manifest the way in which mechanised copies provided optimised formal solutions, which had to be imbued with subjective gestures in order to create new fashions.

Reading this politically, one can observe an established base of rigid patterns upon which liberal gestures could be imprinted, so that modernity could progress through comparatively radical styles while resolutely maintaining its socio-economic superstructure. The *poncif* is not historicist in subjectifying a past style or trend as a singular gesture for a season or a short-lived artistic trend, but is historical-materialist in denoting, literally, outlines and repeat patterns across time. The *poncif* was only effective as a logo or trademark when it was recognised as a repeated gesture within the artist's work, so that the writer or painter could be distinguished stylistically and succeed economically – as well as becoming historicised as an exponent of a style or movement. The repeat patterns that Marx had observed in the reign of Louis Napoléon III, and that Baudelaire with self-effacing cynicism had declared as his artistic mantra, were used by Benjamin, as we have seen, to define the rhythm of modernity in which fashion recreates its own past as a copy by delineating a pattern and then imbuing it with what is purported to be a radical gesture, a transitory revolution that displays the old in the guise of the new.[12]

The *Salon*

From the dialectical structure of couture production in the studio I would like to venture on to the environment of display and reception – not only for fashionable clothing but for the latest trends in art. I want to inquire into the economic context from which the *Salon* emerged as a site and how it contained and synthesised structurally the markets for both art and fashion. Continuing with my method of reading examples from literary production through material environments, I will now discuss another part of Zola's Rougon-Macquart cycle, the novel *L'Œuvre*[13] of 1886, in which the traditional, annual *Salon* of the Académie des Beaux-Arts was used as one setting, in marked contrast to the newly installed *Salon des refusés* for rejected – and implicitly progressive – artists. The official *Salon*, which began as an institution for academic painting in the late eighteenth century, became entrenched in its orthodoxy throughout the nineteenth century. For 1863 the number of artworks that were refused admission to the *Salon* numbered more than 2,200 (out of 5,000 submitted that year).[14] The protests by artists and the negative publicity in the press about this rigid and supposedly rigged process of selection and the associated notion of cultural conservatism, even anti-modernism, worried the government of Louis Napoléon. As mentioned previously, the Second Empire had recast imperial history as grounds for the promotion of a free market and a liberal culture industry. So, the perception of an officially sanctioned *Salon* as unwilling to recognise the latest tendencies in art was anathema to the promotion of fashionable tendencies that had distinguished Paris as a centre for the culture industry. Like the empress Eugénie espousing the new clothes by Worth as a mixture of past silhouettes and new surfaces, her husband, despite an obvious preference for the historicism of royal portraitists such as Franz Xaver Winterhalter or Alexandre Cabanel which he shared with his wife,[15] wanted to be seen as recognising the latest cultural tendencies – provided they did not actually criticise his regime. Thus Louis Napoléon's government let it be known that it was glad to defer the critique of the academic *Salon* to the new, bourgeois consumers of art: 'His majesty, intent on letting the public judge the legitimacy of these reclamations, has decided that the works of art that had been refused are now to be shown in another part of the *Palais de l'Industrie*.'[16]

This *Salon des refusés* had been commissioned already in 1843 at the Musée du Louvre by his predecessor, the *roi bourgeois* Louis Philippe,[17] but now the motivation shifted from ostensive bourgeois liberalism to a free-market application of economics to cultural production. New tendencies needed to be embraced not for their progressive character, let alone for any systemic critique or challenge they might contain, but because they promoted repeat consumption. It follows that paintings were to be reviewed according to the dictates of fashion. Cabanel's official portrait of Louis Napoléon III, which was included in the academic *Salon* of 1865, was condemned not for its sycophantic historicism or retrogressive style but because it showed the sitter's sartorial faux pas:

> Ah! The suit of the portrayed! And his silk stockings? Is this a valet to whom Monsieur Cabanel has lent these threadbare rags? Mme de Sault – Mme Guy de Charnacé, *née* comtesse d'Agoult – who knows her stuff, since she writes about fashion, dispensed in her review in *Le Temps* the following sartorial advice: 'As much as the jury had deliberated before awarding the honorary medal to this portrait, so much had the public assiduously and unanimously expressed its less than favourable judgement of this piece. To whom belongs this "success"? To a pair of silk stockings to which Monsieur Cabanel perhaps owes the cold reception that his portrait has experienced.'[18]

Fashion was materialised in art not simply by being featured within the narrative of a painting or by the style in which the work was executed, but, more succinctly, by the *fashionability* of the cultural commodity as such; by its acceptance into the canon of the latest expressions and its transitory relevance for the present.

The *Salon de refusés* and its subsequent incarnation the *Salon des independents* have been traditionally read by art historians[19] as the birthplaces of modern art through repeated formal challenges by the avant-garde (Realism, Impressionism, Post-Impressionism). Yet these sites were more complex than a binary opposition between academic convention and formal radicalism. What made the institution of the *Salon de refusés*, which Zola had used as an alternative *mise-en-scène* in his artworld novel, so significant was not its oppositional character to an established style in art but the fact that it had been instigated by a regressive, royalist government. The official patronage of new, at that time still marginalised, art was effected in order to generate economic and cultural capital for a city and a nation that wanted to see itself as culturally progressive. For capitalist modernity, a binary contrast did not suffice for analytic purposes; it required the dialectic perception of *modernité* as being made up from the ancient and the modern, from the transitory recasting of the eternal. Thus the review of the first *Salon des refusés* by the French writer-journalist Théophile Thoré/William Bürger was prescient. Thoré's early interest had been in radical political questions and French republicanism during the February Revolution of 1848. But when he attempted to equate contemporary materialism with the utopian socialism of Saint-Simon and Étienne Cabet's Icarian movement, Thoré was publicly criticised by Cabet. The materialist-positivist philosopher took obvious objection to having his promotion of workers' cooperatives as an alternative to capitalist economic structures reduced to frivolous expressions of atheist and excessively liberal communality by an art critic.[20] Despite this criticism from his peers, Thoré's 1863 review of the *Salon* remains one of the more materialist critiques of the culture industry of the Second Empire, notwithstanding the established format of running through a series of painters and their works. The critic observed across the two *Salons* in the main building and the annexe

> two hostile currents, which perpetuate, to put it differently, the ardent struggle between classicists and romantics, or if you will, between conservatives and innovators, between tradition and originality. Do we not find on the one hand Romans in an age of decadence, generating refined pastiches of dead styles, and, on the other hand, naïve barbarians, seeking reality and life?[21]

Thoré's simultaneity of the ancient and the modern, of historicism and material reality, tallied with the emergent discourse on modernity, but his concern was also with how such a dialectic manifested itself in material, technical terms. He subsumed the new artists who featured in what he termed the 'Salon of the Condemned' into a trend without any unifying characteristics:

> A naïve stranger who visits the *salon des Réprouvés*, who believes himself to be in the official exhibition, would suppose without a doubt that the French School, in ostensible unity, concerns itself with the depiction of man and of nature, which it views without any preconceived ideal, without a fixed style, without tradition, and also without any personal inspiration. It seems as if the artists take art back to its origin, without preoccupying themselves with what had come before them in terms of civilization ... The people conceive in their barbarous state, I am not sure how, something sincere, emotive and at the same time burlesque and imperfect. New and singular indeed [*nouveauté et singularité*].

[...]
French art, viewed through these outcast works, seems only to begin, or to begin again ... Instead of looking for contours, what the academy calls *le dessin* [working drawing], instead of labouring on details, what the classical lovers of art had termed *le fini* [finish], the aspiration here is to produce a striking unity of effects, being neither anxious about improvement nor about minutiae of details.[22]

Théophile Gautier, who had pioneered the critical coinage of *modernité* in his democratic halcyon days under Louis Philippe, had become by then the mouthpiece of a regressive empire. His vice-presidency of the Académie des Beaux-Arts, his editorship of the official *Moniteur* and his newly awarded, very substantial pension of 3,000 francs per year[23] had turned Gautier into the prime exponent of what modernity in capitalism had to become: a promotional structure for commodity production and the associated generation of inequalities and repression. Yet the dialectics that Gautier and his erstwhile friend Baudelaire had observed within *mode et modernité* continued to affect cultural production. Thoré was only one in a long line of critics who noted the apparition of ostensibly progressive tendencies within constant repetitions, and wondered what economic and social system would bring forth such self-negating structures.

Zola, as part of this critical lineage,[24] presented the reader with two types of art merchant, one a traditional lover and connoisseur of the works he is representing, the other an exponent of capitalism's speculative accumulation of commodities. Both characters were based on real-life models whom Zola knew and whose business tactics he had analysed – as can be gleaned from his sketches, compiled as *Notes de Guillemet*. The traditional *marchand de tableaux* in Paris before 1848 combined the sale of artworks with items related to their production, for example paper, canvas, paints or frames. After the February Revolution these merchants were succeeded by a new type of entrepreneur who instigated a number of structural changes, especially with regard to communication and promotion. The market for art in France had not developed organically since the Revolution, when the first public museum had been inaugurated and official debates had questioned the need to conserve past court and Church artefacts. Selling and buying artworks appeared to be a radical break with the past, instigated through the political and economic framework that Louis Napoléon implemented after 1851. There was no model yet on which to base the market for art, neither was there a progressively evolving structure for consuming culture, as there had been neither a sufficiently expansive bourgeois class, nor had the mechanisms of a contemporary culture industry been created, in which the latest and most transitory can exist in dialectical relation with the immutable of the classical canon. Zola wrote with undisguised irony in his essay 'Le Moment artistique': 'Such is our time. We are civilised, we have boudoirs and *salons*; whitewash is fine for the bourgeois, we need paintings for the walls of the rich.'[25]

The new market for contemporary art defined itself through capital speculation, *ergo* an economic method that strives to create artificial exchange and surplus values, which in turn can be exponentiated through relevant financial strategies. The art market in the second half of the nineteenth century was preoccupied with incessantly renewing the Baudelairean *poncif*, which allowed the presentation of the old in the guise of the new and showed programmatically its very modernity, attaching itself expressively to the modern material object with regard to both content and form. The *actualistes* or Impressionists with their narratives of hedonistic bourgeois who were portrayed in the latest fashions, their style of painting which expressively emphasised the transitory and ephemeral (changing light conditions, etc.), and their new gallerists and art dealers, represented a resolutely seasonal and contemporary phenomenon.

Zola's *L'Œuvre* presented the art dealer of the Impressionists as a novel type. References for the novelist were new gallery owners such as Georges Petit, Hector Brame and, most pertinently, Paul Durand-Ruel, all united within the fictional character of Naudet: 'A very chic appearance, English jacket, coach waiting by the door, box at the opera, who sells the paintings to the imbecilic amateur, and who does not know anything about art but acquires a canvas like a stock market option.'[26] Naudet (like Durand-Ruel in real life) broke decisively with the tradition of selling art that had been prevalent in the previous generation:

> The ambition grabs hold of him, he wants to sink the Goupils, to beat Brame, to be the first, and to centralise his operations. He builds a townhouse in the rue de Sèze, a veritable palace ... A department store for painting [*les magasins du Louvre*] ... He stocks his gallery and waits for the Americans who come in May [to the annual *Salon*]. He stages exhibitions. He buys for 10,000 francs in order to sell for 50,000 ... A stock market for paintings, a syndicate to show paintings.[27]

Such speculation required the *poncif*, depended on the woman on the haystack whom Zola had ridiculed in his critique. It needed fashion. In order to furnish the walls of the rich with paintings, a mere fulfilling of demand did not suffice, since this demand did not yet exist in the art market. Such demand had to be created first; it had to be generated in an artificial and artful way. This was done either through causing a scarcity of existing artworks – thus Durand-Ruel bought up the entire estate of artists such as Théodore Rousseau, including unfinished and abandoned works, preliminary drawings and sketchbooks, in order to control their release to the market; or it functioned by promoting single artists through the genesis of the solo exhibition in private galleries after 1848, which supported the progressive subjectification of the autonomous artist and the promotion of stylistic movements.[28]

These manoeuvres were based structurally on fashion, especially on the fashion for clothing. The *couturier* or *couturière* was first of all determined through his or her *poncif*; each style was the fashion designer's very own, and despite the early formation of the Chambre syndicale de la haute couture in 1868 under the auspices of Worth, it was not yet the fixed seasonal succession of collections but the single character of the *couturier/couturière* that drew the clientele: the artistic compositions of Worth, the material transparency of Jacques Doucet, the decorative opulence of Émile Pingat, and so on.

The emphasis on subjectivity and individual trademarks was a perfect fit for the ideological as well as social development in France from the 1850s onwards. Yet I would like to eschew a wider discussion of the philosophical discourse on individualism, despite its obvious application to contemporary artistic creation, in favour of its material circumstances. As the sociology of this time analysed, social individualism was extremely rare in modernity,[29] not because of any dominant socially collective structures but, on the contrary, because the apparent liberty of the individual only existed under the *octroi* of the object. Industrial capitalism in France in the second half of the nineteenth century generated the dominance of objectified structures in which the individual was only perceived as an effigy of the totality of her or his society. She or he stands within, and only very rarely outside, a social and cultural form that was determined by political economy and ideology. Thus Baudelaire's call for the *poncif* testified to a desperate and perhaps also cynical realisation that the subject could no longer define or distinguish her-/himself epistemologically, but solely in terms of exchange values in the market: the significance of fashionable form, powers of consumption and dealing in social etiquette. Correspondingly, when the artist admitted to himself that he existed only via the *poncif*, and when the market through feuilleton, gallery or *Salon* structured his existence for him, he simply had to succumb to fashion and had to work alongside it in order to avoid falling behind, out of fashion, or into disrepute. In the salons of the (haute) bourgeoisie, the haystacks of 1868, Worth's satin gown of 1871 and perhaps even the instalments of Zola's novel themselves quickly became old-fashioned, and for the continuous existence of his commodities the artist had to react to or, better, pointedly embrace the very latest in form and content.

At what point was fashion to be recognised as a general phenomenon, as extending from its material manifestation in fabrics and objects, and how did it present itself in the culture industry in Paris after 1860? The fashion for clothing, in the guise of the above-mentioned *couture-création* and the subsequent haute couture, appeared dialectically as structural constant and constantly changing genre picture. The gowns, boots, interior decorations and gestures were changed to be understood as part of a material avant-garde that defined groups who desired to adopt and emulate it. As mentioned in Chapter 2, the sociologists Tarde and Simmel had observed already at the end of the nineteenth century that fashion constantly dies and is reborn within a new, seemingly radical innovation, only to repeat the process shortly afterwards.[30] The same 'avant-garde' was celebrated in the art market. The gallerist provided insider information by means of promoting progressive styles and movements, and the intimate advance of knowledge permitted the subject to remove himself from the societal form and elevated him to the realm of cultural consciousness that appears inaccessible to the other classes. The dealer sold speculation on what was to come in art, the cultural capital that was in the process of being formed. The client trusted in him so as to be able materially to apply this advance knowledge, in the form of direct financial investment – this artist, this movement would be popular and successful – or to establish social status: 'I am buying something that no one else in my class has yet.' For both types of speculation, for both areas of fashion and of art, the general public performed a role which also had to be understood as dialectic. Fashion occupied itself in its desired acceptance simultaneously with its rejection by the public (in the nineteenth century, the theatrical *épater la bourgeoisie*). As long as a gown, a painting, a piece of theatre or a moral position was able to shock and disgust the public, the avant-garde was able to exist. When the work became too obviously bracketed within the consumption of the culture industry, it had to be replaced by a new avant-garde that railed against the 'old', and the cyclical process, the unlocking of new investments, could continue.

However, as detailed above, these 'innovations' or 'revolutions' could not consist of esoteric or marginal styles. If a fashion (for art, for clothing) remained contained in itself, if it was not brought to the public through a self-supporting system of promotion, criticism and reception, it could not partake in the capitalist economic process. The nineteenth-century gallerists in Paris therefore developed a number of structural devices that were to define the modern market for art. I would like briefly to present two of these. The first is the example of the gallery or, better, the enterprise of Adolphe Goupil et Cie., whom the fictional Naudet wanted to trump in Zola's *L'Œuvre*. From 1867 onwards Goupil developed, in adaptation of the Woodbury process, the *photogravure*, which was a direct, photographic, economically lucrative copy of a painting, replacing the erstwhile laborious transposition of the image through lithography or etching. The Goupil enterprise, founded in 1860, exhibited art, acquired works inclusive of their rights of reproduction, distributed these reproductions, and subsequently released the painting – with a significantly enhanced public visibility due to its mechanical reproduction – back into the market. This speculation with the work of art could reap profits through a simple re-sale (although this was a high-risk strategy) but was much more assured through the marketing of reproductions. Zola wrote in one of his art criticisms of 1867:

> Obviously, M. Gérôme [the history painter Jean-Léon Gérôme, son-in-law of Adolphe Goupil] works for the company of Goupil. He creates a painting so that this painting can be reproduced through photography and engraving and be sold in thousands of copies.[31]

The reproduction lent continuity to art, maintaining the impact of the painting long after it had vanished into the hands of a private collector or had been locked into (the vaults of) a museum, where only a social, educational and geographical elite could access it.

Goupil graded the reproductions in terms of exclusivity and price, whereby the cheapest edition in the form of small-scale *cartes de visites* or the more costly, larger *cartes album* were made available to an extensive sector of the bourgeoisie after 1867, whereas the high-quality photographic reproductions in the series 'Musée Goupil' retained an air of exclusivity – and commanded a much higher premium – through their grand format and portfolio presentation.[32] During the Second Empire a comparable process was introduced to sculpture. The renowned photographer Gaspard-Félix Tournachon (better known today under his pseudonym Nadar) took a picture of the figure of Phryne, which had been based in turn on a well-known painting by Gérôme from 1861, entitled *Phryné devant l'Aréopage*. This image was subsequently reproduced in three dimensions through *photosculpture* and widely distributed in France and abroad. Zola commented as late as 1877 on the enduring public impact of the Phryne:

> a tiny, naked, caramel-coloured figure devoured by the eyes of old men; the caramel saves the appearance ... He [Gérôme] is infamous for painting his works just so that they can be photographed: these reproductions serve to decorate thousands of bourgeois *salons*.[33]

Gérôme was fashionable; his works sold through a myriad of reproductions, yet he was not *à la mode* within the parameters of a progressive culture industry, since he had become unable, at least by the time of Zola's critique, to create or maintain a coveted *poncif*. Gérôme produced, if not for the masses, certainly for an expanded public, and it would be the Manets, Renoirs and Degas of gallerists such as Durant-Ruel, Petit and Brame who would monopolise contemporary artistic discourse and attain future speculative value. However, conceptually speaking, the reverse was also true, in that Gérôme, in openly exploiting the latest marketing strategies and techniques, could be said to have been very modern indeed, whereas the Impressionists could be perceived as following old inherited pattern in their artistic production in oil on canvas.

The second structural device I would like to discuss relates to the department stores that from 1850 onwards became temples of consumption for inscribing fashion in the mind of the general public. The department store demarcated an oppositional site to the salon of the *couturier* or the *couturière* in which the subjectivism of individualised commodities was promoted, although both share material (textiles) and form of communication (fashion on display). The department store mediated fashion as a shared experience, not as an exclusive appointment in a secluded room but as a collective display and performance. The movement through, across, up and down the department store was a reification and commodification of social interaction, with which consumers readily and often joyfully engaged. Even more than the Benjaminian arcade lined with replete shop windows, the department store with its counters, display cases and mannequins that were disseminated across floor levels allowed for the commodity to be moved from a composed display of goods to their spatial performance on the body through sartorial fashion – and this transfer from space to body was a prominent material iteration of the process that Marx had observed for commodity fetishism. The female consumer readied herself for the shopping experience, within the scenography of new metal-frame buildings with innovatively moving stairs and novel lighting features, by stepping out in her latest finery to purchase further additions to her wardrobe. And it was no surprise that the fetishistic ritual of consumption spilled over into new pathologies, so that the department stores became sites of increased kleptomania or hyphephilia – sexual satisfaction derived from stealing and touching fabrics.[34]

Commodity fetishism, intensified by the increased circulation and cyclical display of new fashions in clothes and accessories, made it entirely logical for the founders of the first large Parisian department stores to consume recent fashions in the art market. They acquired thus the latest movements and schools of painting as promoted by the galleries of Durand-Ruel or Petit. Aristide Bouçicaut, founder of the Bon Marché department store (1852), bought Realist art (e.g. Courbet); Ernest Cognacq and Louise Jay, after founding La Samaritaine, immediately began to collect the first generation of Impressionist painters; Théophile Bader, the director of the Galeries Lafayette, moved from École de Barbizon painters to the Impressionists; and Ernest Hoschedé, the owner of department stores in the rue de Poissonnière, not only published the journal *L'Art de la mode* but also secured for himself principal Impressionist works even before the first group exhibition at Durand-Ruel had opened its doors in April 1874.[35] Why did these capitalists, who made their money in fashion (in both the narrow and wider sense of the word), feel compelled to buy into an artistic avant-garde by acquiring comparatively unknown painters? While a kinship might have been felt by the retailers of fashion with the fashionable subjects and objects in the 'Actualist'/Impressionist paintings, the merchant and the gallerist were instrumental indeed in stimulating tastes and interests. The owners and directors of the large department stores did not buy from just anybody. In 1862 they sought out Durand-Ruel in the rue de la Paix, the street of luxury retail, where art galleries nestled next to the showrooms of Worth and other couturiers. From 1867 they visited him in the rue Lafitte, the new street for the arts, where adjacent to the town house of the gallerist Petit and the mansion of the collector Hoschedé, one could find the salons of the royal dressmaker Laurent-Richard, of the *modiste* Guichard, and of the *couturière* Palmyre. This neighbourhood in the first arrondissement constituted the spatial and, significantly, structural proximity between the material character of fashion and that of art. Pierre Assouline wrote in his biography of Durand-Ruel:

For art dealers like Durand-Ruel the moment arrives in the middle of the nineteenth century when they can interest art lovers in the entire work of a *créateur*, and not merely in his annual party piece [for the *Salon*]. The price for paintings is now determined, too, by criteria like originality and novelty. The price that is, not the value.[36]

Creations in art and fashion defined themselves, particularly within modernity, through an originality that resided within the concept of novelty itself. New forms of production such as the Impressionist painting-style, novel distribution methods such as Goupil's *photogravure* or the *photosculpture*, and contemporary types of consumption all generated an originality that had moved away, already at its historical point of origin, from the subjectivity or professed autonomy of modern art. The equivalent value which was equated with price – and not only within the context of industrial capitalism in France after 1852 – was not inherent in the work but became determined externally through the very reaction of art to economic and ideological conditions. Impressionism might affect an oppositional tendency – and artists such as Édouard Manet and Camille Pissaro did indeed have strong political convictions – but it derived its originality from the visualisation of fashion that surrounded and enveloped it: in colours, forms, narratives and material application. The fashion for sumptuous, avowedly artistic clothing, the emerging haute couture, simultaneously fuelled and succumbed to the contemporary market in an obvious and direct mode. Despite the creative work of *couturier* and *couturière*, the fashion for designed clothing could not be directed teleologically towards absolute autonomy or a complete, that is, esoteric, subjectivity. In order to exist, fashion had to be allied with consumption within the culture industry. It thus directly mirrored modernity and was not compelled to lose itself in aesthetic transpositions, justify its existence in the market, or critically question itself.

This applied in equal measure to the concrete financial structures within the culture industry of the time. For example, Durand-Ruel borrowed throughout the latter half of the nineteenth century substantial amounts of money from the banker Charles Edwards – his neighbour in the rue Lafitte – in order to finance the rapid rise of his art dealership, in a similar way to Naudet's fictional operations in Zola's *L'Œuvre*. As security for these loans, Durand-Ruel established the 'collection Edwards', which he replenished with the estate of Rousseau and also with works by Delacroix, Dupré, and so on. This

5 View through the window of the Fondazione Bonotto on to the factory floor, Molvena 2016

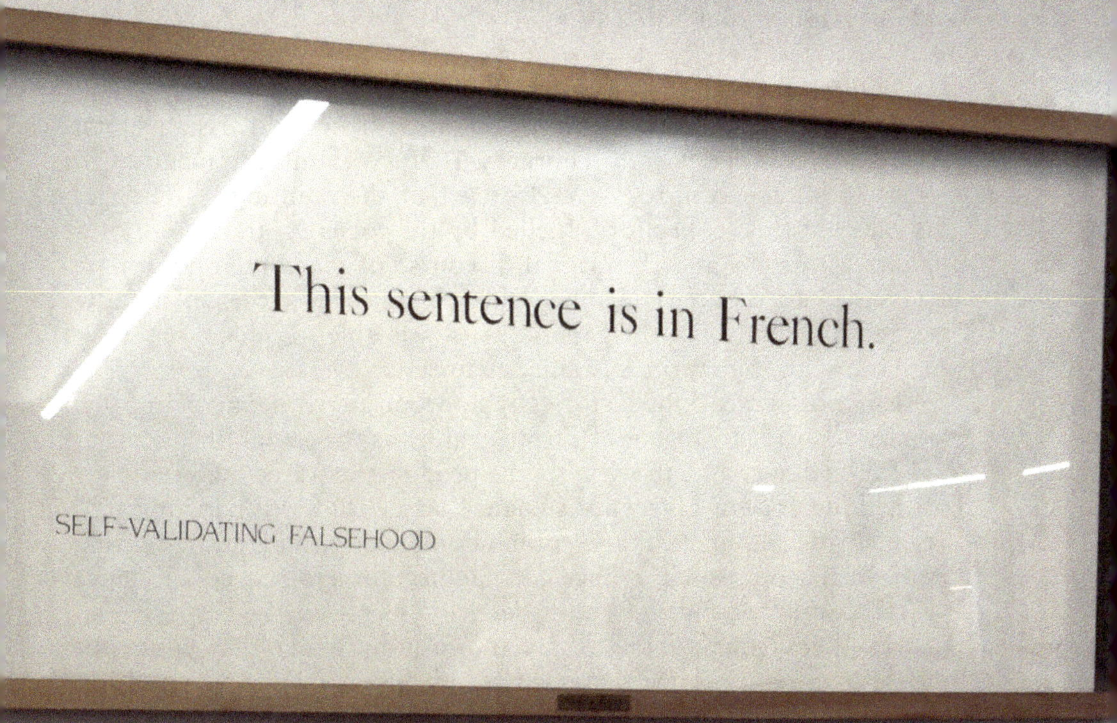

This sentence is in French.

SELF-VALIDATING FALSEHOOD

collection, a fictional construct since it existed only in name and in Durand-Ruel's storage, was auctioned off in the Parisian Hôtel Drouot over three days in February 1870, without any mention to press or audience as to the real owner of the paintings.[37] The rise in value of this 'collection', fuelled by the focus on the *œuvre* of a few select artists and the critical discourse of the contemporary art press, benefited both the banker whose investment in the gallery now reaped dividends and the gallerist who was able to update his stock in hand with even more sustained financial prowess.

It is not cynical but historically appropriate to define art in this context as the fetishising of surplus value; as the social product that was valued over and above what the producer required materially for its making and for his own sustenance. After 1848 this had appeared as a new development that went hand in hand with institutionalising industrial capitalism in France and had become a logical consequence of its economic conditions and practices. Surplus value surpassed an assumed equivalent value for art and fashion, which they could not possess in reality, since they satisfied idealised social needs and not material ones that could be quantified through use value. Speculation within fashion assumed a dimension that resided not simply in direct financial transactions. Fashion was speculation itself; it had to create an object that the subject took to herself as self-determining. The gown, the dinner service, the chaise longue, the new way of showing oneself in the box at the races, all had to appeal to a social stratum in order to be comprehended as fashion. The *créateur*, or the applied or fine artist, could not plan simply how taste would develop, just as the client of the *couturier* or artist would not know if and when his investments would rise in the stock market (unless they had been privy to the above-mentioned insider information). But the designer, as much as the gallerist of the avant-garde, was able to create fashion through particular marketing strategies when he had situated himself as a taste-maker for his clientele and perhaps also in the public eye. Such a making of taste within modernity did not mean developing a cognitive subject but rather the emergence of a material object, a process to which fashion lent its essential rhythm and form.

Notes

1. For a detailed discussion of the coup in its political, economic and social contexts, Karl Marx's *The Eighteenth Brumaire of Louis Bonaparte* [1852] is indispensable. Among the more recent works on the socio-economic environment of the Second Empire are Charles H. Pouthas et

al. (eds), *Démocratie, réaction, capitalisme, 1848–1860* (Paris: Presses Universitaires de France, 1984); Pierre Guiral, *La Vie quotidienne en France à l'âge d'or du capitalisme: 1852–1879* (Paris: Hachette, 1976); and for the production of textiles and fashion, Claude Fohlen, *L'Industrie textile au temps du second empire* (Paris: Plon, 1956).
2. Émile Zola, *La Curée*, in *Les Rougon-Macquart*, vol. 1 (Paris: Lacroix, Verboeckhiven et Cie., 1871), pp. 123–5; Eng. trans. by A. Goldhammer, *The Kill* (New York: The Modern Library, 2005), pp. 98–100 [translation modified].
3. Émile Zola, 'L'Ouverture' [dated 2 May 1868], in *Écrits sur l'art* (Paris: Gallimard, 1991), pp. 191–5, here p. 192.
4. See also Charles Baudelaire's subsequent eulogy on the *l'habit noir* as 'heroism in modern life' and exemplary for the close connection between *mode et modernité* in his review of the art at the 'Salon of 1846'. Charles Baudelaire, 'Salon de 1846: XVIII. De l'héroïsme de la vie moderne', in *Œuvres complètes*, vol. 2 (Paris: Gallimard, 1976), pp. 487–96.
5. Émile Zola, 'Les Actualistes' [dated 24 May 1868], in *Écrits sur l'art*, pp. 206–11, here p. 207.
6. See here also Terry Eagleton on the relationship between the 'literary mode of production' and the 'general mode of production' in his *Marxism and Literary Criticism* (Berkeley: University of California Press, 1976), esp. pp. 50ff. on the production of Victorian novels.
7. *La Curée* appeared first in *La Cloche* on 29 September 1871, and its publication was banned on 5 November. The journal had already been deemed 'hostile to the interests of the Second Empire' in 1869 and its editor, Louis Ulbach, had been imprisoned for six months. After the Commune, when Ulbach directed the building of barricades, the weekly, now wedded to the democratic opposition to the Third Republic, again fell foul of the French authorities. Zola wrote to Ulbach: 'And through these three monstrosities [the main characters of *La Curée*] I have attempted to give an idea of the terrible slough in which France is sinking.' Letter, dated 6 November 1871 and published in *La Cloche* on the 8th; cited after Lionel Acher, 'La Boucle transgénérique de *Phèdre* chez Zola', in Michèle Guéret-Laferté and Daniel Mortier (eds), *D'un genre littéraire à l'autre* (Mont-Saint-Aignan: Publications des Universités de Rouen et du Havre, 2008), p. 249 n. 2.
8. In the second chapter of *La Curée* the scene is set through a detailed, factual account of the property speculation in the period of Haussmann's Paris development, which affords the three protagonists, Aristide Saccard, the speculator, his wife Renée and son Maxime, the utmost luxury – before the housing and stock market bubble burst in May 1873 and led to the economic crisis of *La Grande Dépression* in France between 1873 and 1896.
9. Charles Baudelaire, 'Journaux intimes XIII: Fusées, no. 20', in *Œuvres complètes*, vol. 1 (Paris: Gallimard, 1975), p. 662.

10. See also my essay on the confluence of contemporary fashion and art, 'The Trademark Tracey Emin', in Mandy Merck and Chris Townsend (eds), *Eminent Domain* (London: Thames & Hudson, 2002), pp. 25–45.
11. This is, of course, a reductive view of the couture studios, in so far as tailoring can also be supremely innovative and subjective, while draping on the stand also results eventually in a set clothes pattern, but the initial approach to designing in each studio is certainly distinct: 'free' composition versus the construction of a template.
12. Jeffrey Mehlman has deconstructed the reading of nineteenth-century literature in late materialist and structuralist terms; see his *Revolution and Repetition: Marx/Hugo/Balzac* (Los Angeles: University of California Press, 1977).
13. Translated into English as *The Masterpiece*, the title can also be read more prosaically as *The Work*, as it details the labour of the artist to have his work recognised and exhibited within the context of the cultural politics of the Second Empire.
14. According to numbers cited in Alphonse Tabarant, *La Vie artistique au temps de Baudelaire* [1942] (Paris: Mercure de France, 1963), pp. 299–302, and also in Daniel Wildenstein, 'Le Salon de refusés de 1863', *Gazette des Beaux-Arts*, 66 (September 1965), p. 126.
15. See the critique of Cabanel's portrait of the dictator-emperor in Tabarant, *La Vie artistique au temps de Baudelaire*, p. 352; but also the fact that a copy of Winterhalter's portrait of the empress by one Hortense Bourgeois (a pupil of Cogniet) was featured in the *Salon des refusés* of 1863 – indicating that, literally, a bourgeois remake of a royalist painting was seen as negligible enough to be refused but also as having enough contemporary relevance for it to be hung in the annexe (cf. *Catalogue des ouvrages de peinture, sculpture, gravure, lithographie et architecture, refuses par le jury de 1863, et exposé, par decision de S. M. l'Empereur au Salon Annexe – Palais des Camps-Élysées, le 15 Mai 1863* [Paris: Les Beaux-Arts, Revue de l'art ancient et modern, 1863], p. 7).
16. Official communiqué published prominently on the second page in the governmental journal *Moniteur universel* (24 April 1863), and edited for the introduction to *Catalogue des ouvrages de peinture, sculpture, gravure, lithographie et architecture, refuses par le jury de 1863. . .*, p. 3. The catalogue is reprinted in Pierre Sanchez and Xavier Seydoux (eds), *Les Catalogues des salons, vol. VII (1859-1863)* (Dijon: L'échelle de Jacob, 2004), pp. 408–29. The Palais de l'Industrie stood between 1855 and 1897 on the site of today's Grand Palais. For a detailed account of the emperor's decision-making process, see Tabarant, *La Vie artistique au temps de Baudelaire*, pp. 299–302.
17. According to an account in *Les Beaux-Arts*, 1843, p. 26, cited in Wildenstein, 'Le Salon de refusés de 1863', p. 126.
18. Tabarant, *La Vie artistique au temps de Baudelaire*, p. 352.

19. As exemplary of this tendency, note the essay by Albert Boime, 'The Salon des refusés and the Evolution of Modern Art', *The Art Quarterly*, 32 (winter 1969), pp. 411–26.
20. See Étienne Cabet, *Le Démocrate devenu communiste malgré lui, ou, Réfutation de la brochure de M. Thoré intitulée Du communisme en France* (Paris: Au bureau populaire, 1847).
21. Théophile Thoré, *Les Salons de W. Bürger*, vol. 1 (Paris: Renouard, 1870), pp. 374–5.
22. Ibid., pp. 413, 414.
23. See Gautier's portrait as 'the most reserved and calculating of men' in Tabarant, *La Vie artistique au temps de Baudelaire*, p. 309.
24. See his critique in 'Mon Salon' of 1866, in Émile Zola, *Mes Haines, Mon Salon, Édouard Manet* (Paris: Charpentier/Fasquelle, 1893).
25. Émile Zola, 'Le Moment artistique' [dated 4 May 1866], in *Écrits sur l'art*, pp. 107–11, here p. 110.
26. Folio 350 of the *Notes de Guillemet*, cited after Patrick Brady, *'L'Œuvre' de Émile Zola, roman sur les arts: manifeste, autobiographie, roman à clef* (Geneva: Droz, 1967), p. 164; cf. the published version of this passage on Naudet, which begins by describing him as 'holding himself like a gentleman, embroidered jacket, gleaming white cravat, hair streaked back, polished, varnished', and ends with the lines: 'For the rest, a speculator, a stock marketer, who mocks good art absolutely.' Émile Zola, *L'Œuvre* (Paris: Charpentier, 1886), p. 243.
27. Folios 354–5 of the *Notes de Guillemet*, cited again after Brady, *'L'Œuvre' de Émile Zola*, p. 164; for the published version in the novel, cf. Zola, *L'Œuvre*, p. 390.
28. To understand just how pioneering the acquisition of an artist's estate had been in the 1880s, one has to look at the new millennial obsession of large contemporary art enterprises (for example New York galleries such as Zwirner or Gagosian) with securing the estates of dying or deceased artists. For many galleries, such estates have become economically more significant than finding new artists, as they allow for: 1) controlled release of works into the market; 2) authority over the secondary market by confirming authenticity and authorising resale; 3) the making or remaking of planned or incomplete works by deceased artists; and 4) promoting the historicity of artists in order to increase their exchange value in the culture industry.
29. See here the work by pioneering sociologist Gabriel Tarde, especially *Les Lois d'imitation* (Paris: Alcan, 1890), the philosophical approach and socio-political premises of which influenced the sociological discourses of Werner Sombart, Georg Simmel and Ferdinand Tönnies.
30. See Georg Simmel's original essay on fashion, 'Zur Psychologie der Mode', *Die Zeit*, 12 October 1895, pp. 20–4, here p. 24; and his later 'Fashion', p. 302.
31. Émile Zola, 'Nos peintres au Champ-de-Mars' [dated 1 July 1867], in *Écrits sur l'art*, pp. 177–87, here p. 184.

32. See Helène Lafont-Couturier, 'M. Gérôme travaille pour la maison Goupil', in Helène Lafont-Couturier and Pierre-Lin Renié (eds), *Gérôme et Goupil: art et entreprise* (Paris: Éditions de la réunion des musées nationaux, 2000), pp. 13–29.
33. Émile Zola, 'L'école française de peinture en 1878' [dated July 1878], in *Écrits sur l'art*, pp. 363–94, here p. 374.
34. The French psychiatrist Gaëtan Gatian de Clérambault researched, on behalf of the Parisian *prefecture de police*, old and new criminal pathologies in public places. His own (almost pathological) passion for fabrics was documented in hundreds of photographs of draped and veiled female bodies. See Gaëtan Gatian de Clérambault, *Passion érotique des étoffes chez la femme* (Paris: Les Empêcheurs de penser en rond, 2002); Serge Tisseron, *Gaëtan Gatien de Clérambault, psychiatre et photographe* (Le Plessis-Robinson/Paris: Synthelabo/Les Empêcheurs de penser en rond, 1997); Yolande Papetti et al. (eds), *La Passion des étoffes chez un neuropsychiatre: G.G. de Clérambault, 1872–1934* (Paris: Solin, 1980); and also the film *Le Cri de la soie* by Yvon Marciano from 1996. Zola himself used the department store as the exhaustively researched *mise-en-scène* for his novel of 1883, ironically entitled *Au bonheur des dames*, where new pathologies are dramatically played out in tandem with economic exploitation and social alienation.
35. See Albert Boime, 'Les hommes d'affaires et les arts en France au 19e siècle', *Actes de la Recherche en Sciences Sociales*, 28 (June 1979), pp. 65–8.
36. Pierre Assouline, *Grâces lui soient rendues: Paul Durand-Ruel, le marchand des impressionistes* (Paris: Gallimard, 2004), p. 104.
37. See Nicolas Green, 'Dealing in Temperaments: Economic Transformation of the Artistic Field in France During the Second Half of the Nineteenth Century', *Art History*, 10.1 (1987), pp. 59–78; see also Assouline, *Paul Durand-Ruel*, pp. 122–5, 202–3.

Chapter 5

Structuralism and Materialism: The Language of a Pur(e)Suit

Debating the role that fashion plays in and for materialism has not been the exclusive domain of historical materialists, who, as mentioned in the first chapter with regard to Baudrillard's change of method, tended to regard fashion as an insubstantial and unhelpful bourgeois distraction. A materialist critique of fashion that moved away from its visual or symbolic appearances was furthered, too, by structuralists and post-structuralists, who are active across the fields of sociology, philosophy and material culture. These theorists, schooled in the structural linguistics of Ferdinand Saussure as well as the semiology of Charles Sanders Peirce, in the anthropological approaches of Claude Lévi-Strauss and, especially, in the materialist sociology and philosophy of Henri Lefebvre, began to analyse between the 1940s and 1960s the language(s) of culture and media in structural terms, as well as developing a new concept of the 'everyday'. As part of these attempts to challenge established cultural hierarchies, and through them to critique socio-political power structures as well as probing popular myths and manifestations, theorists looked at fashion in the broader sense of the word: 1) as anthropological signs that appear as objectified human behaviour (customs and costumes); 2) as an independent language with its codified material signifiers and signifieds (the fashion system); and 3) as an ambiguous field of socio-cultural production in which constant novelties and repeated 'revolutions' are propagated under the auspices of solidified social conventions – the aforementioned eternal recurrence of the new. Structuralist and post-structuralist views of fashion are directed by an interest in the transitory but powerful role it asserted in post-war capitalism, with its seemingly unrelenting appetite for materially exclusive creations, which, as we saw in the example of Dior in the second chapter, exist in a carefully cultivated habitat that is theatrically divorced from social reality. This counter-intuitive fascination on the part of a new generation of late materialist thinkers with culturally exclusive objects was qualified by a methodological engagement with fashion's structural aspects, its development of an independent semiotic language that had internal consistency while constantly changing its textual and visual elements. Such an interplay of self-renewing and self-reflexive signifieds within a culture of consumption revealed for these theorists fashion's untapped political potential.

The first direct structural analysis of fashion's expressions came from Roland Barthes who, from 1957 onwards, made the language of clothing and dress a repeated subject in his work. From his early methodological text 'History and Sociology of Clothing' in the socio-economic journal *Annales*[1] to the occasional piece on fashion in the 'Palace' nightclub for *Vogues Hommes* more than three decades later,[2] Barthes is exemplary for the structural analysis of the fashion system and its social semantics. As fashion objectifies and commodifies the subject through material forms such as fabrics, accessories, cut and silhouette, it abstracts individuality and humanism into a system and pattern of signs that can be decoded according to contemporary trends that become manifest in visual and material language. The deciphering of socio-cultural codes is significant for post-structuralists especially, who tend to regard our material culture as a simulacrum, as *not producing* reality but *only representing* it. In this respect fashion is unique in its ostentatious coding of individual human forms as fugitive trends that shape bodies through diet and decoration. Fashion does not disguise the economic and political power structure it represents through its system of signification; it simply displays it as a temporary appearance – with the full knowledge that the self-same structure will continue in substance but in a different form once one fashion has passed on to the next.

In materialism, the analysis of the structure – wherein structure is mainly equated with *social* structure – has a clear historical precedent. As we have seen in Marx, the representation of human relations as analogous to relations between commodities is a central socio-economic fact within modernity: 'capital is not a thing, but a social relation between persons, established by the instrumentality of things'.[3] For historical materialists especially, this structural relation between subjects and commodities establishes patterns of economic dependency, which are grounded concretely in labour conditions as much as abstractly based on the dialectics of production and consumption. The Marxist and structuralist Lefebvre looked in his first book at the critical interplay of lexical signs, commodified objects and related power structures: 'History displays, however, in most great civilizations, a distressing contradiction between the magnificence of ideological justifications, costumes and words, and the monotony of the everyday.'[4] For Lefebvre, Marx's materialism offered the fundamental structure on which to base an understanding of the role of (everyday) objects. 'Material objects intervene in human society,' he wrote, 'they are "goods". They are a stimulus to social activity, to human needs and relations.'[5] And none more so than fashion with its close proximity to and formal imprint on the subject's body. Yet as commodities, these objects, determined in their historical value in part through changing fashion, occur not as neutral signs but as signifieds of ideological operations. Lefebvre explained: 'Once launched on its existence the Commodity involves and envelops the social relations between living men. It develops, however, with its own laws and imposes its own consequences, and then men can enter with one another by way of products.'[6]

Fashion has embraced this mechanism to make the reification and objectification of social relations through commodities a ground for material innovation, where products determine, by virtue of their formal novelty, the position of the wearer vis-à-vis her or his social environment – including, significantly, the conditions of its production. For Lefebvre, the

> relations between things and abstract quantities are only the appearance and expression of human relations in a determinate mode of production, in which individuals (competitors) and groups (classes) are in conflict or contradiction. The direct and immediate relations of human individuals are enveloped and supplanted by mediate and abstract relations which mask them. The objectivity of the commodity, of the market and of money is both an appearance and a reality.[7]

Class conflicts as simultaneously embodied and mediated through fashionable appearances? For structuralists and post-structuralists, such a direct political polemic would be a step too far away from linguistic or semiotic analysis. Here then, materialists began to take issue. Alfred Schmidt, in his study of Marxist conceptions of history which was cited in the previous chapter, refuted the structuralist thesis of an abstract universalism in Marx's economic analyses, in particular the 'historicism' that Louis Althusser and his followers[8] wanted to detect therein. Instead Schmidt credited Marx with a fundamental awareness of how abstract patterns can be developed from concrete historical processes (production). More polemically, the Italian philologist Sebastiano Timpanaro in 1970 critiqued contemporary structuralist positions in his renowned discussion *On Materialism*. Although Timpanaro shared the orthodox Marxist view of temporary appearances as mere manifestations and not as structural elements for political economy, and thus looked upon fashions – whether they are sartorial or intellectual – with distinct suspicion, his critique of the contemporary 'trend' towards structuralism is certainly credible. The central essay in his book took issue with the structuralists because they represented for him a 'fashion',[9] and he reserved particular criticism for Barthes's work on clothing, which represents for him but a 'cultural orientation' of an 'extra-linguistic Structuralism', deemed anti-materialist.

> Roland Barthes's little book *Elements of Semiology* . . . does nothing more in substance than summarise Saussure and linguistics; remaining within the sphere of possible extensions of semiology to the fields of fashion and cuisine . . . [A]lthough Barthes has attempted to develop a Structuralist theory of fashion in another book, and although 'culinary Structuralism' has been amply developed in the latest book by Lévi-Strauss, it seems to me that the future of semiology would be somewhat cloudy should it continue to cavort about with contrasts between skirts and blouses, blouses and pullovers, soups and entrees, etc., learnedly distinguishing 'paradigmatic' relationships from 'syntagmatic' ones.[10]

However cutting Timpanaro's critique of Barthes's efforts on linguistic systems in fashion writing and in the elements of contemporary clothing was, he would have to engage with the substantial advantage that he had discerned within structuralism, namely the debate about the synchronic or diachronic nature of language and cultural systems. And here, unrecognised by the Italian philologist, lies great potential for fashion to exemplify structural change. In the discontinuity of styles and visual movements, which are nevertheless embedded into a rigid socio-economic structure, fashion provided a dialectical form that showed how an essentially diachronic phenomenon supports synchronicity for cultural and social ideologies. Timpanaro's *On Materialism* was concerned with the concept of science – in terms of epistemology as much as historical discipline – and its relation to materialist thought, and for him any tendencies towards championing evolutionary or psychoanalytical structures were to be avoided, as they only emphasised continuity.[11] Yet analyses of the diachronic nature of language and culture still provided a tool that could determine structuralism as anti-historicist.[12] As I discussed in my second chapter on Benjamin, one very substantial critique of historicism's ideological import within a political economy of signs is produced by fashion. So, there is common ground between materialists such as Timpanaro and structuralist thought, even when it appeared back in 1970 as if this was just a fashionable application of Prague School linguistic analysis to everyday culture. We have seen at the end of Chapter 3 which deals with select literary texts on fashion how the structural linguistics of the Prague School were used productively by contemporary French thinkers to reassess modernist writing. Now I would like to continue with structuralism, which Timpanaro discerned, quite rightly in some respects, as yet another expression of bourgeois idealism[13] and discuss how one can use structural analysis for the materialist assessment of cultural phenomena.[14]

One primary reference to materialism in structuralist thought is generated by the focus on commodity relations and the fetish, as well as by the idea of a social system that can be traced within the semantic structures of the culture industry. For Barthes, who was a close friend and correspondent of Lefebvre, the materialism of Marx left an ambiguous residue. Although Barthes noted the focus on production and the need for systematic economic analysis, he rather took from Lefebvre a sociological perspective on the everyday, which he combined with linguistic analyses for his collection *Mythologies* (1957) and *The Fashion System* (1967). In presenting himself as a contemporary thinker who eschewed any singular ideological position, Barthes embraced the expansive commodity culture of his time to an extent that could not avoid complicity with existing ideological power structures. In his biography of Barthes, Louis-Jean Calvet gave a telling example of the structuralist working with the head of France's largest advertising agency on a contract for a state-owned automotive company: 'The fact that Barthes had accepted the Renault contract, that he had used his scientific or intuitive skills, albeit momentarily, to improve car sales might lead to the conclusion that he himself was fascinated by a world which elsewhere he criticized.'[15] Materialism, as evident in the everyday and in popular media, was for Barthes primarily an underlying structural constituent of society, not a methodological tool to prise ideological structures apart. Yet the way in which structuralist (and post-structuralist) approaches implicitly build materialist critique into their analysis, by demonstratively dismantling 'grand narratives' in economy, society and culture, allows for a fruitful combination of the two theoretical positions.[16]

In the following I want to contemporise materialism through the example of a structuralist analysis of a popular medium in which an object of fashion plays a central role. The example is chosen for its ostentatiously ideological position: a Cold War thriller produced in Hollywood where opposing sides were clearly demarcated and the 'happy ending' signalled the demise of a political system that, although unnamed, was connoted as socialist (and thus associated by many with historical materialism). My analysis is not meant to be a simple antithetical operation in which an ideological construct is exposed by the very signs it espouses, but it makes a particular effort to demonstrate how wider cultural production can be distilled via the metaphor of a material clothing item: the male suit. Its simultaneous understanding as object and as metaphor is generated through a hegemonic structure of production – the suit functions as a conservative mainstay in its respective understanding – and through a narrative that complies resolutely with a wider (political) power structure. In this example (post-)structuralism works as an analytical device that, when linked to the materialism of the chosen object's production and the materialism in the critique of the cultural product, reveals the complex ideological operations behind them.

North by Northwest

The example I have chosen is a film by Alfred Hitchcock, *North by Northwest*. For me, this film has a visual cinematic narrative that offers more surface than depth, more disguises than realities and more commodified images than narrative content. I will argue that Hitchcock's film and the role that Cary Grant plays in it are best explained by looking at appearances – precisely because they are deceptive – and not at hermeneutical codes, cinematic quotations or self-referential truths.[17] Because the outermost surface of this film's narrative – I am discounting here cinematic techniques – is occupied by the costume, my argument centres on one of these, namely Grant's suit, which is present continuously throughout the duration of the film and thus stands analogous to the suit's normative presence in men's fashion of the time.

Such exclusive focus on an item of clothing might be seen as highly restrictive, neither discussing sufficiently Hitchcock's cinematic production nor detailing the aspect of consumption in male fashion and its sociological significance. Yet I want to show how Grant's suit allows for a reading of the object simultaneously through its media representation and its materiality as commodity. This commodity is ideological and it functions politically; a bourgeois form of dress that appears in almost every scene of this Cold War thriller. Thus it serves as an apt example for the original application of the (post-)structuralist method of deconstructing dominant narratives. Yet at the same time the suit represents a production process, which allows for its materialist reading alongside the (post-)structuralist one. The care that Hitchcock took in deciding upon the costumes for his films – for *North by Northwest* he spent days at the exclusive New York department store Bergdorf Goodman with his female lead Eve Marie Saint to select her outfits – makes clothes an integral part of the interpretative *mise-en-scène*.[18] I aim to alleviate any concerns about not taking Hitchcock seriously because of the focus on a mere suit by arguing that the director deliberately cultivated surfaces in order to expose the perfunctory character of his subject matter. It has become habitual to praise Hitchcock for the 'psychoanalytical' – and thus anti-materialist – references in his work, as if a cursory reading of Freud marked most of the characters in and of his films. This is suggested in two ways. On the one hand, the characters are caricatures of psychological pathologies, for example the oedipal murderer (*Psycho*), the necrophiliac compelled by a fear of heights (*Vertigo*) or the homosexual narcissist (*Rope*). On the other hand, the filmic narratives are regarded as akin to subconscious thought processes, for example the dream sequence in *Spellbound* or the voyeurism as projection of internalised conflicts in *Rear Window*. Exemplary for such a view of Hitchcock's work are the almost hagiographical interviews by French director François Truffaut, who concluded his book by stating that Hitchcock was 'a neurotic and it must have been hard for him to impose his neuroses onto the whole world'.[19]

The post-Freudian psychoanalyst Lacan, who displayed in his lectures the strong influence of structuralist linguistics and semiology as well as a debt to Marxist terminology, postulated in his 1964 lecture 'The Subject and the Other: Alienation' that the subconscious is structured similarly to language.[20] In Lacan's writing, and in his analytical practice, the subject is confronted by a tripartite separation between 'the imaginary', 'the symbolic' and 'the real' that structures his perception of objects – in linguistic, semantic and indeed in material terms. The anthropologist and Marxist Lucien Sebag, who for many years was an analysand of Lacan,[21] responded in his book *Marxism and Structuralism* (also of 1964) with the argument that the relation of the subject to reality was only rendered problematic through linguistic structures. Sebag maintained that in order to arrive at a systemic understanding of epistemologies as well as cultural manifestations, any structuralist-anthropological reading must be combined with the materialist perception of the object.

Approaching in a structuralist fashion the psychological interpretations that have been fitted to the populism of a Hollywood production, and approaching Hitchcock's cinematic language through the presence of select objects such as the suit, reveals the superficiality of/emphasis on surfaces in the film as a concrete social and political action on part of the director. Sebag wrote:

> In this context language becomes an extreme generality, as it permits the refraction of reality through its associated code; but the object becomes particular when moving across to ideologies. From there we are directed on the one hand to the sender and the conditions of what is being sent, and on the other hand to the receiver and the conditions of reception. There is perhaps no field that is more important for an analysis of the ideological process . . .[22]

Obviously, Hitchcock's position has to be understood through the specific socio-economic conditions under which he produced his work – this applies to any artistic expression, whether populist or elitist, contemporary or traditional, everyday or exclusive. But such a receptive discourse has been eschewed by critics (and audiences) in favour of formal or psychological interpretations; a fact that becomes particularly problematic in case of the 'MacGuffin' which Hitchcock popularised,[23] when the concrete materiality of the object remains unrecognised.

The original structuralist analyses of objects, in mass media and as commodities, undertaken for example in Barthes's essay-collection on modern *Mythologies*, had been politicised to a great degree. Therefore I feel that a Hollywood tale about a spying game at the height of the Cold War offers a convincing case study to which to apply such a concentrated structuralist 'reading' of cinematic images and objects as knowingly *political constructs*, which can readily satirise and subvert their own ideology.

The present approach chooses a dozen scenes from the film, in chronological sequence, in which the suit is a signifier of the cinematic language or a verbalised object of the dialogue that drives the narrative. The suit thereby assumes a role that goes beyond its normative, superficial function as dress within the filmed action.

Method

The sartorial details described in the following are not to be taken as metaphors for behavioural patterns, nor are they meant to be symbolic of the character's psyche. They are read foremost as visual signifiers within a semiotic analysis.

When Barthes first elaborated in 1957 on such an analysis, reversing the dominance of semiotics over linguistics in favour of, perhaps surprisingly, fashion writing, he established a tripartite analogy between fashion and language. In his essay 'History and Sociology of Clothing', Barthes paralleled the linguistic classification of language and the socially commodified significance of clothing items.

In linguistics a differentiation exists between *langage*, the language spoken within an anthropological framework; *langue*, spoken within a cultural group or society; and *parole*, the individual manner of speaking that everybody uses for her- or himself. This classification finds its structural analogy in the differences between *vêtement*, clothing in general; *costume*, as ethnic/national dress or cultural sign of recognition; and *habillement*, individual sartorial expression.[24] Barthes regarded *langue* as an institution, 'an abstract body of constraints', similar to the formalist attire of the suit that constrains the corporeal, whereas *parole* is the part within the institution that is momentarily chosen by the individual and actualised for the purposes of communication, both verbal and sartorial.[25]

A decade later, with the publication of *The Fashion System*, Barthes altered the above distinction and switched the terms *vêtement* and *costume*. The latter was reduced to the most generic meaning, while *vêtement* became an equivalent to the structuralist *langue*.[26] Yet by substituting *vêtement* for *costume*, Barthes lost a significant aspect of his application of clothing to writing in its historical and cultural context: the literal connotation of the male suit – *le costume* in French. Because *langue* is defined as a 'structural institution', its equivalent should be the homonym of the suit, as the main sartorial constituent in men's fashion since the early part of the nineteenth century.[27] This shift, which is critically accounted for in Barthes's publications in the decade after his original essay,[28] covers up the institutional significance of the suit as representing, almost too obviously and logically, the norm of a Western, patriarchal and commodified society. I think it is thus more fitting to retain the terminology of Barthes's first study – quite apart from the fact that 'costume' in the English language denotes the clothes of an actor, which are patently not what Grant wears in Hitchcock's film, as he essentially plays himself and not a character.

Barthes explained in his essay of 1957 that a matter of personal dressing ('un fait d'habillement') constitutes first of all a deteriorated, that is, non-normative state of *costume*. Yet this state can be transformed into a secondary *costume*, when the deterioration functions as a collective sign, as a value: a minimal variation of the suit can become a matter of *costume* itself, the moment it is rendered a normative constituent of a certain group, a notion particularly expressive in dandyism.[29] More recent, 'post'-structuralist writing has qualified assessments such as the above as formalistic. Yet for me, Barthes's text on clothing and fashion – similar to Michel Butor's essay from 1969[30] – remains convincing for exposing structural relations in their material and ideological contexts, rather than losing them in the subsequent, 'postmodernist' fashion for discursive deconstruction and associative word-play.

In the following I want to demonstrate how the suit as sartorial surface functions as a signifier in an old-fashioned narrative that tells of the hero's trials and tribulations, and shows him being pursued, ridiculed and assaulted until he liberates himself from normative constraints to gain first freedom to act, and then love and respect as an individual. That such 'liberation' is ultimately but a perfunctory gesture that remains embedded in the structural confines of traditional cinematic and social language is to be expected from a US production of the 1950s (something Hitchcock also comments upon ironically), and in my view does not conflict with the present formal reading of the suit within the convoluted pursuit of the film's story.

The Film

Scene I (first day, late afternoon; the Oak Room, Plaza Hotel, New York City)

The film *North by Northwest* was scripted by Ernest Lehman, shot by Robert Burks and directed by Alfred Hitchcock for release in July 1959. On the surface, and this is what concerns me here, it is an espionage thriller in the best tradition of Hollywood's Cold War paranoia. The comical or absurd elements and the casting of Cary Grant as a Madison Avenue executive mistaken for a government spy who is constantly chased and attacked until he turns the tables on his foes adds the element of light-hearted entertainment to the improbable tale of pursuit, betrayal and double bluff.

In the opening part of the film – I will adhere to its chronology but, for obvious reasons, will not go through it scene by scene – the viewer encounters Roger Thornhill (played by Cary Grant) meeting with business associates in a Manhattan bar. He is dressed in a lightweight, three-buttoned suit (rolled to the middle button so that the top button hole appears on the left lapel), made from worsted wool in a blue and grey glen plaid pattern. There are darts to the front of the jacket to shape the waist but the overall effect is of a relaxed fit; this is emphasised, too, by the moderately padded and straight shoulders with slightly roped sleeve heads (the armhole of the pattern is high but wide). In a similar mix of the relaxed and the formal, the jacket lacks vents in the back, thus resembling an American sports coat, while retaining more traditional

6 Cary Grant, still from *North by Northwest* (detail), 1959

single-welt, jetted pockets and functioning three-button cuffs. The trousers are cut to a long rise, have double pleats in the front, turn-ups and clasped side adjusters (to fit without a belt). Matching the jacket details, the suit-trousers have slanted side pockets and one single-welt, jetted pocket on the back right. The suit is combined with a white poplin shirt with a soft, slightly pointed collar and French cuffs, accessorised by a tie in grey silk, woven with hardly discernible white dots, light-grey socks and dark brown shoes.

In cinematic chiaroscuro, Thornhill's three companions are attired in dark suits: the character Mr Wade with a white tie and *pochette*, Mr Nelson with a dark tie, and fellow advertising man Mr Welner with a sombre red tie. In this scene, where Grant is seen sitting comparatively still for the first time, the spectator is offered a contrasting reading of Thornhill versus the other male characters, a reading that functions essentially through clothing-signifiers and which is maintained until the very last part of the filmic narrative.[31] These formal and structural contrasts, pertaining as much to the persona as to the actor Grant, of whom Hitchcock asked nothing more than variations on his habitually superficial charm and ironic distance, are established by clothing Thornhill in a bespoke suit made by Arthur Lyons at the Savile Row tailors Kilgour, French & Stanbury – an establishment regularly frequented by Grant.[32] The supporting cast in this scene offer off-the-peg, that is 'manufactured', backgrounds, providing the common sartorial language (*costume*) of the 1950s, so paradigmatically embodied by Gregory Peck's *Man in the Grey Flannel Suit* in the eponymous film of 1956. Grant/Thornhill sits cross-legged and mannered, displaying the (alien, i.e. European) sophistication of matching socks and brown shoes, while the other characters remain stiffly reserved behind their table. His is therefore a *parole*, a subtle but clearly expressed deviation from the norm, which prompts speculations about his social and individual behaviour.[33] In the subsequent dialogue these speculations are fuelled by Lehman and Hitchcock, in the customary ironic subversion of their heroes' roles, by employing an oedipal *spiel* of Grant fussing over getting a message to his mother – a device that rather ridicules the polished *parole/habillement* of the actor and that throws his character into the subsequent turbulence of the narrative.

Scene 2 (first day, early evening; library of country mansion)

Thornhill, having been fatefully mistaken for the government spy George Kaplan,[34] is taken to villain Philip Vandamm (played by

James Mason) who, in the apparent guise of Lester Townsend, eyes up his opponent for a first sparring.

> Vandamm: 'Not what I expected; a little taller, a little more polished than the others.'
> Thornhill [with heavy irony]: 'Oh, I'm so glad you are pleased, Mr Townsend!'

Here, the sartorial surface of the suit begins to assert its dominance over all other epistemological strands in the narrative. Both men mistake each other for somebody else, yet neither makes any apparent effort to look through the respective disguise. On the contrary, they seem to take positive delight in assessing each other's outward appearance.

Vandamm is attired in a three-piece, neo-Edwardian dark suit, and wears a slate-grey tie. He is to be read as somebody who is well-tailored, yet exceedingly so: his sartorial signifiers are too respectable, too elaborately stiff to be telling the truth about the man, in dialectical relation with the relaxed silhouette of Thornhill's suit, as he stands like an actor in front of a (stage) curtain. Consequently, the first dialogue between Townsend/Vandamm and Thornhill concerns acting (by agents) and visits to the theatre. Throughout the course of the entire film Grant never lets the spectator forget that he is acting in more than one sense. As a man in his made-to-measure suit, he is confronted with the task of playing himself – both in the concrete, professional sense (of being an actor) as well as fictitiously (as part of the false identity constructed in the film's narrative) – in a manner that makes it impossible for the spectators *within* the film and *of* the film to accept this construction of the self. Reading him through Barthes and Sebag, Grant/Thornhill is an object that is abstracted and structured by the language of the clothing to such a degree that his reality can only appear within a dramatised ideology.

Scene 2b

Vandamm's sidekick Leonard (played by Martin Landau) enters the library in a fitted navy suit with a blue tie, taking Thornhill's handsome surface for nothing more, but also nothing less, than it is, while protecting his own views behind an equally polished mask; Leonard's reserve will break only in the film's climactic last quarter.

> Vandamm: 'Ah, Leonard. Have you met our distinguished guest?'
> Leonard: 'He is a well-tailored one, isn't he?'

Thornhill's misplaced internalisation of oedipal laws, hinted at in the beginning, finds its projection in his physical approval by a criminal, who by common critical consent is cast as a gay character.[35] In his series of interviews Truffaut praised Hitchcock for his decision to render Vandamm such a debonair character of immaculate dress and manners, because it adds 'the element of homosexual rivalry, with the male secretary [Leonard] clearly jealous of [the heroine Eve Kendall, played by] Eva Marie Saint'.[36] Yet the matter is far from being so well-cut. Fastidiousness in dress here signifies a narcissistic core, which supports the sartorial surface of all three men. Thornhill's elegance is first and foremost to be read as a designed corrective to a loss of moral values: he drinks too much, depends too strongly on his mother, already has two failed marriages behind him and steals other people's taxis. Those who merely glance at him read Thornhill as a well turned-out surface that is hard to resist or criticise. Yet even the comparatively relaxed care in his appearance generates the perception of him as being too groomed and handsome, too polished in all walks of life, and too aloof in the presence of women, especially. All of which puts his conventional masculinity in question – a speculation that pursued Grant as a film star throughout his career, and one that Hitchcock evidently enjoyed playing with.[37]

In Vandamm's case, sartorial elegance is a guise for a more sinister subversion of core values in contemporary society. His suit, as well as his mansion and his assorted entourage, make for a respectable front, masking the espionage whose ultimate aim is to destroy the American way of life. His accent and clothes thus must appear out of place, alien (English in this case) to the eyes and ears of the contemporary audience.

Leonard's suit signifies concealment, too. It is a front for 'immoral' desires: the tailoring accommodates the gun that is later used for intimidation and attempted murder; the sombre and anonymous cloth is used to deflect attention from any effeminate behaviour (shorthand for indulgence in gay sex); and the tight stiffness of the cut emphasises the extreme economy, or even lack, of movement that betrays the single-minded pursuit of an unsocial ideal.

Scene 2c

In the ensuing struggle, Thornhill is forced on to the sofa and plied with Bourbon; the suit is seriously assaulted and soiled for the first time.[38] Indeed, here one begins to read 'the suit' exclusively as the signifier and the character of Thornhill as the signified: the hero is defined through his surface, and the pursuit in the course of the film's narrative concentrates on the garment, whose light grey wool cloth keeps distinguishing, rather absurdly, the fugitive in his pursuit.

The fact that the cloth and shape of the suit show remarkable endurance and make a complete recovery from the pursuits and assaults in the preceding scenes must be read as Hitchcock's effort to present the hero as a stable and identifiable commodity to the audience. Although his superficial *parole* might be suspicious, the actual signifiers, the suit as a sartorial constituent, the pristine white shirt and the straightened tie, must remain intact. Nothing is torn, frayed or irreparably soiled. The hero has a seemingly Kantian or Enlightened categorical imperative: he has always to look such that the form of his clothes, his *costume/langue*, cannot be penetrated as a general sartorial and social norm (*langage*). The American way of life, at least in perfunctory perception, cannot be seriously damaged or turned inside out. While this has an obvious ideological and commercial logic to it, it is far from adhering to a formal logic, since its language has to be constructed anew for each communication, for each novel Hollywood production, in order to be fitted for a new environment and the latest fashion. Although the *langue* is thus ideologically and politically set, it has to remain flexible enough to account for the respective visual, artistic expression. 'The Fashion System', postulated by Barthes, must be adhered to so that the assorted ideology does not appear isolated or dated.

Thornhill escapes by driving intoxicated with turned-up lapels and crumpled suit down a cliff road; he is picked up by the police and spends the rest of the night in jail. The next morning he is questioned, fined and subsequently released. Still wearing the same suit, he then attempts to peel away at least one of the surfaces in the narrative, namely his mistaken identity as George Kaplan.

Scene 3 (second day, around noon; room 796 at the Plaza Hotel, New York City)

Thornhill clandestinely enters Kaplan's room accompanied by his mother Clara Thornhill (played by Jessie Royce Landis). A valet delivers a black suit from the dry cleaner, affirming that his order came via the telephone and not from the owner of the suit in person.

> Thornhill: 'I am beginning to think nobody in the hotel has actually seen Kaplan.'
> Mother: 'Maybe he has his suits mended by invisible weavers.'

This statement appears enigmatic, even for the highly irrational character that the mother embodies (with the absence of a 'father', any hope for a reality principle within this oedipal dependence seems to have been abandoned from the start). However, what Clara Thornhill actually hints at is an invisible power that mends and repairs the surface of the social fabric. In the case of the film's narrative, as the spectator later learns, this power is the government agency dealing in counter-espionage, which eventually assists Thornhill to regain his position in society. The construct of 'George Kaplan' – whom we now suspect, along with Thornhill, of being indecipherable – is signified only by a dark suit whose anonymous and ordinary sartorial language prevents any identification through a personable or characteristic *parole*.

Scene 3b

Thornhill takes the cleaned suit from the wardrobe and slips on the jacket. Awkwardly tailored, it is too wide in the shoulders and waist, whereas the sleeves are much too short for Thornhill's arms. Uneasy about such an affront to his sartorial sensibilities, he shifts his shoulders and looks accusingly at his protruding left shirtsleeve and double cuff.

> Mother: 'I don't think that one does anything for you.'

Scene 3c

Thornhill takes the trousers and holds them in front of him. The waist is too wide, and the cut is conservative, with badly executed turn-ups when compared to the perfect length of his own trouser legs, which fall gracefully on to the polished surface of his shoes.

> Mother [ironically]: 'Ah now, that's much better.'
> Thornhill: 'Obviously, they have mistaken me for a much shorter man.'

Thornhill's/Grant's *parole* is not yet easily subsumed into the clothing mainstream of *langue*, even though his work as an advertising executive should have schooled him to think constantly of new words and sentences to express the self-same commodities, to find new surfaces for old products, so to speak.

The sartorial shell of Kaplan's suit is not distinguished enough for the hero; worse still, it is inadequately short. And it is not necessary to look at Hitchcock's penchant for amateur psychoanalysis and for popularising Freudian ideas in his films to read the shortness of the sleeves and trousers as what they are meant to connote: the inferiority of one male member in contrast to another. The fact that the mother ironically praises the shortness of the trousers indicates how completely oedipal control has been exerted on the hero. Normative *langue* is preferred over individual *parole*. Even if the former is ill-fittingly short, it is sanctioned by societal and maternal judgement precisely because it is impotent, that is, less threatening or suspicious.[39]

Scene 4 (second day, evening; sleeper compartment on the 'Twentieth Century Ltd.' train from New York to Chicago)

Having added the role of murder suspect to his already convoluted assortment of characters, Thornhill is now pursued on to the fast train from New York to Chicago, where he is taken in – in the most improbable manner – by the industrial designer Eve Kendall (Eva Marie Saint), who hides Thornhill in the upper bunk of her compartment. After the immediate danger has passed, the hero is released from his confinement. When the bed is lowered, Thornhill removes a pair of broken sunglasses from the breast pocket of his suit, which, miraculously, appears immaculate despite the cramped conditions. The encounter with Eve might have broken one of the surfaces – the reflecting, concealing one of the sunglasses – but Thornhill's individual sartorial surface still remains untouched.

On the contrary, in embracing Eve, still fully clothed, Thornhill is reminded of what makes him attractive: the fact that he is a well-dressed commodity whose inner feeling or epistemic situation mean less to his surroundings than the sartorial signifier that clothes him.

Scene 5

>Thornhill: 'What else do you know?'
>Eve: 'You've got taste in clothes, taste in food . . .'
>Thornhill: 'And taste in women. I like your flavour.'
>Eve: 'You're very clever with words. Probably can make them do anything for you. You sell people things they don't need . . .'

In the profusion of his various roles, advertising executive, manabouttown, doting son, alleged government spy, suspected murderer and, now, sophisticated lover, the aspirations and dangers within the cultural discourse of 1950s America are projected upon the surface of Thornhill/Grant. There appears to be no conflict between the made-to-measure clothes and the identity that is tailored to each situation of the pursuit.[40]

The three linguistic shifts that Barthes observed in the transposition of sartorial commodity to language are also manifest in the Thornhill character: the 'real' shifts to 'image'; the 'real' shifts to 'language', that is, it is described; and, thirdly, the 'image' itself shifts to 'language'.[41] The linguistic operation that functions in fashion writing applies in equal measure to the narrative around the hero in *North by Northwest*, multifaceted as he is.[42] Instead of Thornhill or Grant – since it is difficult to distinguish an objective or disinterested 'real' in the context of Hollywood – we get an immaculate attire, seemingly indestructible. This 'image' is perpetually thematised in the film. The suit is chased, crumpled and squashed, but also constantly referred to and discussed within the 'language' of the film, both in its visual and dialogue form.

Scene 6 (third day, nine o'clock in the morning; platform at Central Station, Chicago)

When Thornhill leaves the train with Eve, he is (if only for a very brief period) in yet in another guise which has been purchased from a porter. Walking beside her, Thornhill becomes concerned about his 'image' – or rather the real state of his suit.

> Thornhill: 'Which one of these has my suit in it?'
> Eve: 'The small one, underneath your right arm.'
> Thornhill: 'Oh thanks. That ought to do the suit a lot of good.'
> Eve: 'I am sure Mr Kaplan won't mind a few wrinkles.'

The 'image' shifts to 'language' as the perfected surface of the clothing becomes a cause for concern. Never mind the real danger of the situation Thornhill finds himself in, pursued by spies, by detectives and policemen on the concourse, and by Eve, who, unbeknownst to him conspires with Vandamm and Leonard: his concern rests with the creases in his suit. But one has to sympathise with Thornhill; apart from the suit there is nothing left for him. His bourgeois identity has been stripped away during the narrative and his identification, which has been supported so powerfully by his elegance and sense of style, is now entirely dependent on the continuity of his apparel.

Eve's response to this ontological dilemma appears casual. Why indeed should George Kaplan mind creases in the suit? For her part she can be sure that the meeting between Kaplan and Thornhill will never take place, while the latter should deduce from Kaplan's badly tailored suit (not to mention his dandruff) that it is not the state of his appearance that matters, but the fact that it is not detected in the first place.

Yet again Thornhill changes back into the stylistic motif of the grey-blue cloth, which looks as cleaned and pressed as in the first scene, the ironed white shirt and the immaculately straightened tie. As vaguely defined as his character may remain, his pursuers should by now pay particular attention to the sartorial shell as the only means of identification; yet precisely this signifier is still worn by Thornhill for his promised meeting with Kaplan on the plains of rural Illinois.

Scene 7 (third day, early afternoon; Prairie Stop, Highway 41, Illinois)

Thornhill stands alienated through his city suit in empty and open farmland, waiting in the wind and dust of passing vehicles for his meeting with Kaplan. He goes through a well-choreographed sequence of moves, signalling his anticipation. Hands are thrust into trouser pockets only to be taken out again, cuffs are tugged, and the jacket is adjusted and finally unbuttoned.

These preparations are just in time, as a biplane ('dusting crops where there ain't no crops') begins to swoop down and fire on him. Thanks to some impressive sprinting, some headlong dives into the field and a clever escape trick under a truck, which is then hit by the plane, Thornhill manages to survive the most brutal assault on his character so far. The absurd magnitude of this pursuit – why resort to the elaborate plan of chasing a man over an open field in a plane, when you could as easily lure him into a hotel room in Chicago to finish him off? – seems to complete the hero's degradation. His elegant *parole* is subjected to murderous (though cinematically dramatised) reality, and for the first time in the film's narrative an existentialist void is created around, if not within, the character.

Eventually, Thornhill returns to Chicago to seek out Kaplan. In the hotel he becomes aware of Eve's betrayal.[43]

Scene 8 (third day, evening; room 463 in the Ambassador Hotel, Chicago)

Although he is covered in flecks and patches of white and sand-coloured dust, which are disapprovingly noticed by the concierge, Thornhill's appearance is miraculously unaffected in substance. The spectator notices no tears or rents in the cloth; the crease in the trousers is sharp, the lie of the collar immaculate, the shirt remains stubbornly ironed and the tie perfectly in place. Again, the effects of existential danger are merely touching the surface; the essence of the suit, as signifier, stays intact. However, for the first time a sense of inner conflict or drama appears; not enough to affect the sign of Thornhill/Grant, but clearly manifest in the visual communication with Eve's character:

> Eve: 'I want you to leave right now ... So, please: Good-bye, good luck. No conversations; just leave.'
> Thornhill: 'Right away?'
> Eve: 'Yes.'
> Thornhill: 'No questions asked?'
> Eve: 'Yes.'
> Thornhill: 'No, I can't do that.'
> Eve: 'Please!'
> Thornhill: 'After dinner.'
> Eve: 'Now!'
> Thornhill: 'After dinner; fair is fair.'
> Eve: 'All right. On one condition: that you let the hotel valet do something with this suit first. You belong in the stockyards, looking like that.'

What appears as a commonplace metaphor of bourgeois cleanliness suggests that a soiled Thornhill is not a Thornhill to speak of. His identity so much depends on the clothing-'image' that any imperfection immediately shifts it back to the 'real'.

Scene 8b

Thornhill sits on the bed, affecting the same confident position as in the hotel bar at the beginning of the film. He telephones the valet while trying to decipher Eve's notepad to find out her true identity and intentions:

> Thornhill: 'How quickly can you get a suit sponged and pressed? – Yes, fast.'

Thornhill: 'Twenty minutes? – Fine . . .'
– . . . –
Thornhill [to Eve who is in the bathroom]: 'He'll be right up.'
Eve: 'Better take your things off.'

Thornhill empties his pockets – still containing a small amount of banknotes and some personal belongings.

Scene 8c

Thornhill [walks up to Eve from behind]: 'Yeah. Now, what can a man do with his clothes off for twenty minutes? – Could he not have taken an hour?'
Eve [slipping off his jacket]: 'You could always take a cold shower.'
Thornhill: 'That's right. – When I was a little boy, I wouldn't even let my mother undress me.'
Eve: 'You are a big boy now.'
Thornhill [in shirtsleeves]: 'Yes.'

Such an exchange is very much part of Hitchcock's cinematic vocabulary. In order to alter the tempo or ease the tension in a thriller, elements of ironic dialogue are woven into the narrative. In this and other cases, the director and scriptwriter enjoy overt references to Freud, who had pervaded American cultural consciousness in the 1950s through the dissemination of psychoanalytical practice. Obviously, the sexual overture, subsequent rejection and frustration, followed by a transposition of oedipal dependency is introduced to suggest the singularity of Eve's position towards Thornhill. The fact, however, that she is allowed actively to remove part of the suit suggests an actual interest in her peeling away the surface and getting at Thornhill's identity. Ironically, this occurs at the very moment when he himself decides to accept the double guise of an alleged agent.

After having accused Eve of being a tease and guilty of criminal role-play, Thornhill walks into the bathroom and relinquishes the last part of his suit to her.

Scene 8d

Eve: 'Trousers please.'
Thornhill: 'Certainly. – Here you are.'

In handing the suit to the valet, Eve inadvertently assists Thornhill in a sartorial rite of passage into the spying game. Like the fictitious George Kaplan, for whom Vandamm and Leonard still mistake Thornhill, he himself now has his suit cleaned in a hotel, by invisible hands and, one suspects, with the cleaning bill picked up by some imaginary source.

Without his suit, yet still in his shirt and tie (Freud and his disciple Stefan Hollós surely would have commented upon such a display),[44] Thornhill then performs his first act as a spy proper by deciphering Eve's note.

Scene 9 (third day, night; auction room of Shaw & Oppenheim Galleries, 1212 North Michigan Avenue, Chicago)

Thornhill, freshly showered and in his sponged and pressed suit, his shoes polished, enters the auction room to approach Vandamm, standing with Eve and Leonard at the front of the bidding public. Vandamm has now, despite the late hour, changed from black into a light grey suit with a dark tie; an unexpected sartorial faux pas by the fastidious spy. One assumes that Thornhill, who obviously has to continue wearing the same suit, would have known better when to change into dark evening attire.

The contrast in tailoring – Thornhill's fitted suit that relies on the perfect cut of the shoulders and collar, versus Vandamm's suit with its slightly over-cut shoulders and wide sleeves – signifies the conflict of *parole* and *langue*. Grey does not equal grey; Thornhill's cloth is identifiably individual (in its subtle pattern), while Vandamm intends to submit to the general sartorial language that is apparent in the grey-suited men around him (one of them being 'The Professor', who supervises the spying game).

Leonard wears his habitually stiff, dark suit and blue tie, which is tight in the waist and slim in the shoulders, tentatively suggesting the cut of a feminine *tailleur* – underneath which he is sporting his gun.

In a flashback to the 1940s 'screwball' school of comedy, Thornhill upsets proceedings in order to get arrested by the police. In the ensuing punch-up his suit is ruffled once more, his sleeves manhandled again by police officers.

Scene 10 (third day, night; Chicago airport)

'The Professor' (played by Leo G. Carroll) and Thornhill finally get to meet and talk about the past days. He is confronted with an elaborate spy story of bluff and counter-bluff, as well as the fact that, despite the sartorial *langue* discussed in the New York hotel room, there is no such person as George Kaplan:

> Thornhill: 'What do you mean, "There is no such person"? I've been in his hotel room, I tried on his clothes. He has got short sleeves and dandruff.'
> The Professor: 'Believe me Mr Thornhill, he doesn't exist. – Which is why I am going to have to ask you to go on being him for the next twenty-four hours.'[45]

This controlling instantiation of the government agency appears now to accept Thornhill's *parole*, which, although deviating from the social construct they are all meant to uphold, has become a form of *langue*: a value, a sign for the collective, with whom he begins to be identified more and more. By taking him into the societal fold of grey-suited men who are directed towards the same normative material goals and who see themselves as productive of the common good (which the urbane and cynical advertising executive had mocked), Thornhill's suit loses importance as *parole* and begins to relinquish its leading role in the narrative.

Scene 11 (fourth day, morning; self-service restaurant opposite Mount Rushmore, Rapid City, South Dakota)

Thornhill meets with Vandamm, who is absurdly dapper in a 'landed gentry' sort of way, in a light tweed suit and green waistcoat with matching tie and dark hat. Thornhill proposes a trade-off between Eve and a safe passage for the spies. Eve then provokes a public conflict that climaxes with her putting two bullet holes into Thornhill's suit before fleeing screaming from the scene. Leonard, ever suspicious of the surfaces presented to him, is confronted with a layer of fake blood on the Professor's hand. Eventually, Thornhill's body is carried away, covered by a matching grey blanket, to a clearing in a wood, where he meets Eve.

Despite this last and most violent assault, the shooting from close range, the suit is as immaculate as ever. Undamaged, it signifies once again the deceptive surface of the narrative; and the viewer understands that the blank bullets were just another 'reality' that has turned out to be a fictional construct. In the dialogue that follows Thornhill asks Eve whether her life has been 'like that', that is, superficial and devoid of meaning, which she affirms in saying that her spying on Vandamm for the US government has been the first 'worthwhile' thing she has done.[46] Eve's and Thornhill's political/ideological positions within the narrative, which they would have to regard as existential for their survival, given the situation they have found themselves in thus far, are thus denoted as being directed solely towards surfaces. The insubstantial aspect of the clothes, of the spoken language and of its synthesis, namely the language of clothing, is now abandoned in favour of an ideologically embellished materiality. Life gets serious and the comedic elements of the film vanish. Obviously, the existing structure, which grants the language of governmental power legitimacy and also clothes in a formal *langue* the suits and *tailleurs* of the protagonists, is not questioned. In order to demonstrate an ontological or existential perspective for the heroes, although their duty to risk their lives in working for their country is not actually spelled out, the film is reduced to brute symbolism: opposing ideological forces battle it out on Mount Rushmore's sculpted heads of historic US presidents.

In this context Leonard's verbal unmasking ('call it my woman's intuition') of Eve becomes significant for the first and only use in the film of the term 'the other side' – the geopolitical equivalent of Lacan's 'the big other' – and for describing the type of fake execution deployed by the US government as 'an old Gestapo trick'. The spectator is thus offered in the end a coagulated materiality that cannot have as subjects the surfaces of the cinematic narrative, and which should render redundant any structuralist analysis.

In order to prevent Thornhill from joining Eve in her final roleplay, the Professor instructs a state trooper to punch Thornhill out. The scene where he hits the pine needles is the last instance when we see the suit.[47]

Scene 12 (fourth day, afternoon; hospital room)

We see Thornhill without his clothes for the first time, pacing restlessly in a towel before a radio. The Professor unlocks the door to the hospital room.

> The Professor: 'Here we are.'
> Thornhill: 'Hello.'

The Professor [throwing a box on the bed where Thornhill rests]: 'Slacks and a shirt . . .' [waving a shoe box] – 'And these . . .'
Thornhill: 'Thank you.'
The Professor: 'That'll do for you around here, for the next couple of days.'

From this moment on, and ironically in his confinement, Thornhill is initiated officially into the spying game. A few hours ago he had, for the first time, played a part that was not for him, that was not made to impress or deceive other members of his social set; this time his role-play was designed to assist society at large. He has been drafted into the ranks of the government. Logically, this needs to be ritualised by a change of clothing. Thus the Professor, as representing normative society, has bought for him sartorial signifiers that are perfect examples of the popular American *costume/langue*: a very wide-cut, button-down Brooks Brothers shirt, slate-grey pleated trousers, black leather belt and black penny loafers.

Yet the outfit is not 'respectable' in terms of bourgeois apparel; it appears disconcertingly casual. The Professor qualifies his choice with the line: 'That'll do for you around here' – meaning the hospital room to which Thornhill has to confine himself in order not to expose Eve as a fraud. Nevertheless, this outfit provides him with the security of a socially sanctioned *costume/langue* – although in the guise of leisurewear – which he requires in order to step out of his previous egotistical character (with its signifier, the polished *parole/habillement* of the bespoke suit) and, after his escape act, to become active in saving 'his girl', the American way of life and Western civilisation as a whole.

Next to such an inherent 'logic', there are also technical, cinematic reasons for a change in Thornhill's clothing: Hitchcock himself said that he required a voluminous white shirt to distinguish Grant from the other actors during the long shots and tracking movements on the dark setting of Mount Rushmore. Indeed, given Thornhill's/Grant's acrobatics in the latter part of the film, it makes more sense to dress him in casual wear than in a suit, although the latter had not prevented his character from performing stunts and engaging in fights beforehand.

Conclusion

It would be simplistic to read the eventual change in attire, from conservative mainstay to casualwear, from timeless Savile Row to fifties Americana, or from individualised bespoke suit to mass-produced clothing, as a sartorial *éducation sentimentale* that heralds a change of attitude in the hero. Granted, the narrative (or indeed moral of the story?) seems to suggest that Thornhill learns to assume responsibility in the end, that he recognises the need for commitment to relationships, and perhaps even to society at large, and that he appears determined henceforth to fulfil his role as an altruistic and engaged citizen. But is this not again another surface? Is there anything in his vague characterisation to show us a glimpse of what can be termed Thornhill's 'identity', that is, his psychological drive, his relationships with people that go deeper than clichés of filial piety, fighting communism or fornicating with young women?

The dictates of the culture industry decreed that a Hollywood film had to end on a moral high note, and Hitchcock abided by such narrative norms. However, the emphasis that has been placed throughout the greater part of the film on the suit, the *parole*, which appears deliberately, even cynically, superficial, suggests a concrete focus on the material surface in preference to any concerted attempt on the part of the writer and director to account for the character's internal development or any changes in his psychological make-up.

Barthes's reading of fashion can be extended to the appearance of Thornhill/Grant in Hitchcock's film because commodified products surround and clothe the character. One of these products develops in a manner analogous to that of a linguistic constituent in (visual) language; not for metaphorical or symbolic reasons – after all, it is just a grey suit – but as an integral part of the narrative, as a visual lead that constructs thematic coherence. My structural analysis in this chapter was put forward in order to look at the materiality of objects and their representation in the media. In this case study a piece of clothing, instrumental for both the look and the storyline of a film, was moved away from symbolic or iconic interpretation towards a concrete analysis of its material and social production. While the actual making of the wool fabric or the suit itself is not shown in the film, its material properties, for instance its being 'well tailored', getting 'mended' or creased and stained, is a continuous part of the film's narrative and a principal subject of the dialogue. This demonstrates how meaning is constructed *within* the structure of an object and how it is read as part of a culture industry and culture of consumption. The sartorial motif in *North by Northwest* has to be shown and talked about as material because it represents material class and wealth – the informed choice by an affluent consumer of made-to-measure suits, and the indestructible concrete presence of an ideological standpoint that is part of the very fabric of the society that consumes it, or at least aspires to consuming it. The materiality of the suit is important because it provides a measure of the materiality of the system that is shown as winning the Cold War, an overall ideological dispute, and as assuming a superior moral standpoint – the killing of the enemy occurs not through a gun fired by the hero but by proxy, through his falling off the monumental forehead of a historic US president. The pursuit of the suit is a very material one, uniting the consumer's desire to emulate the hero's elegance and sophistication with the fiction and fabrication that the cloth and shape of such a suit can never be destroyed or defeated. The textile needs to be read as a text, in the way that structuralism had learned from materialism: as the inquiry into the equation of an object with its concrete socio-economic meaning.

Notes

1. Roland Barthes, 'Histoire et sociologie du vêtement: Quelques observations méthodologiques', *Annales: Economie, Sociétés, Civilisations*, 12.3 (1957), pp. 430–41.
2. Roland Barthes, 'Au Palace ce soir', *Vogues Hommes*, 10 (1 May 1978), reprinted in *Œuvres complètes*, vol. 3 (Paris: Seuil, 1995), pp. 824–6.
3. Karl Marx, *Capital*, Vol. 1 [1867/1890], in Marx and Engels, *Collected Works*, vol. 35 (London: Lawrence & Wishart, 1996), p. 753. Marx had made this fundamental observation already in his article 'Lohnarbeit und Kapital' (Wage Labour and Capital) of 1849.
4. Henri Lefebvre, *Dialectical Materialism* [1939] (Minneapolis: University of Minnesota Press, 2009), p. 142.
5. Ibid., p. 134.
6. Ibid., p. 80.
7. Ibid.
8. See Louis Althusser, *For Marx* [1965] (London: Verso, 2005); and Louis Althusser and Étienne Balibar, *Reading Capital* [1968] (London: Verso, 2009). Alfred Schmidt's critique can be found in *History and Structure*, pp. 61–6, 84–93.
9. Sebastiano Timpanaro, 'Structuralism and its Successors', in *On Materialism* [1970] (London: New Left Books, 1973), p. 209.
10. Timpanaro, 'Structuralism and its Successors', p. 183. He is referring to Barthes's *Fashion System* of 1967 and Claude Lévi-Strauss's *The Raw and the Cooked* of 1964.
11. See the discussion of Timpanaro's *On Materialism* in Raymond Williams, 'Problems of Materialism', *New Left Review*, 1.109 (1978), pp. 3–17, especially pp. 13–16.
12. Timpanaro, 'Structuralism and its Successors', p. 191.
13. Ibid., p. 198.

14. Within his critique of 'Structuralism and its Successors', Timpanaro remains affirmative of the impact of Lefebvre and others; what he manifestly cannot abide is the 'neo-positivism' in post-structuralist writing by Lévi-Strauss, Michel Foucault and Jacques Lacan. See Timpanaro, 'Structuralism and its Successors', pp. 188 and 194, n. 134.
15. Louis-Jean Calvet, *Roland Barthes: A Biography* [1990] (Cambridge: Polity, 1994), p. 143.
16. In one of his early books Fredric Jameson had critiqued Soviet formalism and structuralism in France from a neo-Marxist cultural perspective; see *The Prison-House of Language* (Princeton: Princeton University Press, 1972).
17. See Geoffrey H. Hartman's essay on *North by Northwest* for a reference to Alain Resnais's *Last Year in Marienbad*: 'The face of those worded images remains smooth, slippery: they are pictures determined not to be words; they insist on a pictographic as well as semiotic content, a nonsensous visual stenography.' Hartman, 'Plenty of Nothing: Hitchcock's *North by Northwest*', *The Yale Review*, 71.1 (1981), p. 14. While this is a commonly held view of the formal artificiality of European art house cinema, it can be applied in equal measure to Hitchcock's smoothed-down cinematic products of the 1950s and 1960s. Fredric Jameson contrasts the stylistic and structural elements in Hitchcock's films as 'dialectically related projections of the two poles of the dilemma of modernist form'. Jameson, 'Spatial Systems in *North by Northwest*', in Slavoj Žižek (ed.), *Everything You Always Wanted to Know about Lacan (But Were Afraid to Ask Hitchcock)* (London: Verso, 1992), p. 48. A structuralist reading of *North by Northwest* can be found in Raymond Bellour's essay, 'Le Blocage symbolique', *Communications*, 23 ('Psychanalyse et cinéma') (1975), pp. 235–63, which moves from the textual to the psychoanalytical. A later version of this essay contains a frame-by-frame reading of the sequence on the Illinois plains. See Bellour, *L'Analyse du film* (Paris: Albatros, 1979), pp. 131–246.
18. A 'clutch' evening handbag with the prominent label of 'Bergdorf Goodman' can be seen in the Chicago hotel room scene. This can be regarded simultaneously as an example of early product placement and as a reference to the stylistic language of commodities that is so pervasive in the film.
19. François Truffaut (with Helen G. Scott), *Hitchcock by Truffaut: The Definitive Study* [1966] (London: Paladin, 1978), p. 534.
20. 'If psycho-analysis is to be constituted as a science of the unconscious, one must set out from the notion that the unconscious is structured like a language.' Jacques Lacan, 'The Subject and the Other: Alienation' [lecture of 1964], in *The Four Fundamental Concepts of Psycho-Analysis* [1973] (New York: Norton, 1978), p. 203.
21. Sebag shot himself reportedly because of his unrequited love for Lacan's daughter, Judith.

22. Lucien Sebag, *Marxisme et Structuralisme* (Paris: Payot, 1964), p. 111.
23. The MacGuffin is an object that prompts or advances a filmic narrative without having any actual significance in itself. In *North by Northwest* the statue containing the microfilms is a typical MacGuffin – as, indeed, is the suit of the main protagonist. Hitchcock himself adjudged that 'my best MacGuffin, and by that I mean the emptiest, the most non-existent, and the most absurd, is the one we used in *North by Northwest*' (Truffaut, *Hitchcock by Truffaut*, p. 194). It would be interesting, if one were to take this causal remark by the director at face value, to extend the thesis so that the non-existent object, the void, becomes the most significant in formal terms. This matches modernist artistic linguistics in which the pause/silence/void between letters is more important than the spoken or written word.
24. For the original definition, see Barthes, 'Histoire et sociologie du vêtement'. For a recent translation that converts the early terminology into English, see Barthes, 'History and Sociology of Clothing: Some Methodological Observations', in *The Language of Fashion* (Oxford: Berg, 2006), pp. 3–20.
25. Roland Barthes, *The Fashion System* [1967] (London: Cape, 1985), pp. 17–18.
26. Ibid., p. 18.
27. See, for example, John Harvey, *Men in Black* (London: Reaktion, 1995); or Christopher Breward, *The Hidden Consumer: Masculinity, Fashion and City Life 1860–1914* (Manchester: Manchester University Press, 1999).
28. The changing of *vêtement* and *costume* can be traced back to one of the earliest essays by Barthes, entitled 'Les Maladies du costume de théâtre', which he republished in 1964 in conjunction with his programmatic text 'L'Activité Structuraliste'. This essay used the term *costume* exclusively to denote costumes on stage or in film. See Roland Barthes, 'Les Maladies du costume de théâtre', *Théâtre populaire*, 12 (March/April 1955), and 'L'Activité Structuraliste', *Lettres nouvelles*, 32 (February 1963); both republished in Barthes, *Essais critiques* (Paris: Seuil, 1964), pp. 53–62, 213–20. Introducing Barthes to an Anglo-American readership, the *Partisan Review* published these two essays together: 'The Structuralist Activity' and 'The Disease of the Costume', *Partisan Review*, 34.1 (1967), pp. 82–8, 89–97.
29. Barthes, 'History and Sociology of Clothing', p. 10.
30. Michel Butor, 'Fashion and the Modern' [1969], *Art in Translation*, 7.3 (2015), pp. 266–81.
31. See James Naremore, 'Cary Grant in *North by Northwest* (1959)', in *Acting in the Cinema* (Berkeley: University of California Press, 1988), pp. 213–35, especially pp. 214–17 for an enthusiastic celebration of Grant's fashion sense.
32. The film and media scholar William Rothman wrote: 'But a further joke is in the idea that Cary Grant could ever be mistaken for a "Roger

Thornhill" in the first place. Roger Thornhill is only a fictional character, created by Hitchcock and subject to his authorship – no more real than the non-existent decoy "George Kaplan". Hitchcock's real agent is – Cary Grant. Grant's complete visibility in the world of *North by Northwest* is an acknowledgement of his familiar way of inhabiting the screen.' William Rothman, 'North by Northwest: Hitchcock's Monument to the Hitchcock Film', *North Dakota Quarterly*, 51 (summer 1983), pp. 11–13.

33. Stanley Cavell in his equation of *North by Northwest* with the theme of Hamlet locates a similar observation in the auction room comedy halfway through the film. The demand on Thornhill is to 'be decorous, be socialized; but society has been forcing an identity and a guilt upon him that he does not recognize as his own, so the natural hope for a way out is to abdicate from that society'. Stanley Cavell, 'North by Northwest', *Critical Inquiry*, 7 (summer 1981), p. 766.

34. This is reinforced in the German synchronisation of the film, realised at Metro-Goldwyn-Mayer's studios at Berlin-Tempelhof in 1959, when the dialogue was changed so that Grant first asks the two henchmen who threaten him in the bar: 'What do you want from me? Are you objecting to my suit?'

35. In an interview, Martin Landau recalled being taken by Hitchcock himself to Grant's tailor Quintino of Beverly Hills, to be measured for the tight-fitting suit. Tim Burrows, 'Martin Landau: "I chose to play Leonard as gay"', *The Telegraph*, 12 October 2012, http://www.telegraph.co.uk/culture/film/starsandstories/9601547/Martin-Landau-I-chose-to-play-Leonard-as-gay.html (last accessed 23 March 2017).

36. Truffaut, *Hitchcock by Truffaut*, p. 143. See also Robert J. Corber, *In the Name of National Security: Hitchcock, Homophobia, and the Political Construction of Gender in Postwar America* (Durham, NC: Duke University Press, 1993), p. 253, n. 12; Robin Wood, 'The Murderous Gays: Hitchcock's Homophobia', in *Hitchcock's Films Revisited* (London: Faber & Faber, 1991), pp. 336–57, 365. Lesley Brill sartorially connects the villains: 'With their dark suits and cold refinement, VanDamm [sic] and Leonard are strongly linked when they first appear in Townsend's library.' Brill, 'North by Northwest and Romance', in *The Hitchcock Romance: Love and Irony in Hitchcock's Films* (Princeton: Princeton University Press, 1988), p. 9.

37. Grant rejected the leading part of Rupert Cadell in Hitchcock's film *Rope* because it appeared to him as too gay. After Montgomery Clift's pitch for the role had been rejected (since his homosexuality was an open secret), James Stewart finally accepted the part.

38. Quintino's of Beverly Hills produced numerous extra copies of the bespoke Savile Row suit to be used for action sequences. In the later scene in the Chicago hotel room when Eve removes Thornhill's jacket, the 'Quintino' label can be glimpsed.

39. See Bellour's 'psychoanalytical' reading of the suit in this hotel room

scene and the later one of Thornhill and Eve in Chicago, when he is perhaps springing the 'trap' that Lehman and Hitchcock laid out in view of such a suggested interpretation. Bellour, 'Le Blocage symbolique', p. 255.
40. 'That film is almost too healthy. Roger learns vigilance without being traumatised. The psyche is not involved, or not as a perverse emptiness, always escaping from being watched and therefore ever wary'; Hartman, 'Plenty of Nothing', p. 23. The professional role of the Eve character as an industrial designer can be read as a subsidiary stage in the production process of modern commodities: Eve designs new, fashionable objects while Thornhill communicates them for consumption.
41. See Barthes, *The Fashion System*, pp. 6–7.
42. A less structuralist reading of the 'image' comes from Jameson: 'The main body of the film can then be seen as a quest or a test, trial by fire, struggle with the adversary, the experience of betrayal, action not with images but within images . . .' Jameson, 'Spatial Systems in *North by Northwest*', p. 48.
43. The scriptwriter could not deny himself this allusion to the name of the perpetrator of the original sin.
44. See, for example, Sigmund Freud, *The Interpretation of Dreams* [1900] (London: Hogarth Press, 1940), pp. 357–8; Stephan Hollós, 'Schlangen und Krawattensymbolik', *Internationale Zeitschrift für Psychoanalyse*, 9 (1923), pp. 73–4; and Joh[an]n Carl Flügel, *The Psychology of Clothes* (London: Hogarth, 1930), p. 27.
45. A dialectical pun by the scriptwriter; 'determinatio est negatio', Spinoza would have said. Kaplan does not exist, yet his existence has to be continuous.
46. Suggesting that industrial design, like advertising (and unlike film-making?), is but a vacuous, unproductive occupation.
47. Although the suit does return in the last but one scene of the film in reduced form (jacket and tie are out of shot) on the bed of the sleeper compartment on the train back to New York.

Chapter 6

Dialectics in C.C.P.[1]

This chapter marks a leap from a historical assessment of materialism as a method and of materialist *praxis* in the study of fashion towards an analysis of contemporary approaches to making garment pieces and accessories. The transitional aspect resides in the combination of fashion design practice and philosophical ideas, whereby the latter look at the way in which materialism has been filtered through the object–subject relationship and the hermeneutics of objectivity and objecthood (*Gegenständlichkeit*). The relation between the acting, socially and historically conscious subject and the products of his and her environment – as objects that are produced by the social relation of production – is crucial for a critical assessment of fashion. I will describe in the following how a *dialectical* view of this relationship provides for me the most sustained and nuanced basis for such a critique.

In the approach for this chapter I would also like to discuss the role of *representation* in the study of fashion. Since materialism and materiality determine the present interpretation of fashion's historic and conceptual values, recourse to representation could be regarded as counter-productive. It might be argued that when fashion does not appear as fashion in the physically conditioned sense of garments and accessories that are worn on the body, but in the form of fashion as theoretical, in particular philosophical, text, as something that is conceptualised as a reflection only of its form and appearance, it loses the very materiality that is at stake here. Therefore an effort is sustained in this book to describe fashion in its materialisation, as developed product, as designed object, as a commodity within systems of exchange and, in its finality, as an embodied performance of power structures. In my view fashion should not be shown essentially through photographs or drawings but needs to be articulated as processes of making. This view, as I will explain further below, determined the choice of my case study of one particular design studio and manufacturer.

At the same time, an object – not only in fashion, but particularly so, due to its proximity to the body – *represents itself to the subject*. The object–subject relationship implies for fashion that a garment or accessory, but equally a novel, a new figure of speech, an innovative form of transportation or a progressive image in the media, is experienced by the subject not merely in its material form but as a representation. Sometimes this representation is a poor substitute for the real thing; at times it is everything in itself. In fashion the representative value has been debated often as to what degree a text, drawing, performance or photograph might represent the actual objecthood of, say, a piece of clothing. Yet this is not a question only of accuracy (of depiction) but a conceptual problem. If the representation depicts the object but equally represents an image in itself, what is the dynamic relationship to the material qualities of the piece, which extend outward from the representation through surface qualities, weight, size and so forth? A polemical argument has emerged from late modernist theories that an all-pervasive media substitutes materiality with images, replaces originals with simulacra and simulates erstwhile concrete, productive relationships. One political consequence of this argument is the view that modernity has entered its 'post'-condition in which materialism is progressively diffused by anti-materialism, so that, for instance, the significance of labour conditions in existing industries has been surpassed by new forms of speculation and entrepreneurship in the virtual realm.

It is significant for the discussion in this chapter that objecthood and, by extension, objectivity are, at least initially, not seen as confrontational but as complementary to the subject. In contrast to the actual piece of clothing, its representation does not oppose subject to object but mediates the object for the subject, suggesting an *a priori* interpretation that allows easier access to the supposed meaning of the actual object, whereas the real garment or accessory might indeed remain opposite to the subject. The represented object as distinct from the material one vis-à-vis the subject suggests already the necessary dialectics within any analysis of the object–subject relationship. It indicates the extent to which shifts and movements in this relationship have to be acknowledged not as mediating 'compromises' or as obfuscating inclusivity but as dynamics that critically pitch elements against one another in order to demonstrate historical changes in economic and social production.

In German the term *Gegenstand* – literally, a thing standing against another – is apt for developing and understanding historical trajectories; from mechanical to dialectical and historical materialism, and onward to contemporary hermeneutics. This is the first time in this book that a hermeneutical approach has been singled out, although I have interpreted literary and political/philosophical texts in previous chapters. But these interpretations were working mainly as textual exegeses, not as part of a delineated philosophical system of understanding. I would like now to introduce hermeneutics, the law of understanding representation, as a system that appears to challenge materialism and, at least in the minds of its bourgeois practitioners, actually overcomes it. However, I would like to argue that these interpretations have to return always to the essentialism of diverse modes and means of production that determine economic and social relations and must therefore point towards materialism. But this does not mean that hermeneutic or phenomenological approaches are not useful and constructive in critically assessing materialism and fashion. It is rather the historical trajectory of these contrasting ideas that reveals again shifting dynamics and changing positions, which become productive in analysing the relationship between object and subject.

Object and Subject

In Chapter 2 I wrote about the way in which Benjamin used fashion to challenge a concept of history and offer an activation of the past through sartorial quotations that, dialectically, rupture the timeline while at the same time preparing the ground for continuity (in consumption). For Benjamin, the dialectic inherent in (historical) materialism and the formulation of the commodity fetish referred back to Marx but, in fact, the ideas had been prepared already by G. W. F. Hegel's dialectics, in both his philosophy of history and in the method of his *Phenomenology of Spirit* – the latter written in 1805/06, during the continuing aftershock of the French Revolution and Napoleon's march through Europe. I would like to spend a bit more time with Hegel (and Marx) in looking at the subject–object debate in relation to the sartorial object that covers and clothes the human subject. I propose to contextualise this debate in what I hope to be fitting phenomenological terms such as *Bewußtsein* (consciousness) *Erfahrung* (experience) and *Gegenstand* (object), which I am reading in materialist fashion as concrete social and political aspects within a framework of production. Methodologically, this means glancing at twentieth-century phenomenology (Husserl, Heidegger, Merleau-Ponty) and its interpretative adjunct hermeneutics (Heidegger, Gadamer) in such a way that metaphysics are made concrete in the relationship between subject and object, man and nature, *Erkenntnis* (knowledge, cognition) and *Gegenstand*, self and material, that is, through social relationships of production – something that had already been inherent in Hegel.

As a theoretical position, phenomenology has suffered from the paradox that it proclaims a return to the things themselves but remains idealist rather than realist (let alone materialist) in its approach. Phenomenology considers things insofar as they appear to our senses, with turn-of-the-last-century proponents such as Franz Brentano having singled out a psychologically tinged 'intentionality' towards objects. He defined consciousness from a first-person point of view while asking for a philosophical method to match the analytical rigour of the natural sciences. Brentano's most famous pupil, Edmund Husserl, at the start of the twentieth century drew a distinction between accidental and essential qualities of things. For Husserl, there existed structures that generated an attitude towards objects as entities perceived in everyday life and the ordinary sciences (not yet quantum theory), which he thought to overcome by declaring that things constituted themselves in consciousness – in brief, a constructive focus on objects, which neglected Hegel as much as most of nineteenth-century materialism as method, and thus had to remain idealist in its subject-centrism.

The subject–object debate, habitually denoted as a hyphenated compound that puts the conscious being before the thing, has a long tradition in Western thought – too long to go into in detail here. I want to condense its origin by starting with Hegel's writing as the first substantial effort to eschew the previous duality of the two terms in order to promote an understanding that integrates subject into object and object into subject. For Hegel, as the philosopher Ernst Bloch observed in his 1949 book on the *Subjekt-Objekt*, method and concrete object are one and the same, namely 'spirit that develops' (*entwickelnder Geist*). They are both propelled by the same thing: dialectics as instrumental to historical development. Bloch wrote:

> It is the history of the subject which corrects itself through its respective object, the object that corrects itself through its subject, in ascending steps, in ever more elevated designs of history and the world, until at last the subject has experienced all its externalising articulations [*Entäußerungen*] and objectifications, and removes itself from these externalising articulations and becomes history as truly understood or as absolute knowledge.[2]

An ideal method and philosophical system must show themselves as a progressive, dialectical process. This means that the dynamic of contradiction and negation within dialectics does not determine a cumulative process of stacking corrections on top of each other, but demonstrates how conflicts such as class wars and systemic changes through revolts and revolutions are structurally integral to a historical trajectory – and not interruptions in a positivist teleology of progress, as bourgeois historians maintain.[3] The dynamic also goes against the notion that contradictions or negations are raised to a quasi-ontological level, as objectively existing independent of the individual subject. On the contrary, the development of historical structures in Hegel and Marx is inconceivable without the acting subject in history and the way in which he or she becomes active or even embodies a resolution within such contradictions.

At its end of the dialectic process stands an actual understanding of historical processes that Bloch, after Marx's left-Hegelian reading, determined as social and political *praxis*. Experience in history is but a dialectical mediation, when conflicts are acknowledged as historical drivers that prompt social change. In this mediation consciousness continuously corrects itself in the *Gegenstand*, in the object that confronts it and, conversely, in the way in which the object corrects itself in the subject that experiences, uses, even wears it.[4] The perception of the object as an external, alienating thing that objectifies us and reifies our social relations is acknowledged, but this realisation is qualified by the way in which the subject acts upon the object to mobilise political action. The dialectic in the object–subject relation is highly dynamic across history. It can be observed for sartorial fashion by the way in which sumptuary laws have not only codified classes but faced, often almost simultaneously, challenges to such codification under the auspices of style changes that allowed a lower, disenfranchised or alienated class to adapt, after a certain, progressively intensifying time lapse, the dress code of a higher class through material transfer, subversion or, less often, outright copy. The clothes of the middle class are adapted for the 'Sunday Best' of the worker who customises hand-me-downs, copies styles in cheaper, often more expressive patterns or subverts the code by combining garments from different classes and for different occasions in one outfit.

It is important to understand that Hegel, and Marx and Bloch after him, never lost sight of the concrete object within a system of thought; furthermore that the *production* of the object through labour is defined as a conscious process for social change. In his *Phenomenology of Spirit* Hegel wrote: '*Inasmuch as the new true object issues from it*, this *dialectical* movement which consciousness exercises on itself and which affects both its knowledge and its object, is precisely what is called *experience* [*Erfahrung*].'[5] Bloch has rightly pointed out in his interpretation of Hegel's philosophy of history, which had been so instrumental for the nineteenth-century debate on historicity, historicism and historical materialism, that this new object is not simply negating or replacing the old one but, as part of the dialectical process, preserves it.[6] The old, negating element is part of the new object and this makes it stand against the initially puzzled and suspicious subject who, only when realising the revolutionary potential of the old object (cf. Benjamin and the Surrealists), can appreciate the new. The past is mobilised in the new object, as part of a historical conflict that needs to be overcome. This view allows for a perception of fashion as acknowledging class conflicts through past styles within new trends. What once was esoteric or 'high' fashion is now made popular through being integrated into a different class or economic sphere via novel production processes and materials that permit an erstwhile expensive object to become affordable and diffused. Once this new object has become fashionable it needs to change again by developing in turn new forms or making or adapting the past.

I have analysed the process of mobilising the past in the dialectic of object and subject that correct each other across history in the second chapter of this book through Benjamin's *Tigersprung*, which rephrased Marx's interpretation of Hegel's *Umschlag* (folding) as *Sprung* (leap): the unfolding from progressive quantitative change to a radical qualitative one, as the leap in historical, political *praxis*. Inequalities become more obvious across time, class conflicts become more pronounced and violent, until a revolution changes the social system – after which the same process continues anew. Hegel saw this in the French Revolution and Napoleon's subsequent reign but, significantly, observed it also in production.[7] The qualitative changes that occurred throughout the early nineteenth century in experimenting with new manufacturing techniques and materials (in France, for instance, a confluence of artisanal workshop tradition and the division of labour in large factories) had been foreshadowed by the instigation of the factory process in the second half of the eighteenth century (for example, mechanised weaving looms powered by steam), which changed the quantities in which textiles, and subsequently clothes, were produced. In Hegel, such historical patterns in moving from quantitative to qualitative change still possess a natural quality; in Marx, they become part of the overall method of dialectical materialism that pitched radical changes in production (from manufacturer to factory) or exchange (from increase in value to accumulation of capital) against social development (from feudalism to the capitalism of competition and monopolies).

There is no static opposition between subject and object. Admittedly, the *Gegenstand* progressively stands against the subject in the course of industry. Yet it is part of a historical dynamic that unlocks patterns and systems and leads to conscious recognition of how object relations (e.g. in exchange processes) mirror the social relations of production and, as postulated in Marx's commodity fetishism, are able even to simulate such social relations per se. The subject is mirrored by the object as a material and materialist reflection of the economic system in which she finds herself, but the object also mirrors the subject within this reflection – her material and social aspiration, her consciousness.[8] For fashion these dynamic reflections become a codifying aspect of modern capitalism. The sartorial object not only provides a utilitarian or decorative covering for the subject but reflects it as a commodified body, with codified clothing, accessories, hairstyles, make-up and so on, which determines the place of the fashion object within a political economy.

Marx made this integration of object into subject and subject into object via mutual reflection a main argument of his early *Economic and Philosophical Manuscripts* (1844). In them he developed Hegel's *Phenomenology* into a demand for the reform of economic structures and social conditions from the ground up. As the composite title of the work indicates, Marx began by critically assessing the abstract foundations of thought and then rendering them concrete.

> The appropriation of man's essential powers, which have become objects – indeed, alien objects – is thus in the *first place* only an *appropriation* occurring in *consciousness*, in *pure thought*, i.e., in *abstraction*: it is the appropriation of these objects as *thoughts* and as *movements of thought*. [. . .]
>
> The outstanding achievement of Hegel's *Phenomenology* and of its final outcome, the dialectic of negativity as the moving and generating principle, is thus in the first place that Hegel conceives the self-creation of man as a process, conceives objectification as loss of the object, as alienation and as transcendence of this alienation; that he thus grasps the essence of *labour* and comprehends objective man – true because real man – as the outcome of man's *own labour*. The *real, active* orientation of man to himself as a species-being, or his manifestation as a real species-being (i.e., as a human being), is only possible if he really brings out all his *species-powers* – something which in turn is only possible through the cooperative action of all of mankind, only as the result of history – and treats these powers as objects: and this, to begin with, is again only possible in the form of estrangement.[9]

The object stands for Marx in one form outside the subject, is representative of the other that opposes the organic body. The object appears as artifice, mechanised nature, means of production, as a fashioned product that provides a covering for woman so that she can be socialised into a system. Such opposition leads to estrangement and alienation, which are made conscious, and therefore can be overcome historically, by the subject appropriating the means of production and thereby gaining in a concrete economic and political sense control over output.

Soviet clothing, as demonstrated during the New Economic Policy (NEP) of 1921–28, which was meant to stimulate consumption after the White Terror, acknowledged the structure of fashion by putting out new styles and novel accessories – even commissioning artists of the Constructivist movement such as Varvara Stepanova, Liubov Popova and Aleksandra Exter to design avant-garde graphic patterns for fabrics and garments. Yet these fashion products were bound up into a nationalised textile production, for which printed cottons and simplified, geometric pattern cuts were developed, as well as experiments in proto-sportswear, in order to provide economical solutions for large-scale consumption.[10] This consumption was not based on class differences through genres of clothing or types of dress, but on the dissemination of a new aesthetic – partly based on revolutionary motifs, partly based on prevailing fashion trends elsewhere in Europe – independent of income or rank. Although the NEP was primarily geared towards agricultural production, its effect in the big cities such as Moscow, Petrograd/Leningrad and Kiev was felt in the way people began to consume objects, not essentially as commodities but as objects made by cooperative, industrial production that embodied technological and social progress.[11] Aleksandr Deineka's numerous images of textile workers, in particular his painting *Textile Women* of 1927 in the Russian Museum in St Petersburg, show the intimate connection between producing and wearing fashion during the Soviet NEP: the women at the spinning and weaving machines are idealised as highly fashionable figures of feminism. A new generation of women workers who are producing for the common good is assembled on canvas through three versions of the modern female body, clothed in cotton dresses that are cut from a simple pattern and customised by either a slight gathering at the waist, a skirt puffed-up through folds, or as a sleeveless versus short-sleeved option. The geometrically bobbed hair, the absence of make-up and the bare feet reduce the female figure and her adornment to the minimum, while the stylised factory environment and the forcefully concentrated action of the women in their off-white or grey dresses render Deineka's figures epitomes of modernity: they are not only women but 'textile women' – simultaneously making the material object and being defined by it.[12] Hegel's postulate of the subject with her consciousness and experience as being transformed by the object is represented here in the female textile workers who are making, through modern manufacture, modern dresses which they can afford to wear themselves and which come to define their modernity through the cloth and cut of the activated, mobilised body politic.

Marx also understood in Hegel's dialectic that the object does not stand against the subject but is developed by the interaction itself. Hegel had fundamentalised this as consciousness and its experience in the introduction to his *Phenomenology*:

> This is the moment of transition from the first object and the knowledge of it, to the other object, which experience is said to be about. Our account implied that our knowledge of the first object, or the being-*for*-consciousness of the first in-itself, itself becomes the second object. [...] From the present point of view, however, the new object shows itself to have come about through a *reversal of consciousness itself*. This way of looking at the matter is something contributed by *us*, by means of which the succession of experiences through which consciousness passes is raised into a scientific progression – but it is not known to the consciousness that we are observing.[13]

Bloch adjudged therefore that the object question is 'dialectically resolved through the model of an already total mediation'[14] between object and subject. Furthermore, this mediation is a historical process: the movement and mediation between subject and object, between self and material, is, for Hegel, both episteme and constituent of history. The subject represents for herself the object in the same way in which the object, within this representation, represents the subject. This act of representing allows for a successively greater immersion into historical events. The subject is not opposed or alienated by the object but attains greater consciousness over time; it is enlightened – not in the metaphysical Kantian sense but in terms of concrete socio-political awareness. This dialectical 'oscillation' (Bloch) is what Marx found as a progressive movement in history in which, through the changing materiality of the subject's productive environment, the subject emancipates herself. The emancipation does not come at the cost of the object, but the *Gegenstand* takes its position as a reflected element within the historical process. Unlike its appearance as a commodity, it is not always alienating in its production, nor constantly fetishised in its consumption; potentially, it becomes a true representation of the objective world.

In a Conscious Fashion

What impact does a reflection on the subject–object relationship have for fashion, in particular for fashion in clothes and accessories? When, as outlined above, this relationship is understood as a dynamic process across history, when the subject sees herself reflected in the object, which in this very reflection reflects its own form as contingent on the consciousness and experience of the subject, and so on in dialectical fashion across progressive stages of self-articulation, then the essential function of fashion as corporeal covering becomes its actual epistemology. Fashion in clothes represents in obvious material terms the way in which a subject reflects herself in an object. The clothing of the body as an objectified, even reified representation of the physical form is, then, in this subjective reflection, dialectically objectified again as an articulation of what is appropriate as bodily covering in a particular time and space. This appropriateness can be filtered, in anthropological terms, through social customs or, in the political economy of capitalism, through, for example, the work of a textile company or a designer who is deemed to be 'fashionable' at a given point and therefore sells well in the market. The articulation of an object through the subject who is wearing particular clothes or accessories is subsequently reflected in the subject who accepts or rejects this fashion for herself and, in a process marked by increased consciousness or experience (even if it is merely the repeated experience of consumption), provides the demand for a new object that in turn influences again the posture, gestures, walk and so on of the subject wearing the clothes. A dialectical oscillation between subject and object continues across time. This process, it is important to remember, continues to occur before the spectre of technical and material innovations that, in reflecting social relationships within the social relations of production, lead to objectifications of the body as fetish commodity and further the alienation of the labourer who makes the textiles, garments and other fashion objects.

The subject–object relationship in Hegel, where the duality between nature and man, phenomenological spirit and material is overcome by integrating one into the other, is not just a metaphysically positivist process in raising consciousness and providing experience. As Marx determined in his reading of Hegel from the *Economic and Philosophical Manuscripts* via *Grundrisse* and *German Ideology* to *Capital*, the economic, social and political consequences of the dialectics in the subject–object relationship can promise progress only before the concrete reality of exploitative labour practices and powerful capitalist monopolies. Marx's and Engels' work on textile production in Manchester laid bare the inequalities and alienation that dominated the making of the *Gegenstand* as commodity-object. In order to understand the object properly, as Hegel had postulated in his *Phenomenology*, it needs to be to be *worked upon* – and by this he meant materially also. Bloch extracted this very modern meaning from Hegel's philosophy which had been conceived back at the start of the nineteenth century.

> When we understand an object [*Gegenstand*] it is changed – at least in our relation to it. Furthermore, after Hegel, it is also the very object itself that has changed: when worked upon, when understood, it changes its own estrangement or alienation, in the same way in which consciousness changes its estrangement from the object. In Hegel the philosopher is not always seen as a productive force, but his view has indeed something continuative, something that makes the subject–object relationship knowable.[15]

In fashion the understanding of clothes does not imply that we read them first as symbolic things, social markers or structural signifieds, but that we understand them as material objects that are produced by the subject as reflection of the subject – materially through systems of production, epistemologically through a historically continuous, dialectical process of experiencing them. It is certainly true that we are all objectified to a greater or lesser degree by clothing. Women's bodies in particular have been subject to the most pathological forms of objectification through fashions across time and geographies. Correspondingly, forms of mass manufacture and the industrial production of textiles and clothing have led to excess alienation of labour within the making of garments. Such factors are certainly present when the object is reflecting back on to the subject, in the way in which we show ourselves sharing and wearing the same selection of multinational brands across the globe.

Hermeneutics have fashioned the subject–object dynamic as a movement between the *Gegenstand* and its interpretation as discourse. This means that *Bewußtsein* and *Erfahrung*, consciousness and experience, are mediated – often in exclusive art forms – and not seen as direct sensory impressions. Objects are objects of experience, something Hegel had already postulated, and the subject attempts to rise to or to match (*entsprechen*) what is there. In order to do so one has to be able to 'read' the object, and this is where hermeneutics as a method of interpretation becomes structurally important. It is equally significant for our reading of phenomenology that it emerges epistemologically from action, not from passive sensual impressions. Woman is an acting subject and the objecthood of a thing, what arch-phenomenologist Edmund Husserl in his *Ideas Pertaining to a Pure Phenomenology* termed less materialistically *Dinglichkeit*, is her reality.[16] For Heidegger, following Husserl, the reading of the object in hermeneutics is not conceived principally as a matter of understanding objecthood but of understanding the subject, the Self through the engagement with the thing. Hermeneutics, like phenomenology, comprehends itself in ontological terms, concerned with the very nature of being. Converted into the currency of clothing, one might thus understand the wearing of clothes in hermeneutical terms not as reading the object (as a sartorial narrative of gender, race, class, etc.) but as experiencing the subject's attempt to match the object that she is wearing through posture, bodily movements, more or less controlled gestures and facial expressions.

Maurice Merleau-Ponty, who incorporated visual perception and physical habitus in his modern phenomenology, pointed back in his last book towards the dialectics of subject and object:

> We say therefore that our body is a being of two leaves, from one side a thing among things and otherwise what sees them and touches them; we say, because it is evident, that it unites these two properties within itself, and its double belongingness to the order of the 'object' and to the order of the 'subject' reveals to us quite unexpected relations between the two orders.[17]

When fashion points beyond the physical experience, beyond the tactility of fabrics, the weight of textiles, the restrictions of the cut, does it become a representation of the body or can it continue to exist as object in itself? Is the perception and realisation of fashion's autonomy not simply material fact (not skin but cloth) or economic factor (commodity production) but read as conceptual: to separate clothing from the body allows for an object-based perception of the sartorial product? As we have seen in Hegel (and Marx's and Bloch's reading thereof), surpassing objecthood is a progressive principle of phenomenology, and one that it shared with hermeneutics. For Hegel, the object that needed to be attained was not only a materially produced thing but also a concept, a thought (or interpreted) fact, while for Marx, this idea became most concrete in his demand that the subject attain ownership of the means of production so that the subject can free itself in and as a social experience. In both cases, as well as in later hermeneutics, there is a progression from the subject's initial standing against the *Gegenstand* to a truly dialectic relationship. For fashion, this might imply the integration of clothing into the body, a material fusion heightened by future molecular engineering or nanotechnology – not a working composition of organic and inorganic matter (the banal fantasy of cyborgs) but a new ontology of the body as composite with the object and therefore not merely debating the traditional law of subjectivity but demonstrating a physiological acceptance of the growing amount of control that the object can exert over us.

In the following case study such a final synthetic event does not occur. The antithesis to and negation of the subject is positioned here as a material contrast that does not need to be overcome or resolved but is active in the very experience of the (fashion) object.

Negation, Part I

Carol Christian Poell is a Milan-based, progressive maker of garments and accessories. His company, studio and label designates itself as C.C.P. srl to avoid fetishising the figure of the designer and to eschew foregrounding his subjectivity – and this hiding behind the work has a conceptual as well as a creative rationale. Poell said a few years ago: 'The *negation* of creative possibilities creates the type, the form and the design of a piece in the first place.'[18] This dialectic of creating from negation is central to understanding the logical reduction and deduction of formal possibilities in C.C.P. Arthur Conan Doyle once credited his fictional detective Sherlock Holmes with the processual approach to finding a solution: 'Eliminate all other factors, and the one which remains must be the truth.'[19] So, in testing out all possible hypotheses to a creative solution, the one that remains at the end must be the right one, no matter how absurd or false it might appear.

Although such *reduction as deduction* might at first appear only as the hyper-rational working method of an obsessive (and fictional) investigator, when it is applied to a process of design over time it offers a comparable logical outcome. Economising on materials, refining a technique to avoid previous unwanted aspects in production (not necessarily omitting mistakes) and honing formal elements demonstrates a clear creative process that leads to an optimised result. Yet in many creative processes that are subject to fashion, such optimising is an absolute anathema. The *octroi* of fashion does not condone an approach through which designed products are engineered towards an optimised form and usage, as this would compromise, even prevent, further changes in style, altered appearances and modified forms of consumption. General acceptance of the ultimate pair of trousers or perfected cut of a boiler suit, as promoted by modernists such as Aleksandr Rodchenko, Thayaht or Federico García Lorca,[20] would put an end to fashion.

Although fashion advertises its wares at every turn with the promise of the best and most advantageous use, producers and consumers alike understand it as a transitory materialisation that can change at any instant. The ultimate pair of trousers is only perfected within the moment of its genesis as a fashion item, not according to any material or empirical rationale. This is perfectly understandable, since the perfection of the trousers is wholly subjective within its time and place. For a season in a certain setting a specific pair of trousers might indeed display a temporary creative pinnacle, but the designer, the retailer and the consumer are all conscious that the next 'ultimate' sartorial solution is just around the corner, waiting to be styled and sold. Empiricism in fashion is a problematic approach, since very few overarching or objective categories are discerned to assess the significance of a designed piece according to its function or longevity. In fashion the shorthand term of a 'classic' is used to describe manifestations that appear to transcend seasonal trends and the vagaries of time. Yet looking closely at such pieces reveals an obvious cultural hegemony at work. The three-piece suit, for instance, has long been decreed as a sartorial staple in embodying the objectified and rationalised (male) body in modernity: it is the cover of the financier, statesman, entrepreneur and government agent who best represents the power structures in capitalism. And when we add psychoanalytical to materialist interpretations, the pairing of such a suit with the phallic symbol of the tie marks another step towards the ultimate form of the hegemonic display of the (male) body – espousing written or unwritten sumptuary laws of dress in industrialised societies.

If, empirically speaking, we cannot discern the ultimate piece of design in fashion, we can nevertheless attempt to analyse the optimising of forms and materials. Research into the best use of materials, the least abrasive seaming or the most flexible or breathable fabric can easily become a hallmark of production. In sportswear, reduction (of wind resistance, of chafing against the skin, etc.) presents a clear teleology in design. The manufacturer works towards the most economical use of material that allows the athlete to optimise her or his performance within quantifiable, measurable parameters. It is understood that this design approach, even when resulting in the rather esoteric skin-tight suits of bobsleigh teams or the obsessively lightweight materials of cyclists or competitive sailors, must be formalised by visual and stylistic trends, to approximate a fashion for performance. Indeed, like motor sport's impact on the design of saloon cars, the transposition of ideas from sportswear, via leisurewear, to everyday fashion has a considerable historical trajectory. From jersey *tricotage* and raglan sleeves to the seamless synthetic tube-knits for the uppers of running shoes, the designed objects for professional sportspeople have influenced much of what we wear today. If optimised performance can be measured in professional sport – this particular suit reduces the drag of the athlete's body by x per cent, the scaled-down weight of that shoe saves y amount of muscular energy – the empirical value of an everyday sartorial object is much more difficult to assess. The way in which a social performance can be optimised by a particular suit or dress depends on time and place and on the subjectivity of the audience that observes such a performance. Do they consider the evening gown appropriate for the occasion and is the three-piece suit actually lending credibility to the wearer? If so, the dress and the suit indeed are 'best in show', but this depends on the way in which fashion is negotiated within an environment that is predisposed towards comprehending the classical as symbolising cultural hegemonies: the suit dresses up the rational character of modernity, the evening gown the marginalising of women through their objectification. Such temporal subjectivity is evident in the way in which the 'classical' is reconfigured within style subcultures or progressive sartorial trends that show a theatrical performance of the body that is supremely conscious of its transitoriness (the Teddy Boy's neo-Edwardian three-piece suit in the 1950s, the deconstructed men's white shirt in Japanese womenswear of the late 1980s).

Today, being 'in fashion' can only be understood as ironic, when it playfully acknowledges the notion of an immediacy that is transitory only, without any impulse to generate lasting impact. The use of branding and logos (visual *poncifs*) as stylistic features on fashionable clothing – derived from sportswear for the most part – acts as an obvious display of the self-conscious relegation of the wearer's subjectivity to the ephemerality of the object that signifies her for a moment and then moves on to the next, without an opportunity for such alienation of the subject to become fully conscious or politically pointed.

The anti-empiricism of fashion and its refusal to consider optimising its structures is evident in the way in which the industry has operated since the latter half of the nineteenth century, with its formalised design process in couture studios and seasonal displays in metropolitan fashion weeks. The development process through mood-board, sketch, working drawing, *toile* and final garment, the six-monthly show of a 'collection',[21] the temporary and ever-changing communication in the media, all work against a process of making that aims at optimisation in material terms. Obviously, manufacturers in the fashion industry aim at economising on their production, but this is directed first towards reducing labour costs and import duties through outsourcing, rather than towards a reduction in material wastage or the innovating of new recycling/remaking techniques for outmoded garments. In fashion, when a product is designed to sell at a high price through the narrative of a complex, time-intensive or even wasteful process of making (evident in so-called luxury goods), this will be visualised in the object and its representation through non-temporary design features with signifiers of 'the classic', such as increased materiality (multi-directional weaving or unusual cut of fabrics, solid precious metals, thick leather, etc.), subdued patterns or reduced colour schemes.[22]

In this respect, fashion is *gegenständlich* as anti-materialist; it stands against a material evaluation of its production that principally runs along the lines of optimised manufacture and the reduction of time and waste.[23] But, as mentioned before, fashion is also supremely materialist in the objectification of the process of exchange. So, the economic relevance of reducing costs is ameliorated through speeding up the succession of product series and sartorial commodities. More and more 'diffusion lines' are added to the portfolio of fashion brands (from cheaper clothing via homeware to furniture) and vertically integrated manufacturing allows for the turnaround of a garment design to reach the shop within the space of six weeks. Instead of formally optimising the object, merely a profusion of variants are offered, which in their multitude construct the mirage of complete choice, so that the consumer feels that across her continuous rhythm of purchasing an optimal equilibrium of combined commodities can be found.

In order to introduce C.C.P.'s work proper I propose to walk the reader through his workshop – which, by the time you read this book, will have been abandoned after seventeen years of occupancy. The workshop serves not only as a place of production but as a productive site that constitutes the phenomenological basis for the work: an environment read and experienced as an immersive object for the subject. Furthermore, in material terms the studio denotes the adaptation of traditional small-scale manufacturing, in particular the in-house control of an artisanal process, to a shifting industrial landscape of production. C.C.P. is ostensibly using the structure of the fashion industry to produce an extremely limited number of 'pieces'[24] that act as experimental templates to innovate wider production processes. I will give a detailed example of how this synergetic process works in the next chapter on textile production, but as a general rule C.C.P. develops with select innovative manufacturers radically new techniques or materials, which, after he has researched and explored them in his own pieces, are adapted and simplified by larger (luxury) brands – mostly in collaboration with the same manufacturers who had originally worked with C.C.P.[25] For example, a US brand (which shall remain nameless) is in the habit of acquiring selections of pieces by C.C.P. from the experimental fashion store Lift in Tokyo. The brand then simplifies and formally reduces these pieces, or even entire outfits, for its mainstream collections, while also using fabrics that were commissioned from the weaver Bonotto (see next chapter), who had developed them originally with C.C.P. It is hardly surprising that this particular brand appears as a watered-down, infinitely reproduced version of C.C.P.'s original design ideas. Such outright copying would be noted negatively were it not for the 'law of visibility' in our culture industry. The brand that is most visible retains the best claim to originality, since the initial design idea went unnoticed by the mainstream media and therefore does not exist in the dominant system of exchange.

C.C.P.'s workshop is situated on the second floor of an industrial building in the southern part of Milan. It had been used as scenographic workshop for the Milan Opera, and the old metal runners built into the ceiling, which held up the scenographies painted on paper as backdrops for performances, now suspend samples and, at the far end of the shop, the paper patterns that C.C.P. has produced over the years. These patterns serve as a structural archive of shapes and forms, slightly shifting in the breeze from open windows and muffling the sound from the studio floor. The room is lit by large windows in thin metal frames along the longitudinal walls of the workshop. The glass of the windows alternates between clear and opaque panes to filter out the glare of daylight. The shop's interior is lined with rows of freestanding shelves that house rolls of fabric and other materials. The front of the workshop connects through two metal sliding doors with an office and a reception room. A massive, battered old workbench dominates the former, while a large, felt-covered metal table and two benches occupy the latter. Between the sliding doors stand a large display case and a metal dresser, both lined with tissue paper to house metal and leather objects.

Against the left wall, looking out on to a courtyard, stands a row of three large pattern-cutting tables that are separated by shelves of samples and fabric swatches. The opposite wall opens to a kitchen, two restrooms and a secluded research library in the designer's office. Outside the right wall hangs a conveyor belt that had been installed many decades ago and which is used to transport materials from C.C.P.'s painting and tanning workshop in the courtyard up to the workshop. The walls of the shop are rough, whitewashed brickwork while the floor is tiled in dark red, covered in traces of age-old studio work with paint, dyes and other chemicals. Window- and doorframes have been stripped of some of their greyish paint, in a gesture of unwillingness to mask the air of rough wear and tear that pervades the space. The combination of sparse, minimal elements in the building and the warmth and odour of yarns, textiles, hides and leather that permeates the air appears a fitting metaphor for the conversion of an industrial space into an experimental designer's workshop. C.C.P.'s studio has retained the workshop's original connection to labour, artisanal craft as well as small-scale manufacturing, as a site that produces materials as much as working them into finished objects. Many design studios are able to produce intricate samples, and indeed the seamstresses and *premiers mains* of ateliers in alta moda or haute couture can complete outfits on site, but as a rule these workshops do not develop their own materials but obtain them from weavers or auxiliary manufacturers (button-makers, embroiderers, etc.). In contrast, the team at C.C.P. produce the greater part of their materials themselves, beginning with the development of yarns and threads, then negotiating weaving, spinning, dyeing and tanning, in addition to cutting and sewing their finished materials. For this, a back and forth between the workshop in Milan and manufacturers in northern Italy is required: when one stage in the making of the garment or accessory in the studio is completed, the object is sent out for a secondary stage of addition or modification, before it returns to C.C.P.'s workshop for another stage to contrast or fuse with the previous ones. Although carefully planned, these stages of the process are not necessarily conceived according to optimised or economic logistics, but instead work with the innate qualities of the material and the object, for instance consciously reversing a habitual production process to lessen the impact of the subject on the organic character of the object, or building up layers in the production in order to be able to partially take them away later, in a material demonstration of making.

I would like to briefly describe an example of how such a back and forth between stages of manufacture emphasises materiality and, through this materiality, exposes the material autonomy of the object. Furthermore, it shows how the manufacturing process, as executed by various workers and artisans (i.e. subjects), is concretely *represented* in the object. In 2010 C.C.P. started to produce a series of leather shoes and ankle boots, denoted as 'prosthetic'. This adjective seemingly foregrounds a subject-related (additive, implanted) characteristic, but the pieces are, in fact, the result of a complex oscillation between stages of manufacture. First, an ankle boot – upper, sole, lining – is sewn together from a raw hide without being exposed to a dyeing or tanning process. The size of the object must be calculated with an excess of 10–15 per cent in order to accommodate the shrinkage across subsequent production stages. Pieces of sanded titanium are inserted at neuralgic points in the object, between hide and lining, positioned where the subject's (wearer's) ankle or toe will be. The titanium pieces are manufactured by a metal workshop in nearby Vicenza that normally produces toe-caps and other safety elements for workwear. The shoe is then 'object-tanned' and 'object-dyed', denoted as a holistic process that materially integrates hide, ply yarn, lining and metal through a reverse method of making. After the shoe has been finished as an object, C.C.P. takes an industrial sander to the leather surface in order to destroy the area on top of the titanium, so that the metal is brutally revealed – akin to the arthritic joint breaking through the skin or an implant/prosthesis being revealed by a dramatic accident.[26] The notion of an organic pathology is here represented through the unorthodox producing of an object, whereby negation becomes a dramatic, self-reflexive and thus constructive process of violent intervention in design production.

Die Entziehung

A literal translation of *Entziehung* is 'withdrawal', when self-generated by the subject, or 'privation' or 'suspension', when imposed on the subject by an external object or force. Poell used this word to identify the psychological and literary technique of his fellow Austrian, writer Thomas Bernhard, who had employed it as a subtitle for the second part of his series of autobiographical novels, *Der Keller* (The Basement), published in 1976.[27] *Entziehung* is syntactically very close to the term *Erziehung* – education or upbringing – and this relational meaning is significant both for Bernhard's account of his youth and for C.C.P.'s heuristic methods in testing out techniques of investigation and design. For Poell, *Entziehung* describes simultaneously a creative, material approach – moving away from codification or typology – and a self-reflexive socio-political position, in which alienation and isolation are converted from economic disparity and individual pathology to aesthetic concept. Like Bernhard, the pared-down language, repetition and deliberate isolation of the work through complex semantics and

7 Carol Christian Poell, object-dyed lined one-piece, prosthetic Goodyear boots (detail), 2010, male Dead-End Collection

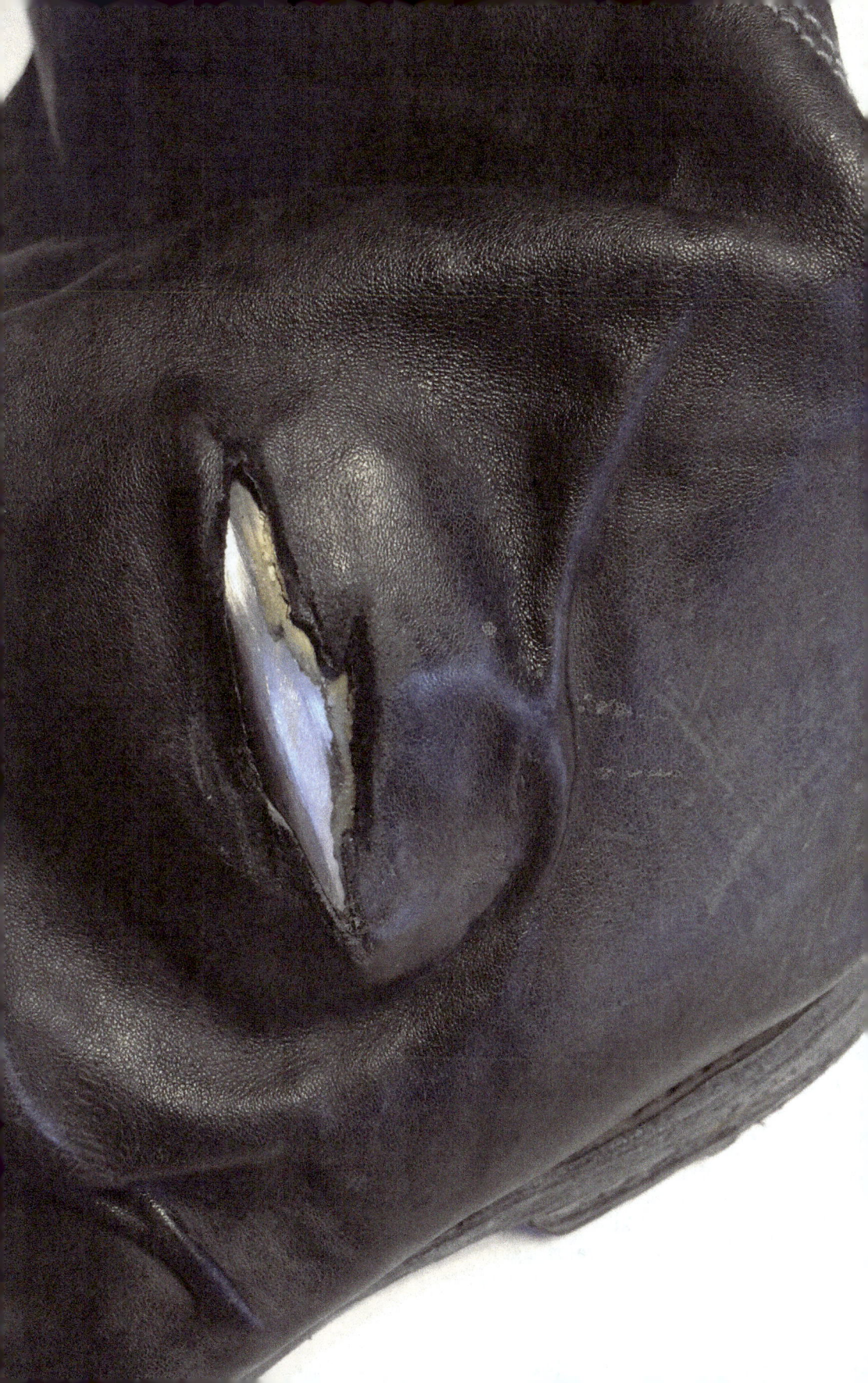

syntax become hallmarks for the strategy of negation that is central to the work of C.C.P.

As suggested above, C.C.P.'s developing of a garment is geared towards optimising a process of making. Poell has quipped that: 'I endeavour to make Marx's coat fit better and better.'[28] The research into yarns, fabrics, leather, or metal as base materials, the inversion and subversion of habitual working techniques in fashion, the innovative and complex pattern cuts, all are conducted contrary to the seasonal rhythm of the industry and displayed anti-cyclically only when deemed complete. The negation of established forms, the eschewing of any promotional activities, the deliberate anonymity of the designer[29] and the refusal to release new work at recognisable intervals have evolved over time and could be regarded now as a dramatic teleology of anti-progress. In fact, the refusal or withdrawal is the result of a complex interaction of conceptual, economic and material reasoning. First of all, one can document a quantifiable economic advantage that has resulted from removing the studio from the fashion system and its cycle. In 2010 C.C.P. stopped producing new garments or accessories. Since then the company's turnover has increased year on year, despite its limiting its output to the greatest degree: it only works with a handful of stores around the world and even these retailers are often given only a quarter of the pieces they would like to order from the studio. There is now a two-year waiting list for each client, and since C.C.P. does not provide garments for photo-shoots or the red carpet, not even fashion 'insiders' or the rich and famous are able to jump the queue.[30]

This economic advantage did not arise from a strategy to artificially generate demand by limiting access (often attempted in 'art' or 'luxury' production), but resulted from a number of interconnected causes. Back in 2010 C.C.P. was ready to cease production because of the lack of mobility and development that could be perceived in the fashion industry at large. Poell says that he 'wants to work outside the market', that he intends to 'avoid any dependency' on the existing economic structure of the fashion industry.[31] And he states outright: 'I produce by questioning the capitalist system.'[32] He does not mean to work outside the economic, social and ideological structures of capitalism, but to approach them differently through his work so that negation, withdrawal, subversion and critique provide a synthetic alternative. But merely questioning the capitalist system is already a notable approach, when one considers the way in which the all-pervasive fashion system exploits workers in the textile industry, operates against efforts towards sustainability (cotton monocultures or water waste in dyeing) and produces huge surplus stock, a large portion of which ends up in landfill. Questioning and critique also reflect on the social relationships that the system creates in its production. Fashion is currently so much subject to constantly renewed consumption that the system itself has become entrenched and sclerotic, and so any real challenges to the structure must appear as rather striking. Yet these challenges remain difficult to realise, or are kept concealed, within a field of strongly vested economic and ideological interests, and one which, as mentioned in previous chapters, acts as an essential rhythm for a culture of capitalism.

Hence C.C.P.'s questioning cannot work by postulating theatrical alternatives to consumptive behaviour, but rather the studio needs to produce in such a way that reflection on the object's making and communication falls back on to the subject – so that it gains the experience that Hegel and Marx (as well as Bloch) demanded. In this context, C.C.P.'s restricting or even negating access is born from concrete material limitations, since garments and accessories can be made only through a time-consuming, self-limiting process. The increasing complexity of the material production and the progressive optimising of designs had put a huge demand on C.C.P.'s studio and staff. Pieces would be subject to ever more intricate and self-limiting processes,[33] until early in 2010 C.C.P. deemed that the apex of garment design and construction had been reached and no further development was necessary. This brought a halt to the design process, and C.C.P. decided from then on to release only existing designs. Therefore the consumer will not find any clothes from the studio that have a date after 2010 inscribed on their label – should there be at some point a new series of works, they will bear the date '2011', notwithstanding the actual year of origin. For the retailers and consumers of C.C.P. the issue of identifying the latest 'collection' has never really mattered, and you will find in a Berlin or Tokyo store garments made back in 2007 and 2008 mixed with work that has just arrived from Milan. Independence from seasonal styles is obviously easier in the more homogeneous formal language of menswear, although gender and sex differences in dress codes have been progressively effaced within the fashion system, especially in occidental countries. In C.C.P. independence from trends and styles is a complex manoeuvre, achieved through setting templates for the gradual transformation of formal ideas that have been established over time. A vocabulary of markers has been established which are not simple stylistic signifiers, but material and technical solutions that are optimised in the workshop.

'I am using capitalism but simultaneously withdraw from it [*ich entziehe mich*]', says Poell.[34] Such *Entziehung* is akin to a hermeneutic experience of objecthood, when the object is perceived across an interpretative distance from the subject. In the case of fashion, the representation of the body is made by a communality of phenomenological experiences that seem to optimise the object in a particular time and space, as the result of interpreting the best possible way in which the body should appear now. Obviously, this tallies with the materialist view of a codification of the body through prevailing object relations in capitalism, and as a reflection of productive relationships in labour (textile weavers, garment industry, design workshops, etc.) – although this is rephrased considerably, of course, when it appears as a political standpoint.

Separating clothing from the body allows for an *object-based perception* of the sartorial product; its autonomy also represents the subject as more liberated. If fashion is not a fetish within a system of capitalist societal norms and mores but a product of a conscious and self-reflexive process of making, its impact turns from codification to manifestation, and the phenomenological import of the *Gegenstand* turns from opposition to a Hegelian integration of subject into object and vice versa. The fashion object can thus become a true representation of temporal consciousness, be it aesthetic (designed artefact), ecological (sustainable thing), economic (lasting and affordable item) or political (manifest ideal of the equality of gender, class, etc.).

C.C.P.'s progressive move towards an unchanging, consciously reflected object in fashion, which manifests itself in its considered and reflexive form of making – reflexive of industry demands as well as materials and techniques – allows for a representation of the subject as subject proper in the hermeneutical sense, which overcomes objecthood (*Gegenständlichkeit*) while, through the notably unorthodox forms of production, showing the object as an idealised reflection of the subject – for a fleeting but significant moment in time. Putting on a piece by C.C.P., the wearer alters his posture and gestures according to the tight cut of the trousers, the small armholes of the jacket, the weight of the overcoat or the metal inserts on top of elbows, ankles or toes. The autonomy of the object imposes itself on him – not as a restriction but as a dialectic production of form in its negation: the piece is not 'new', it is not comfortable, nor it is flattering, but, in these negations, it becomes all three. It is independent of seasonal demand, thus always new; it elongates and trims the wearer, thus aestheticising the body.

Negation, Part 2

In his book on objectivity – or perhaps *objecthood* would be a better translation of *Gegenständlichkeit* – as a principle of phenomenology, the philosopher Günter Figal wrote in 2006:

> In objectivity [*Gegenständlichkeit*], the exteriority of things not longer comes into focus on the basis of conduct and its context. It also does not show itself due to the fact that something falls outside the scope of one's conduct and its context. Rather, it steps across from. The objectivity is what steps across from, and then, at least for a moment, *stands over against*.[35]

The close-fitting, raw objects with metal inserts and oddly processed materials confront the subject with her notion of what fashion is, in the objecthood of what is worn. Since 1995, when Poell began to develop his tendency towards reducing the appearance of clothing and towards manifesting the materiality of making, he was conscious of how such a process can lead to the final disappearance of the work within its own reduction. At C.C.P. the materialism of design has grown in significance such that experimentation with working processes takes up a vast amount of time and is expanded across seasons, so that nothing is shown in public for years. Furthermore, the honing of material processes of making is rarely made visible on the outside of garments or visualised by surfaces or colours. It remains hidden, concealed, only visible when a piece is turned inside out so that, for example, the unlined jacket shows its intricately perfected construction or a nylon parka with taped seams is pulled out and over a long woollen jacket.[36] Small changes over time are imperceptible – except when worn, when the body of the wearer experiences the object and matches this experience in a changed posture and habitus; for example, when the flexible yarn that connects the French seam on the side of a pair of trousers expands and contracts with the wearer's movements, revealing and concealing glimpses of the body underneath.[37]

The materiality is to be understood as the primary object, and the completed garment only as secondary object. This explains, too, C.C.P.'s lack of fashion communication, since the essential character of the object is destined to remain unarticulated, while the fashionable commodity that could be presented is seen as less significant within the overall process of making. In turn this means that the dialectical movement across history back and forth between subject and object does not lead to a teleological goal (any instantaneous 'perfect look'), but rather the wearer progressively experiences C.C.P.'s garments over time and takes part in an ageing process that adds material patina as well as symbolic substance. This experience can be seen in the everyday process of wearing, but I would argue that it is more essential than this, as it offers a previously impossible ontology of the clothing object through its dialectic relationship with the subject: being used and simultaneously reflecting back on this use. I would caution the reader to understand this in terms of the old adage 'clothes maketh the man',[38] since this is not a social phenomenon but an existentialist one, heightened by the fact that C.C.P.'s clothes are difficult to obtain and do not conform readily in shape or form to the existing fashion system. 'The object,' summarises Poell regarding the autonomy of his garments and accessories, 'like the personality of the wearer both have their own identity.'[39]

In this context I will describe two further examples from C.C.P.'s workshop. The first is a coat shown in 2009 in the slaughterhouses of Milan's abandoned meat market, in a series of tiled rooms where gutters for draining blood are cut deep into the floors and rusting meat hooks run on ceiling rails – the latter used on this occasion to display the sample garments. The coat was made from glass fibre in a voluminous shape with slightly rounded shoulders. Woven from a yarn that was loosely twisted from dangerously sharp glass and very brittle filaments, the fabric had a structure that was similar to ordinary canvas, whereas its production was experimental as well as restricted in the most dramatic way. Glass fibres are used in the form of woven material in the building trade for insulation, where they are habitually covered by layers of other stuff (concrete, resin) to hold the weave together and protect users. C.C.P. twisted the microscopic glass shards to produce a yarn with a very short staple length that was sprayed for hold and lined with a polyester/cotton mix for protection and substantiation alike. The cutting and sewing of the weave had to be done wearing gloves, mask and goggles, since the filaments would shred the surface of the skin before the seamstress would even notice.

This garment is indeed a *Gegenstand*, an object that stands against the subject, since it can neither be worn (unless with a complete under layer of body and face covering), nor is it construed as fashion, since it could not appear in a social setting: any touch or accidental brushing against the coat would result in severe injury to the neighbouring body. The coat was an exercise in material research: how can glass fibres be woven into a usable textile and then how can this be cut and tailored into a garment?[40]

8 Carol Christian Poell, glue-taped unlined jacket (detail), 2008, male Off-Scene Collection Photo: Deepti Barth

The result of this research was acknowledged to be unwearable in practice (despite fulfilling all the basic functions of a coat), but it was a staging post on a dialectical route to experience – although in this instance a negative, physiologically negating one.

When the coat was displayed in the tiled room, buyers wandered around it, describing a perimeter around the object, resisting the impulse to touch and drape the garment over their bodies. Yet two orders were made for the coat, prompting C.C.P. to construct another version and ship it within protective layers to the buyer, who, it must be assumed, stored it at the back of his wardrobe, unable ever actually to put it on. We can see here a fundamental dialectic of making: the negation of creative possibilities generates the type, form and nature of the design. This is not a reductive process of filtering out formal or aesthetic ideas, but an emphasis from the outset on one principal idea, namely that of negation, that is, the role of the coat-object as *not* being worn by the subject. It demonstrates the object's independence from the subject, as a reflection of the subject in the process of making and as reflecting back on to the subject the material quality of its objecthood. In the latter context, the object is born from the relationship between material and function, which might negate each other but which also need each other for mutual constitution. Here, the coat's fibreglass filaments negate its function of being used as a covering for the body (although it would be protective indeed), while its shape and cut remain dependent on the subject that prompted its original form as a piece of clothing.

As C.C.P. suggests across its pieces, fibre composition, yarn and fabric constitute objects in themselves in the context of material conception, and they are thus not subordinate to the garment-object, as one might surmise from the successive stages of the production process. The conception of the first object negates the second (no garment is envisaged initially), but through the formal application to the body as an eventual garment the secondary object negates the first. This in turn moves the secondary object away from its temporality as fashion object for finite consumption and denotes it as a form generated by material and technique, thus as abstracted and independent from time- or site-specific consumption. Again, the notion of temporal independence is very different from the cliché of the fashion 'classic', which merely reprises a traditional shape or appearance of an object typology in clothing. The materiality of the glass-fibre coat situates it away from the subject, and this move, despite the subsequent technological innovation of progression, renders the object – a combination of primary and secondary material objects – an abstraction of the type of 'coat', forever unworn but coveted nonetheless by collectors as a significant autonomous work.

The second example distinguishes the object from the subject not through its materiality but through its production process. Another coat, this one developed between 2006 and 2007, is fashioned from material that is cut and tailored in its raw state, not in the worked-upon form in which it customarily features in the making of garments and accessories. The base material for the 'Tanned Coat', similar to C.C.P.'s shoes and boots, is raw hide – in this case horse – treated with lime and sodium sulphate (to remove the hair) and rendered ph neutral. The sodium 'pickles' the hide so that decomposition does not occur after a couple of days or so but is arrested until the process of making the coat is complete. The hide is already cut into precise pattern pieces and sewn together, such that the eventual wearer's size only provides a reference point of sorts. Because the material shrinks after tanning and dyeing, the pattern pieces have to be calculated with an excess of at least 10–15 per cent, so that the proportions will eventually relate back to the wearer's (clothing) size – although this is very approximate, and the fitted coat is more likely to mould the body into a posture rather than accommodating the existing individual body-shape. The workers at C.C.P.'s studio have to wear chainmail gloves or thumb protectors when piercing the raw hide with their awls and wedge-point needles for seaming, sewing on buttons and attaching the lining. The latter is an actual part of the design concept; as mentioned above, C.C.P. does not use lining in the conventional way to conceal the inner workings of the garment, but rather any cloth inside must constitute a concrete feature. In the case of this coat, a nylon lining can be unbuttoned, detached all the way down to the bottom seam and then pulled over the coat as a separate layer. Elements such as additional fabric pieces or horn buttons, as well as the thread used to sew the pattern pieces together, have to be selected carefully to withstand the chemical reactions resulting from the eventual tanning and dyeing processes. In the research phase a wastage of some 50–60 per cent of all samples (as well as quite a few of the final garments and accessories) has to be taken into account, since the chemical composition of the tanning liquid in combination with various dyes cannot be calculated absolutely, so yarns and threads often deteriorate and dissolve unpredictably. This is a good example of the supremely materialist primacy of matter that, for C.C.P. and Bonotto, is crucial in allowing chance into the making and in developing autonomous textile or clothing objects.[41]

On the studio floor, next to the sewing machines, water-soaked mattresses were installed to rest the raw coat on so as to prevent it from drying out, which would fossilise the material into mummified animal skin. For the same reason the raw coats are hung in refrigerators overnight. The needles for the sewing machines have to be prepared to withstand the sodium in the pickling and the moist state of the hide. Only when all the original parts of the coat are sewn together is the piece 'object-tanned' and 'object-dyed'. These terms are used by the studio to denote a process that is unlike a final surface treatment, gloss or coloration, which are customarily employed to fuse pattern pieces, and hide seams, darts or indeed imperfections and mistakes in the manufacturing. Instead the process is determined as integral to the very function of the material. Object-tanning allows for hides of different weights and thicknesses to be combined fully together, as the eventual contraction of the hide during the complex tanning stages integrates the seam into the resultant leather – while the thread actually stays 'raw' inside the seam.

The object is taken for itself, understood as an autonomous piece that does not comply with the restrictive manner in which traditional patterns are cut from pre-tanned and -dyed leather to create an outer covering for the subject, the wearer and consumer. Here instead, the quality of the original material is preserved until the very last stage and the object remains self-contained for as long as possible. But in fashion the object can never be fully removed from the subject. Were it not tanned or dyed, the raw coat would undergo an organic fossilising process; it would quickly harden to a shell – the studio has preserved one such mummified specimen – and become brittle. The object has to be turned into a garment for the human body so that it is not a document or monument to a process. The leather coat is shrunk by the object-tanning and -dyeing to a size that is appropriate for use, and functional elements such as buttons can be used eventually to close the garment around the wearer's body. The dialectical relationship of object and subject reflecting each other independently is maintained here in the very making of the piece.

One of the fundamental postulates of C.C.P. is that 'function remains independent of the wearer (not one wearer or one body type), but the garment is conceived to be worn in the abstract'.[42] So, what becomes of the relationship between subject and object, of the reconciliation sought by occidental philosophy at least since Hegel? When we understand the fashion object as autonomous in its conception in order to allow for a hermeneutical understanding – what Gadamer and his followers such as Figal have exemplified in literature, classical music and fine art – we tend

9 Carol Christian Poell, pickled leather jacket (detail), 2007, male Disjointed Collection Photo: Deepti Barth

to separate out its reflection of the subject and relegate the latter's experience to a sensual impression. Conversely, if we look at the materialist conception of favouring a progressive integration of subject into object and object into subject over time, across successive stages of historical experience, we might conflate the sartorial covering with the identity of the subject. The fetish commodity can be felt to exert its ever-increasing power on the subject in denoting social aspiration, spending power, leisure time, privileged cultural information, movement through travel, and so on. In this context the outmoded refrain of clothes making the man can function indeed as an outward, formalised substitution, but not as an ontological synthesis of consciousness and material form.

'Negation in itself should be seen as conceptual' is how Poell defines his credo.[43] In art practice such a statement would not raise any eyebrows.[44] In the making of clothes and accessories, however, negation implies not simply eschewing representational or pictorial values but abstracting the body itself. Such abstraction can occur formally within adornment, as one principal function of clothing, but when it appears centred on the subject it becomes a much more radical infringement of the phenomenology of (self-)perception than any art installation or performance. This is heightened by the close connection of garments and accessories to everyday experience, in comparison to the disinterested consumption of artworks in cultural institutions, so that radical infringement is felt within the familiar, not separated out spatially or temporally as an occasional experience. When the object is read historically and phenomenologically in the left-Hegelian, materialist sense as ideally reflecting the subject rather than as *Gegenstand* (as standing in opposition to it), the 'conceptual negation' extends outwards from the subject to sartorial covering or to adornment through accessories. C.C.P.'s designs become a form of social positioning that negates – through their abstraction – economic dependencies and ideological power structures; they question social relations of production in their making and even social relations *tout court*. The autonomy of the fashion object at C.C.P. abstracts its form from the context of the fetish commodity that is primed for consumption and allies it with ways of forming the subject, physically and mentally.

Wearing the garment does not always mean accepting the object's abstraction of the body; the details in the making of the garment can lead to an unconscious acceptance of organic or physical references that are built into the design. In 2014 C.C.P. received an email from a heart surgeon to solicit a correspondence about the stitching techniques that have informed the connection of materials.[45] At

C.C.P. the notion of the scar, as a raised seam across or between pieces of leather or fabric, has been important in the abstracting of the organic body.[46] The principle of stitching things together extends across subject and object so that one is reflected in the other through a heuristic technique, that is, a method of addressing and solving problems that draws not on logic but on experience, learning and testing. In this regard, stories and fictional narratives can be heuristic devices in acting as ideal models that are not to be emulated but that help to situate characters, actions and objects, so that Bernhard's *Entziehung*, for instance, is a work to which hermeneutics can be applied not only to interpret an autobiographical narrative but to serve as a model structure to understand a particular form of consciousness or experience. Indeed, 'scar-stitched' is an object description that is detailed in a number of more recent pieces by C.C.P.

Like the above-mentioned 'prosthetic' elbow and toe titanium inserts, the 'orthopaedic' boots and bowler hats that began as a series in 2001, or the 'piss-tanned' leather pieces from 2000, the 'scar-stitch' references the physiology of the subject as a dialectic: it approximates organic aspects of the wearer in the abstracted form of the clothing, while, in appropriating these for the fashion object, establishing an autonomy of the *Gegenstand*. The object does not need the subject because it takes its organic components and abstracts them for its making and form. I come back to Bloch, for whom, as discussed at the start of this chapter, such affirming and negating of the subject through the object had been a central thesis in evaluating Hegel's dialectic of history:

> Thus Hegel's dialectical process, when progressing step by step through abolitions [*Aufhebungen*], is not 'abolition' in the destructive sense of liquidating, it is also *Aufhebung*[47] in the sense of setting aside and conserving. This constitutes the loyal side, the backward-looking Janus face in Hegelian dialectic. It is the side that is mainly concerned with synthesis, which, aside from negation, renders it suitable as *historical legacy*. This, too, is part of the dialectical process: its result is not merely the step that has just been reached but also all previous steps.[48]

In fashion this restitution of the past in the form of the latest garment or accessory is not only the result of a general lack of innovation but of the finite variations that are possible for clothing and adorning the subject's body. When all sartorial forms have been considered, only variants can be renewed. For C.C.P. this progress through readily acknowledged past steps led to arrested development (since 2010). It also means remaining within a given formal vocabulary that is grounded in absolute material innovation and, more significantly perhaps, in the negation of the subject's autonomy vis-à-vis the fashion object. The *Gegenstand* stands, in contrast, as an abstraction of the wearer that is autonomous and does not depend on the body for its meaning. 'The first attempt always concerns the material, in being curious about the material', says Poell[49] and such a strait-laced focus is as much a matter of making and manufacturing as it is a socio-political position.

Notes

1. Союз Советских Социалистических Республик, the Union of Soviet Socialist Republics, abbreviated as СССР – adapted here for the title minus one 'С'. The СССР's founder V. I. Lenin defined Hegelian dialectics in 1914 as follows: '1) the objectivity of consideration (not examples, not divergencies, but the Thing-in-itself); 2) the entire totality of the manifold relations of this thing to others; 3) the development of this thing (phenomenon, respectively), its own movement, its own life; 4) the internally contradictory *tendencies* (*and* sides) in this thing; 5) the thing (phenomenon, etc.) as the sum *and unity of opposites*; 6) the *struggle*, respectively unfolding, of these opposites, contradictory strivings, etc.; 7) the union of analysis and synthesis – the break-down of the separate parts and the totality, the summation of these parts; 8) the relations of each thing (phenomenon, etc.) are not only manifold, but general, universal. Each thing (phenomenon, process, etc.) is connected with *every other*; 9) not only the unity of opposites, but the *transitions* of *every* determination, quality, feature, side, property into *every* other [into its opposite?]; 10) the endless process of the discovery of *new* sides, relations, etc.; 11) the endless process of the deepening of man's knowledge of the thing, of phenomena, processes, etc., from appearance to essence and from less profound to more profound essence; 12) from co-existence to causality and from one form of connection and reciprocal dependence to another, deeper, more general form; 13) the repetition at a higher stage of certain features, properties, etc., of the lower and; 14) the apparent return to the old (negation of the negation); 15) the struggle of content with form and conversely the throwing off of the form, the transformation of the content; 16) the transition of quantity into quality and *vice versa* ((*15* and *16* are *examples* of *9*)).' Vladimir Ilyich Lenin, 'Summary of Dialectics' [1914], in *Collected Works*, vol. 38 (Moscow: Progress, 1961), p. 220.
2. Ernst Bloch, *Subjekt-Objekt: Erläuterungen zu Hegel* [1949] (Frankfurt a.M.: Suhrkamp, 1962), p. 68.
3. See, for example, the studies by François Furet on the French Revolution

(followed by other historians such as Simon Schama), for whom the events of 1789 and 1791 merely arrested the unrelenting march towards bourgeois capitalism that had been initiated by industrialisation and parliamentary monarchies.
4. See Bloch, *Subjekt-Objekt*, p. 80.
5. G. W. F. Hegel, 'Introduction, §86', in *Phenomenology of Spirit* [1807], trans. A. V. Miller (Oxford: Oxford University Press, 1977), p. 55.
6. Bloch, *Subjekt-Objekt*, pp. 125–6.
7. On the first aspect, see the series of essays by Joachim Ritter, *Hegel and the French Revolution* [1957] (Cambridge, MA: MIT Press, 1982); on the second aspect, see, for example, Hans-Peter Krüger, *Heroismus und Arbeit in der Entstehung der Hegelschen Philosophie (1973–1806)* [1979] (Berlin: Akademie/de Gruyter, 2014) – a work that was written in the mid-1970s as a dissertation at the Humboldt Universität in Berlin, influenced by the materialist historians of the Leipziger Schule, and was published decades later in the context of non-materialist Hegel studies in the West.
8. The subject is denoted as feminine throughout this chapter, as I think befits the topic of fashion. This is not to mirror gender orthodoxy or show a clichéd view of the sexes' respective types of consumption, but is a simple reflection of fashion's historical trajectory.
9. Karl Marx, 'Economic and Philosophical Manuscripts of 1844', in Karl Marx and Friedrich Engels, *Collected Works*, vol. 3 (New York: International Publishers, 2005), pp. 331, 332–3.
10. For an overview, see Tatiana Strijenova, *La Mode en union soviétique 1917–1945* (Paris: Flammarion, 1991).
11. A great visual document of this period is Dziga Vertov's film *Man with a Movie Camera* of 1929, edited by his wife Elizaveta Svilova, depicting metropolitan life in four unnamed Soviet cities (Kiev, Kharkov, Moscow and Odessa).
12. In the preparatory sketch of 1927 Deineka still had an 'old-fashioned' figure in headscarf, peasant blouse and skirt exit the picture plane to the right, as well the woman in the centre preening and grooming herself like a fashion plate, rather than working at the loom. In the final version these reminders of the old are banished in favour of resolutely modern dress and mores.
13. Hegel, 'Introduction, §87', *Phenomenology of Spirit*, pp. 55–6.
14. Bloch, *Subjekt-Objekt*, p. 194.
15. Ibid., p. 357.
16. Edmund Husserl, *Ideen zu einer reinen Phänomenologie und phänomenologischen Philosophie. Erstes Buch: Allgemeine Einführung in die reine Phänomenologie*, in *Jahrbuch für Philosophie und phänomenologische Forschung* (Halle: Niemeyer, 1913), pp. 70, 279. Husserl, of course, used only the male gender (*der Mensch, der Mann, man*) for human beings in general.
17. Maurice Merleau-Ponty, *Le Visible et l'invisible* [1959/60] (Paris:

Gallimard, 1964), p. 178; Eng. trans. by A. Lingis, *The Visible and the Invisible* (Evanston: Northwestern University Press, 1968), p. 137.
18. Conversation with the author, Milan, 20 June 2014.
19. Arthur Conan Doyle, *The Sign of the Four* [1890] (New York: Quality Paperback Club, 1994), p. 6; the opening chapter is fittingly entitled 'The Science of Deduction'.
20. See, for example, Rodchenko's 'productivist' outfit of 1921, cut from wool-tweed with leather patches on the pockets and adjustable ankle straps to guard against wet, cold or the spillage of harmful materials at work; Thayaht's (Ernesto Michahelles) Futurist 'TuTa' of 1920, the unisex linen overall, with a pattern cut that minimised fabric waste; and 'el mono azul', the hyper-functional blue cotton boiler suit worn by both men and women of the republican militia in their fight against fascism during the Spanish Civil War, 1936–39.
21. In the last decade the seasonal showing has been fragmented by 'Cruise', 'Resort' and pre-collections for select buyers, and the immediacy of the internet has resulted in the present instigation of the 'See Now, Buy Now' shows by global brands.
22. On luxury, capital and labour, see my essay 'The Luxury Duality: From Economic Fact to Cultural Capital', in John Armitage and Joan Roberts (eds), *Critical Luxury Studies: Art, Design, Media* (Edinburgh: Edinburgh University Press, 2016), pp. 67–87.
23. Obviously, industrial manufacturers and investors aim at reducing costs where possible, so economising on material must be a principal concern. But this is not put forward as a rationale for making fashion, for example selling a dress under the tagline that it wastes the least amount of fabric in its pattern cut (as occurred with the kimono template or utilitarian clothing in Europe during the Second World War).
24. 'Pieces' is a neutral term that is employed to define all parts of the output at C.C.P. and suggests the exploratory and fragmented understanding of the development process.
25. Repeatedly, experiments by C.C.P. which required an artisanal or small-scale industrial manufacturer to adapt its machinery or production technique have prompted more mainstream fashion companies to seek them out and commission similar work – allowing the manufacturer to redeploy the adapted machines, even when the actual process had to be simplified to accommodate lower costs and higher outputs.
26. C.C.P. uses the same technique to reveal titanium 'elbows' in object-dyed jackets, poking through overlock seams.
27. Conversation with the author, Milan, 29 May 2016.
28. Ibid.; see the opening chapter of this book, pp. 49–50.
29. This is not a tactic akin to the (later rather theatrical) approach by designers such as Martin Margiela, who based his expansive communication strategy on the ostensible refusal to be identified or interviewed face to face. In contrast, C.C.P. does not release any photographs of objects or designer(s), and so no longer communicates its existence

in the industry through representation, but only in production. As a Società a responsabilità limitata it also remains a privately owned company that does need to publish financial details, while its capital is divided into stakes that can be bought or sold only through a laborious notarial act.
30. There are numerous tales of pop musicians and stylists for US movie stars asking for (free) samples from C.C.P. so that their clients can wear the pieces on special occasions – all to no avail.
31. Conversation with the author, Milan, 29 May 2016.
32. Ibid.
33. One instance was the 'self-edge' series of garments (begun in 2009) that used the selvage of tightly woven wool as an absolute guideline for each pattern piece: an extremely complex and materially expensive way of determining forms. There is more about this example in the next chapter.
34. Conversation with the author, Milan, 29 May 2016.
35. Günter Figal, *Gegenständlichkeit* (Tübingen: Mohr Siebeck, 2006), p. 135; Eng. trans. by Th. D. George, *Objectivity: The Hermeneutical and Philosophy* (Albany, NY: State University of New York Press, 2010), p. 114. For me, Figal makes for an interesting reference, combining a focus on Heidegger with its apparent political and systemic opposite, namely critical theory – attempting a synthesis of phenomenology and Gadamer's hermeneutics with elements of a materialist tradition without, alas, bringing them back to their shared origin in Hegel.
36. Jacket from the 'Instant' series begun in 2004, and the piece 'GM 2385-LEICHT4', first made in 2008.
37. PM 2417-NORM4, first made in 2008.
38. Apparently this saying came into fashion through a translation of Erasmus's 'vestis virum facit' in *Adagia*, Erasmus's collection of Greek and Latin proverbs, begun in 1500 and completed in 1536. See *Collected Works of Erasmus*, vol. 34 (Toronto: University of Toronto Press, 1992), pp. 204–5 (adage III I 60).
39. Conversation with the author, Milan, 29 May 2016.
40. In his conversation with the author, Milan, 29 May 2016, Poell said that the coat was used to find out whether yarns with glass-fibre properties could be woven and cut to tailor a garment. Indeed, a weave that is very similar in character to the glass-fibres has been used as fabric for C.C.P.'s recent garment pieces.
41. More on this aspect can be found in the next chapter.
42. Conversation with the author, Milan, 20 June 2014.
43. Ibid.
44. This goes for denying the character of an artwork as autonomous in the sense of its being independent of its context (cf. Clement Greenberg's formalism or Michael Fried's late modernist iteration of subjectivity); but conversely also for negating the production of art through subject-centred essentialism or even atavism, as in Butoh

or Viennese Aktionism – the latter an obvious reference point for C.C.P.
45. Conversation with the author, Milan, 20 June 2014.
46. On the stitch as a medium between scar and seam, see Christian Michel, 'Thought Without Concept: Carol Christian Poell's Paradoxical Aesthetics', in Giovanni Matteucci and Stefano Marino (eds), *Philosophical Perspectives on Fashion* (London: Bloomsbury, 2016), pp. 121–9.
47. Bloch here adopts from the first part of Hegel's *Encyclopaedia of Philosophical Sciences* the dichotomous meaning of the German verb *aufheben*: to sublate, metaphorically to cancel or abolish something, but also literally to pick something up, to set aside and preserve. This meaning marked the basis for Hegel's coining of the dialectical method.
48. Bloch, *Subjekt-Objekt*, p. 126.
49. Conversation with the author, Milan, 20 June 2014.

Chapter 7

Primary Material

The previous chapter concluded with Carol Christian Poell extolling the virtue of matter as the foundation of the design process. I want to show in the present chapter that this is not a reductionist statement in the tradition of mechanical materialism, but particular to a considered form of production, which Poell often realises together with Italian weavers Bonotto SpA, who are the subject of this chapter. The case study of such production, its environment and labour conditions underscores the main tenet of this book that materialism is simultaneously concerned with forms of making and political economy, with creative as well as socio-political ideas.

Like many small to medium-sized manufacturers in Italy, Bonotto is a family-owned business, presently in its fourth generation. When I visited the company at the beginning of October 2016 the brothers Lorenzo and Giovanni Bonotto just had sold 60 per cent of their spinning and weaving factory, 30 per cent of their factory for finishing textiles and 13 per cent of Bonotto Editions, their experimental showcase in Milan, to the Ermenegildo Zegna Group.[1] According to Giovanni Bonotto, this was for structural as well as personal reasons.[2] The structural aspect pertains to the steady demise of small and medium-sized textile, fashion and accessory manufacturing across Italy. Only thirty years ago, around the town of Molvena in the Veneto region where Bonotto is based, some fifty family-owned companies were producing or finishing textiles. Today there are but two: one is Bonotto, the other Marzotto; the latter is now focused exclusively on spinning woollen yarns under its own name and for three subsidiaries in the textile province of Biella, in the Piedmont. The personal reason was not to burden his children with the need to take over the family business into a fifth generation, coupled with the opportunity to transfer Bonotto's productive capital to a company like Zegna that, albeit on a much larger scale, retains the workings of a family-owned business. The Bonotto and Zegna families are indeed friends and the sale of a large portion of the business is therefore intended to preserve an independent tradition, rather than having to sell out at a later point in the company's future.³ This danger of 'selling out' remains very real in the current Italian economy.

Bonotto's immediate neighbours in Molvena were Lino Dainese, head of the high-tech company that has produced, since 1972, motorcycle clothing, helmets and shoes, and Renzo Russo, who developed the Diesel brand in 1978 and has contributed significantly to the innovation of global fashion communication over the past decades with his ironic and irreverent advertisements for denim clothes and other goods.⁴ Only a few years ago Bonotto approached his neighbours to broker a collaboration that would unite experimental weaving, high-tech leather and plastic manufacture with progressive fashion communication in Molvena, to create a mutually supportive local infrastructure. His efforts were unsuccessful, and Dianese was sold in 2015 to a Bahrain-based investment company while Diesel has moved its design and communication headquarters down the road towards Thiene and for a few years now has struggled with its various subsidiaries and licences.⁵ This unsuccessful attempt to unite local manufacturing pointed to the structural problem of maintaining the infrastructure necessary for a real ecology of artisanal production, which allows primary materials to be produced in the vicinity of processing and manufacturing industry. As I will discuss further below, this ecology is crucial for makers such as Bonotto to innovate their manufacturing from the ground up, as a structural as well as an economic alternative to the present production of (fast) fashion.

'I studied with Umberto Eco,' said Giovanni Bonotto, 'and thus became contaminated [*inquinato*] with semiotics. When it comes to fashion, I consider Carol Christian Poell "il mio maestro".'⁶ These two reference figures came together when Bonotto held seminars in semiotics at the Domus academy in Milan, where he first met Poell, and they have informed his strategies in developing the social conditions of production within frameworks of vertically integrated manufacturing as well as the culture industry. For Bonotto, signs are significant in connoting his work as 'objects', not as 'commodities'. Although they are produced for the market and, in the main, for profit, the material is understood as oscillating between signifier and signified to create the sign, as forming value within the exchange process yet simultaneously as standing for a process of making. Vertically integrated manufacturing for him is not a simple logistical and economic measure to speed up production through in-house facilities, but a means of controlling the ecology of production, from primary material to finished product, whereby, in Bonotto's case, the final product depends a lot on further construction processes and, in an ideal scenario, on collaboration with a designer of clothing and accessories. When the material is integrated into the process it implies that the formation of productive structures follows the path of the matter, from fibre to yarn, to weave, and via finishing methods on to fabric and cloth (and, finally, to garments and accessories). This can be observed in the set-up of Bonotto's factory at Molvena and F2, his facility for finishing in nearby Schio, where the natural water-flow from the foothills of the Alps determines both the location and arrangement of the manufacturing process. Concrete, effective structural changes in the conditions of production and therefore in the social conditions of labour, as well as the wider definition of labour within economic and cultural production, can only occur when the primary material is considered from the start. It marks a fundamental, cumulative analysis of building up material and sequencing the steps of production – without the fragmentation and decentralisation that has determined so much of the economic output of the textile and fashion industry in northern Italy since the 1980s.

The economist Giuseppe Nardin, who headed the socio-economic research institute Poster in Vicenza and who has occupied himself with local textile and fashion manufacturing, completed a study of Benetton in 1985. In this study the almost ontologically sounding *materie prime* (primary matter) was singled out as determining Benetton's restructuring of the enterprise, from localised textile manufacture to a system of decentralising, outsourcing, franchising and speculative financial services for its subcontractors and suppliers. Ironically, Nardin credited the resolutely diversifying Benetton system with a multitude of industrial ontogeneses: 'In fact, every division of production develops and processes internally each phase of storage and quality control of the primary material.'[7] Yet in the separation of this divisional labour, no one production facility can understand the concrete linkage of its material development to that of another; they are simply positioned as various points along chains of supply and production. Although materiality is at stake in each of these phases, it is not connected through an ecology of matter but merely through industrial logistics. Benetton's yarns are spun away from the places of weaving and finishing, and the 'controllo delle materie prime' is through an administrative system that evaluates processes almost exclusively in economic terms. This produces a move towards a form of vertically integrated production, as can be seen in Benetton's attempt to group the vast majority of its subcontractors in the north-east of Italy. But this decentralisation of economic output to ever smaller subsidiaries – which, moreover, must rely on Benetton's dispensing of credit and financial services (through a number of banks in which it has acquired shares and which have now been subsumed by Italy's lingering banking crisis of 2016)[8] – is far from generating a material integration of labour, nor is it conducive to inclusive social conditions of production. In contrast, and at a much smaller scale compared to the global player Benetton SpA, Giovanni Bonotto and his brother Lorenzo have centralised production around a site and locality that permits their 300 plus workers to see the material interconnections within production – through shared spaces, joint expertise, and the collective potential for intervention and integration.

Considering the significance of the sign (as representation, index or cypher) in favour of the material and the social-politically concrete, Giovanni Bonotto has declared: 'Umberto Eco, whom I had as professor at [the university of] Bologna, was saying to me: "Chi legge il cartello non mangia il vitello". Therefore I had to try and subvert the rules.'[9] Literally, this saying means 'he who reads the menu never gets to eat the veal' – emphasising that semantic rules and the primacy of the discursive over the material are to be challenged, and even ignored, if one is to get to the meat of a problem. This perspective illuminates Bonotto's engagement with productive practice rather than with speculative capital.

Reliance on the primacy of material can also be demonstrated in the way in which Bonotto uses mistakes, akin to the outcome of C.C.P's negation-as-deduction technique discussed in the previous chapter, as creative means to initiate processes. The crucial element here, however, is that the worker at the loom or at the dyeing vat participates in this idea as the actual executive. He or she has to embrace the notion of the mistake as going against the set-up or function of the machine and standing in dialectic relationship with any prior training or acquired skill. The worker acknowledges that there is an aberration, a fault-line or mistake – yet this is not to negate the process but is the very thing to be developed through existing skills and a mechanical process that had been pre-installed in order to further the development of craft and manufacture. The creative customisation and changing of the machine – mostly via its initial set-up and interventions through chemical or material additions – becomes a mode of operation. The production process remains sufficiently flexible, and the communication of intermediate

10 Specification sheet used during the production process at the Bonotto textile factory in Molvena, October 2016

070	APRICORDA CON TAGLIERINA	
602	CESTO LANA COTTA	α 4/10 (27' h 125-127)
330	APRICORDA	cu.
480	ASCIUGARE H 150 cm SOVR 30 %	
630	CIMARE	
805	VISITA FINITO FALDA/FALDA	
660	VAPORIZZO	
700	ALZATRICE	

H. Finita 135.0 14

DATI PEZZA FINITA	Metraggio	Peso	Altezza	Gr./Mt.	Supplemento Prezzi		
					Metraggio	Peso	Fe
	Osservazioni:				Colore		

results and initial outcomes is kept close in order to embrace the unexpected and aberrant. This can be seen in Bonotto's particular specification sheet, which details through a list of types and names and through attached samples the combination of spun fibres to be used and the way in which yarns of varying staple lengths are to be woven together. Furthermore, the sheet specifies which weaving loom to use and determines the spatial relationship between individual, movable warping creels on which the bobbins with their spun yarns are kept and the looms, which are fed with a diverse selections of yarns. This is of particular interest for Bonotto's production at Molvena, as it is distinguished by experimental set-ups and endeavours to card and spin yarns from rare and hard-to-process fibres and to combine them in complex weaves in which vastly diverse degrees of density, elasticity and staple length are combined. Such complex set-ups and spatial arrangements almost invite problems, and they demand creative solutions. Significantly, the specification sheets leave blank a large space at the bottom of the page for the worker at the loom to note her or his observations and, in case of concerns, to suggest alternative forms of production. The sheets are checked and collected at the end of the day, and a system is established at Molvena in which weavers talk to supervisors, who in turn talk to Bonotto, who then checks back with workers after changing or editing the specifications, where necessary, in order to work out possible ways forward. As Bonotto proudly affirms:

> Our semi-automatic machines are capable of great results with textile matter, of manipulating materials in such a way that the fabrics we release on the market sell like hot cakes. I do not go where expected in order to sell, but our clients come to us to buy, since we are unique in Europe in terms of our working processes. 80% of our production is scientifically generated, while 20% is left to the worker who is thus asked to intervene in a creative fashion and open new doors. Today, factories are no longer these pyramidal structures: the web has instilled a sense of community, not understood in the cooperative-Marxist sense but as constructed around collaboration. This is an epochal change but, alas, a lot of time passes before industry has the courage to appreciate it.[10]

This is not a teleological process of optimising production or perfecting manufacture, but an organisational set-up of labour that allows for the development of new fabrics and embracing chance in the making of patterns, so that, for instance, what might constitute an individual mistake becomes, across the length and width of the cloth, a contrasting motif that is repeated as a distinct intervention. In turn, this subsequently challenges the designer to use such errors or mistakes in the weave as compositional aspects and visual foci when cutting and sewing the fabric into clothes. In an analogy to historical materialism, and despite Bonotto's protestation that his method is not Marxist, it could be said that recognising repeat fault-lines across an expanse (of space or time) and, moreover, comprehending them as patterns, allows for turning apparent mistakes into creative markers and rendering problems productive through considered forms of labour.

The Conditions of Production

In order to outline further how the conditions of production, and the social conditions of labour that are related to them, are determined, I would like briefly to outline the manufacturing space and the machine-architecture in Bonotto's factories at Molvena and Schio. Like the description of C.C.P.'s workshop-cum-factory in Milan, my description is meant to suggest a phenomenological reading of space that remains materialist in placing workers within material conditions of labour while suggesting subjective agency vis-à-vis the object of production.

The factory at Molvena is situated in one of the industrial districts that were established in the early 1970s across northern Italy. The political scientist Antonio Negri wrote another study of Benetton, some four years after Nardin, in which the company stood as exemplary for the entire textile and clothing sector in Italy. Negri detailed how the 1970s saw labour disputes as well as de-industrialisation across various manufacturing sectors, and how the conservative Italian government employed market structures to try and redevelop local centres of manufacture – partly based on traditionally sites for craft production, partly based on the existing infrastructure across the centre of the European Union in which trans-Alpine trade played a major role.[11] Territory became a mark of existing expertise and skill sets on the part of a local workforce, and part of an expanded industrialised network, which allowed Benetton, for instance, to decentralise its production from 1972 onwards across small subsidiaries. It allowed Bonotto, in the same year, to move from making straw hats into textile production, developing and expanding the cottage industry at Molvena into a modern factory, which was eventually preserved and turned back – as I will discuss below – against progressive automation.

In Molvena a small country road passes the neighbouring factories of Diesel and Dainese before settling in a gentle curve before two large houses that front expansive warehouse and manufacturing spaces. The house on the left contains Bonotto's administration and, on the lower ground floor, a *centro stile* (style centre) that is concerned with developing new textile ideas and designs. The building on the right houses the Fondazione Bonotto with Luigi Bonotto's collection of Fluxus art. These rooms and studios all have direct and unrestricted access to the factory behind them, while the Fluxus collection is distributed across all the buildings, especially in the factory, where the walls are covered with multiples, posters, assemblages, video-screens and prints, all visible and accessible to the workers, who thus work around the art and visual poetry. A window the size of a medium-format painting is cut into one wall, occupying the space between some Fluxus works and allowing a view down into the weaving section of the factory; spatially and visually the 'image' of the factory, as sign of labour conditions and production, is equated with the lexical signs and indices of the works around it, including George Maciunas's US genocide-data-flag, Henry Flynt's 'sentence' and Allan Kaprow's speech-bubbled tire-'Yard'. Luigi Bonotto's idealised intention of having his family factory read and understood as 'a total work of art'[12] is perhaps to be taken with a grain of salt, but certain productive features such as the aforementioned integration of accidents and mistakes or the free experimentation with materials certainly invite comparisons with a congenial Fluxus approach to art production. Giovanni Bonotto has spoken more prosaically of the desire 'to impregnate manufacture with art'[13] and he explained repeatedly how his youthful encounters with artists such as Joseph Beuys, John Cage and Yoko Ono shaped his attitude towards chance and experiment and towards the integration of art and life, industry and culture.[14] So, the everyday material of objects and the casual and ironic engagement with art practices in Fluxus could indeed serve as a good model for experimental spinning and weaving in Bonotto's factory. The director of the Bonotto foundation, Patrizio Peterlini, showed me videos of workers echoing Fluxus processes in their work at the looms, and while this seemed more playful than conceptually rigorous, it is exactly this free engagement with processes that artists such as George Brecht, Dick Higgins, Daniel Spoerri and Ben Vautier continually extolled. Peterlini also coined the description of Fluxus as 'the prêt-à-porter of art', and while this might be read as a light-hearted, even throwaway remark, there remains a profound, alternative ethic in the use of multiplication and the adaptation of mass-production for artworks by the Fluxus artists, and in their ready embrace of commercial techniques to subvert productive structures in capitalism.¹⁵ Reflecting on Fluxus and his father's collection, Giovanni Bonotto loftily declared, at a time when the global financial crisis was hitting manufacturing across northern Italy hardest: 'I could say we have always worked at random.'¹⁶

The shop floor of the building that occupies the majority of Bonotto's site is arranged so that one progresses from the style centre, via the vast multi-coloured storage space/archive for fibres, yarns, fabric samples and cloth, straight on to the spinning section with its repair and maintenance workshops in the back. The spinning section of the building is more transparent and airy, since here fibres are twisted into yarns on open machines that keep them rigorously separate, before they are brought together in the subsequent warping and weaving processes. Individual colourful yarns are produced initially as distinct entities to be composed together in the neighbouring section of the factory. Fixed and movable creels, sorting the bobbin cones, structure the space into vertical grids with serial arrangements across creel boards, which can either be selected and removed by hand and brought over for starching or warping, or can be electronically accessed when set up for warping on spools or drums. The positioning of these drums for the parallel winding-up of ends from many winding packages (cones) on to a common package (drum) connects – productively and spatially – this section to the part of the factory where the weaving looms are housed. Bonotto mainly employs the technique of sectional or pattern warping, where diverse yarns are wound up in sections to prepare for complex colour patterns – in contrast to the direct, high-speed beam warping that is used in less costly production set-ups for single colours or for warp ends from one material only.

On a connecting wall, between an arrangement of spare spools and warp drums awaiting use, Bonotto has installed four video screens that display elements of a visual poem (*Poema Bonotto*) made by the Italian artist Giovanni Fontana in 2016, in which words are semantically as well as tonally deconstructed, serialised and then spoken over the rhythmical noise of the warp beams and looms – a reference to Fluxus, as well as to Futurist *intonarumori*, in particular Luigi Russolo's noise machines of 1913/14. Factory sounds, also present in the work of another Italian composer, Luigi Nono, who used voices and tape recordings for *La fabbrica illuminata* (1964), provide Fontana with a historical and continuous sonic background for the formulation of narratives and aesthetics, in which industrial noise constitutes a notable element in the progressively complex canon of sounds at the disposal and for the consumption of modern man and woman. Such an interpretation might read as a passive cultural mediation of labour processes that obfuscates their social and economic realities. Yet observing the materiality of the warping beams in the factory space and seeing how they dwarf the screens between them brought home the subjugation of culture to the materialism of machinery and labour at Bonotto. It demonstrates clearly what is central to production and what is an auxiliary reflection.

From the storage space and library/archive of yarns and weaves, via the warping area of the factory, the space extends at a right angle to the weaving section building, where all the looms are housed. The two buildings, of approximately the same size but of different heights, mirror the arrangement of the two houses facing the street before them, and also provide quite distinct production spaces. While the smaller style centre, the colour-saturated archive and the warping section appear relatively calm and open, the weaving section with its many double-height looms running at full speed is much more crowded and noisy. Indeed, boxes full of ear plugs are distributed around the place and the air seems heavy with microscopic bits of fibre that coat the parts of the looms that are more abrasive to loosely woven surfaces, like lint residue from an overactive tumble dryer. The corridor that links the two parts of the factory serves to spatially separate the warping from the weaving, while heavy plastic curtains at the top of a small metal staircase shield the archive from the noise of the looms – distinguishing not simply working processes but equally *materie prime* from manufactured product.

The arrangement of the spaces principally follows the logic of the weaving process. First yarns are spun from fibres and treated to enhance natural colours or dyed. The yarns are arranged parallel on drums to form, as yet unstarched, warp. These warps can then be starched, if required, or used in their original materiality. Starching is here a generic term for synthesis and holistic treatment of all parallel yarns together on the drum or spool. The drums are then put into the loom where other yarns, constituting the weft, are shot through them to form woven cloth. The weaving process is as varied as the infinite number of combinations of warp and weft suggests. It can provide a minimal-looking cloth from one material in uniform colours, which nevertheless can contain the most intricate patterns or structures within it, or it can expressively interlock yarns from very diverse materials, which are woven into multi-coloured patterns of varying textures.

The vast majority of today's weavers use looms that are mechanically powered and work on distinct

11 Two of four screens installed between spare spools and warp drums, showing the work by Giovanni Fontana, *Poema Bonotto*, 2016

variations of how they move the warp in order to have the weft pass through. In principle, Dobby looms use harnesses or shafts that move the warp yarns up and down in groups, as sets of threads. Since only a limited number of these harnesses can be held by one loom, due to the size of the machine and its arrangement on the shop floor, this limits the complexity of the woven pattern somewhat. In contrast, Jacquard heads on looms can move warp yarns via a punch-card system that was developed in 1800 and is now computerised. Jacquard looms are structurally defined by a control system that automates the patterning and employs thousands of hooks to move the warp threads up and down individually, so the patterns can become extremely complex. This impacts on the speed of production: Dobby looms generally run much faster than those with Jacquard heads – both in terms of set-up as well as in the actual weaving process. The movement of warp yarns, together with the selection of weft insertions that are provided at Bonotto across his selection of vintage machinery with shuttle, air and water jet, rapier and projectile looms, renders the forms of interlocking yarns vast indeed. The Belgian company Bonas launched the first electronic Jacquard loom in Milan in the early 1980s, to cater for a market, mainly in northern Italy and across Europe, in which production is distinguished by high versatility and intricacy, yet still has to achieve rapid output. Such computer-controlled machines economise significantly on the time it takes to set up punched paper designs, so that a company can realise smaller sizes of samples more quickly, advance more variations and, as is important at Bonotto, experiment with interventions and 'faults'. Yet these machines are very expensive to acquire and run, so larger machines with Jacquard heads that allow for individual control of up to 10,000 warp ends only make sense for producers who distinguish themselves by developing specialised textile designs.

In fact, specialisation and choice play essential roles in the weaving processes at Molvena. The looms produce samples of intricate woven fabrics that are presented in two 'collections' each year, thus adhering to the orthodoxy of the fashion industry in separating modern existence into spring/summer and autumn/winter clothing. Each season offers about 600 samples, averaging more than three million square metres of textile in all conceivable threads: worsted woollens, silk, linen, cotton, viscose, polyester, elastics, etc. – many of which are sourced from very rare animals whose hair can only be spun into very small batches of yarn. Four broad categories determine the textiles: fabrics for the elevated market of ready-to-wear fashion, including some of the most famous global brand names such as Armani, Prada, Marni and Gucci; sportswear fabrics (especially for men) for companies such as Moncler; luxury fabrics for houses such as Chanel Haute Couture or Christian Dior Couture, which accounted in 2014 for 43 per cent of Bonotto's turnover;[17] and a small production by *la fabbrica lenta* (the slow factory) executed on old looms to artisanal standards.[18] I will further describe this latter part of the production later in this chapter, as a case study for particular looms and weaving processes. The samples are woven initially to around twenty-five metres in length (instead of the customary 200 metres at other companies), which takes an entire day or more, due to the complexity of the machine set-up. Even the comparatively small size of the sample allows for an appropriate amount of fabric to be presented to buyers, so that aspects such as tensile strength, pliability and weight can be assessed in relation to possible patterns or draping around the body.

Yet weaving is not the ultimate part of the process that the sample has to go through before it is deemed complete and can be offered to designers and companies. Once a sample of the desired cloth is woven – and the specification sheet at Molvena has been completed – the woven fabric is transferred a few miles up the road to Bonotto's F2 (pronounced 'effe due', standing for factory two or finishing stage two) in Schio. Here the long or short chains of the yarns that have been woven are finished, a step in the production that materialist designers such as Poell regard as accounting for 60–70 per cent of the textile's character.[19] Finishing can take a number of forms, depending on the type of woven cloth – whether it is yarn-dyed or whether it needs to be piece-dyed after weaving – and the essential quality of the material. F2 is housed in a rectangular building, which covers just over 25,000 square metres, roughly half the size of the factory in Molvena. Some 200 workers are employed at Molvena and another 70 or so at Schio. Work is generally arranged in two shifts from 5:00 a.m. to 8:00 p.m., though some of the complex and time-consuming processes for dyeing and finishing at F2 cannot be interrupted and therefore require working in four shifts around the clock.

When I visited Schio in October 2016 it was a warm day and the F2 building was open and airy, with surprisingly little noise and smell, given the amount of heavy machinery and the use of chemical processes. The space is structured as a rectangle with a large goods entrance on the south side into which the fabrics from Molvena (and from four small weavers in the vicinity that Bonotto uses for less complex sampling work) are delivered and from which they progress through the finishing processes in a clockwise direction to the packing and shipping stations, after having come full circle through the building. The progression works along the perimeter of the rectangle but also ventures inside it, where specialised machines are positioned in relation to working processes at the edge. The arrangement of the machinery conforms to the shape and length of the operations, but equally allows for structured human interaction with the processes, for instance quality control and revision. Very few of the machines are lined up to suggest a large, uninterrupted automated process, which would undoubtedly speed things up but would not permit the aforementioned interaction and intervention that Bonotto (and C.C.P.) deem vital for realising the material quality of the textiles.

First the woven cloth from Molvena is unrolled over large spools to form loose folds. The fabric is aired and animated; it is given space to move – an aspect that is integral to Bonotto's idea of production on a whole but is particularly pertinent to the finishing process. Giovanni Bonotto wants 'a factory that respects the material' and uses processes that 'draw out the good from the material'; therefore the cloth is not simply given a prescribed character (in texture, flow, etc.) but is allowed to expand and develop by itself throughout the finishing – again, with the possible incorporation of chance and accidents into the finished product.[20] In practical terms, animating the cloth and giving it space also supports the drawing out or creating of plastic values in two- or three-dimensional textiles, where flatness or, conversely, volume become crucial. A machine that is unique to Italy employs a flow of some 20,000 litres of water to wash the fabrics so that they can freely move and expand, grow or shrink in three dimensions, without stress to the weave or to its fibres. Listening to Giovanni Bonotto, one gets the sense almost of an 'anthropomorphising' of textiles, imbuing fabrics, especially when made from organic fibres and yarns, with a character that needs to be 'preserved', 'awoken' or 'set free'. The shrinking occurs in large old washing machines with circular drums, or else the textiles are run through longer automatic washes where they are pulled along under pressure through the water. There is also provision for a felting process during the initial wash with a 'very old machine', which uses steam, warm water and soap to press wool fibres together to form long, blanket-like textiles. Next in line is the drying process that, in a similar way to the washing, can be divided between mechanical drying where long sheets are pulled along under pressure, and methods where the fabric is giving three-dimensional character by being tumbled about or blown along under no stress and with very little direction (often turned in circles in a drum).

12 View of F2 finishing factory at Schio, 2016

Bonotto's machines are also specialised in lessening abrasion, so certain fabrics are dried for hours in delicate cycles.

In contrast to the emphasis on reusing traditional machinery that is so typical of Bonotto at Molvena, most of the machines for dyeing fabrics have been bought new in order to guarantee processes that are both economical and ecological. Giovanni Bonotto says 'here the fabric eats the colour' to describe the way in which cloth is dipped in and out of the liquid colours and chemicals at the bottom of large stainless steel tubes/vats set up at an angle.

He also states in this context that 'matter makes matter work' – and this is not just a scientific issue of chemical reactions or of changing aggregate states or molecular structures inside the textile or yarn or fibres. The combination of different matter (diverse yarns) through weaving is articulated in the finishing by bringing out the characteristics of one fibre vis-à-vis another, so that they create tensions or open up to show their particular characteristics, which, in turn, are then appreciated by the subject as softness to touch, floating across the skin, or enveloping the body with stored warmth. The principle of 'matter makes matter work' obviously cannot be fully controlled, since Bonotto, like C.C.P., wants matter to develop autonomously or at least independently, despite being subject to production stages in industrial manufacture. Here, again, an analogy can be established between the rational, scientific principle, which provides a fundamental epistemology for materialism, and the practice of manufacturing as well as the social conditions of labour that derive from it. The object (fabric) directs the behaviour of the subject (producer, worker), not in the alienating process of objectifying the body through commodities (clothing codifying the appearance of the consumer), but in dialectical fashion, where labour appears as the considered outcome of the material character of the raw or finished product. The subject produces the object through spinning, weaving, dyeing, etc., while the material quality of the object produces the subject through his or her work, where materiality is subject to autonomous processes of accident, chance and creative intervention. Such (textile) work is iterated subsequently as intimate surfaces that produce the subject in a different fashion, in garments or accessories.

Another step in the finishing process involves machines that cut the pile of certain fabrics or, through roughening, raise the pile by scraping it with either metal or carbon brushes. High pressure can be applied at the pressing stage to produce a silk effect on the surface of the textile. At the end, another stage of drying is introduced where the textile is chemically treated and then run on a type of assembly line through a long and wide oven, while another drying machine creates a 'perfect storm' in which the fabric is blown along, turned and tumbled to puff the fibres up. This particular transport by hot air is quite different from the traditional drying process in which the fabric is pulled along by hooks that exert pressure on the sides and across the weave. Drying at Bonotto also occurs by 'vapourising', when hot steam dries the fabric while it is either dragged along under pressure or moving freely in folds. These drying processes create the final shrinkage, after which quality control looks at the finished fabric, which has returned to the entrance of the rectangular factory building, after which it is rolled up again to be stored and shipped out. At F2 there is a principal contrast between controlled transport across tightly regulated stages of production and the free-floating movement within other processes. This contrast is used to determine the finishing as a whole: fabrics are controlled or liberated at certain stages for different periods of time, and these stages succeed one another in particular sequences so that the same fabric can be processed into a vast array of different characters.

Giovanni Bonotto has spoken about an 'archaic nature' that needs to be given back to the finishing process, as if one were back at a river bank, washing, beating and drying the fabric by hand in water and the open air. This ambition, although sounding nostalgic and somewhat displaced, is certainly given expression by the airy confines of the F2 factory building and the sequence of its work but, equally, by the use of old-fashioned machinery and the deliberate decelerating of working processes. Slowing down, too, lies at the very heart of innovation at Molvena.

The Slow Factory

Within the set-up of Bonotto's factory a very particular feature needs to be distinguished. This feature is material in essence; it pertains to specific machinery and a changed tempo of production but equally marks a move away from an economic and social strategy that had informed textile production in northern Italy since the late 1970s. So, in order to explain the significance of Bonotto's material gesture, I would like to provide some context before going into detail about his actual production method and output, and thereby demonstrating how much researching and understanding properly the eventual manifestation of fashion derives from its primary material.

Political scientists and economists such as Negri on the left of centre or Nardin on the right agree in situating the development of the textile industry in northern Italy within shifts in government directives and mainstream political philosophies. Their histories of Benetton, published in the second half of the 1980s, demonstrate their reading of a move towards vertically integrated production, the expansion of a manufacturing-based company into the financial sector and the overarching championing of entrepreneurship as a direct outcome of political developments instigated by successive right-of-centre governments in Italy – and by extension wider free market philosophies in Western industrialism such as Thatcherism and Reaganomics. Retrospectively, it is tempting to judge Nardin, Negri et al. as direct products of their time, getting caught up in mapping economic detail on to more general social movements. Certainly, the economic conditions set by the Italian Christian Democrats in the 1970s and early 1980s mirror the strategies of Margaret Thatcher, Helmut Kohl, Ronald Reagan and their economic ministries to usher in a free market in which regulations are reduced and considerable tax breaks are made available to speculative financial operations and large-scale entrepreneurship.[21] However, even in the politically heated conditions of these years[22] the fundamental structure of the Italian *Mittelstand*, the small to medium-sized family enterprise (SMEs in English, PMI in Italian),[23] as the non-subsidiary, independent firm that has traditionally resided at the heart of textile and fashion production across Italy continued to assert its significance. Although the German term *Mittelstand* encompasses a particular emphasis on export, whereas family businesses in Italy have often been directed towards an internal market, the focus on innovative production, research and development certainly has many equivalents on both sides of the Alps. Such is the case at Bonotto, where the heads of the factory and the senior employees (outside management) have advanced degrees of education from polytechnics and universities, and where up to 8 per cent of the profits is reinvested directly into research.[24] This research is not simply concerned with material or technical optimising but can be quite abstract. As Giovanni Bonotto acknowledges, a large portion of the research does not yield a concrete economic output but rather contributes to a philosophy of experimentation, utilising the aforementioned faults and errors. When the German *Mittelstand* model is applied concretely to the manufacturers in the Trentino/Alto Adige, Lombardy and Veneto regions in regard to their structures and conditions of production, it also means that these family enterprises now share very similar economic and social challenges across Europe's centre, including the particular demand on the textile industries to reposition their output as distinct from mass-manufactured fabrics and fast fashion. The Italian PMIs can mix traditions of artisanal manufacture with technical innovation, due to the quality of their machinery and their educated workforce, as well as building on a strong socio-economic foundation that is based on indexed wage increases, and health- and pension benefits.

Negri, in his analysis of the entrepreneurial structure of Benetton and the figure of the CEO within it, proposed a methodology of mapping the company's new internal structures on to a changed landscape of economic structures, in which entrepreneurship purportedly altered the relationship of capital and labour. For Negri, people such as Lucciano Benetton embodied a 'new paradigm for the head of an enterprise'. They 'inscribe a creative function within social co-operation, within an productively autonomous process that is reinforced in society, in the wider social *ensemble*'.[25] Constructing an analogy between relations of production and social relations finds its methodological precedent in Marx, as we have seen, but what is significant here is that the structural composition within a manufacturer is regarded as dialectically *reflecting* as well as *proposing* social composition. For Negri, structural change occurs inside the enterprise and is not imposed by an external economic structure as before. Labour works not only inside capital but is more ambiguously positioned in a liminal space where a director or entrepreneur himself becomes 'part of the force of social labour'.[26] In my view, this odd ambiguity reveals itself also at a methodological level, since the head of a manufacturer remains the owner of the means of production (even in the outsourcing system of Benetton) and, more significantly, accumulates and holds capital. Hence the owner and their investment, holdings, facilities and machinery must be subject to the rule of economic exchange processes that continue to be determined by mercantile capitalism. Obviously, Negri reinforces this idea through his mapping of the entrepreneur, yet his shifting of the process inside the factory or manufacture marks a suggestive departure from structuralist tendencies in contemporary materialism and Marxism and progresses to a more ambivalent, subject-orientated perspective, which, one could argue, might allocate more agency to those inside the production rather than the exclusive determinism of labour relations by social relations in capitalism.

In terms of Bonotto's enterprise, this can be seen as symptomatic of a new generation of entrepreneurs who studied sociology or semiotics rather than economics[27] and thus produced a more structural and interdependent understanding of the relationship between their firm and the local ecology around them. Their restructuring of the conditions of labour can be seen perhaps as a genuine desire for (a degree of) emancipation of the workers; yet this appears somewhat impotent, in only reflecting internal structures on the outside, rather than allowing for social activism or political action to challenge the economic system. Yet Negri's definition of the 'restructured worker' seems important enough to pursue for a moment. He wrote in 1989:

> To sum up, in the conditions of production that are determined by the new productive social cooperation, *the restructured worker positions himself to ultimately reveal and realise social power structures.* The restructured worker is the *expression of the new productive social cooperation*. The quality of his labour, that is the quality of the very high productivity of socially unified labour: the quality of the surplus value that he allows to be pushed to the highest level during the production process, *has nothing to do with the reduction of running costs or ancillary expenses of production* [« faux frais »] that operates by rationalising the social: on the contrary it is creating value that is linked to the new social cooperation. The productive social cooperation is the basis for a productive leap determined by the restructured worker.[28]

In this slightly tautological definition, the restructured worker is both the expression as well as the actor in the 'new productive social cooperation', which, following Negri's and Nardin's exploration of the new entrepreneur, is governed by distinct social conditions of production, marked by collaboration – as we have seen Bonotto emphasising, too, in regard to the percentage of creative intervention, the epistemology of change and the material function of the specification sheet.

Bonotto has talked pointedly about the Industrial Revolution subjugating, through its processes of making, the object, such as nature (cotton, wool, etc.), by the subject (the industrial worker). He cites C.C.P. as teaching him about the 'primacy of material' and about 'freeing material' as significant forms of turning around this historical process.[29] In historical-materialist fashion, Bonotto regards the subjugation of nature, of object by subject, as the reason for the alienation of the worker from his work, for the progressive lessening of options and opportunities for intervention, and for the passive role of pushing buttons on and off. All these phenomena are meant to be addressed by *la fabbrica lenta* (the slow factory), which Bonotto instigated in 2007. He intended thereby 'to give the worker a new spirit', and as esoteric as this might appear in the context of weaving and spinning, such a notion has historical precedents in the early nineteenth-century silk weaving industry in Lyon (and also in Lombardy), in which the workers' interventions were rendered redundant, and they were alienated and transformed from independent artisans to wage labour and economic servitude in the space of a few decades. In this period, from the 1810s to the 1850s, labour activists, social reformers and liberal politicians uttered demands similar to Bonotto's, asking for the spirit of labour to be returned to the worker in order to usher in a period of cooperation, creative intervention and innovation that would bring quality and high productivity to the luxury textile sector. In conversations about his firm, Giovanni Bonotto has railed against alienation and has emphasised that his workers are given back responsibility. Yet since these are not the demands of a political economist or a materialist philosopher, but are carried out by the actual head of a manufacture, concrete measures can be applied and tested in the workplace.[30]

The worker, for Bonotto, should not be overseeing the automatism of the fast machine but should interact and intervene in the process through deliberate set-up, fine tuning and intervention. The worker can restructure her- or himself as a 'craftsman' or 'artisan', and these often rather meaningless terms attest to a significant process of reintroducing handiwork and learning into even large manufactures. The following case study of looms and production at Molvena bears this out.

Two paths led to *la fabbrica lenta*. The first starts out from the financial crisis of 2007/08, which led to a nadir in Bonotto's turnover of 20.6 million euros[31] – a dramatic decrease of 20 per cent[32] – and a year later required the company to lay off a quarter of its workforce.[33] The second has its origins in the work with C.C.P., which gave centrality to primary matter and prompted Bonotto to state that 'I went in search of the matter to restore its dignity'[34] – whereby matter, in Italian *materia*, designates particularly the raw material for production. The global financial crisis impacted on family-owned manufacturers across northern Italy, with a dearth of credit/investment and an almost complete state of hibernation on the part of luxury brands that dramatically reduced their orders post-2008. Less money could be found to acquire select raw materials, invest time in complex manufacturing and finishing processes, as well as exploring markets for expensive, specialist products. This prompted Giovanni Bonotto to rethink his entire production set-up.

> The development of Made in Italy as glamour and of capitalism as celebrating money was symbolically closed on the 11th September 2001 with the crash of the Twin Towers. Since then, day on day, we have been trying to pick off the fruits of an epoch, yet we all know that the system is saturated and dead. Then came last year's financial crisis and the return to what I and others have termed the 'new Middle Ages'.[35]

This blunt assessment also has positive overtones in that Bonotto indeed favours a return to the studio workshop of the Renaissance and the education and creative practice of the artisan-worker associated with it. This might not necessarily comply with Negri's definition of the 'restructured worker' in cooperative associations, but it goes some way to addressing the failings of capitalism with its propensity for the rapid turnover of fast fashion.

Two types of looms are of particular note at Bonotto, and both have long ceased to be produced or employed in modern textile manufacture. Yet they are integral to understanding the concept of the 'slow factory': the first was made by Picañol in the mid-1950s, the second by Vamatex in the 1990s. In the collaboration between C.C.P. and Bonotto the designer suggested a new type of research and development with the textile producer that required a new structure of production, determined by intensive preparation and set-up, and demanding a collective understanding of primary matter and material properties from worker, company head and user-designer. Bonotto agreed to these demands since they allowed him and his brother to reposition the company after 2009 and to develop samples that could eventually be commercialised in larger quantities for clients such as Rick Owens, Gucci, Marni and Chanel. For instance, C.C.P. gave his consent for Bonotto to retain options on their joint textile development, which were later 'adopted' (to use a neutral term) by companies that are more visible in the market. As mentioned in Chapter 6, a certain US-based designer is known to buy an entire range of C.C.P. at a Tokyo retailer in order to harvest stylistic and material ideas, which are then taken to Bonotto in order to be realised at a faster rate – and in much higher quantities – than in their original experimental phase with C.C.P. Since copyright infringements are notoriously difficult to pursue in fashion and moralising about the originality of design ideas certainly does not abound in the industry, such examples are tolerated for their mutual benefit: if there is enough capital and production capacity to go around, weavers and designers might feel that they need to accept imitation as the sincerest form of flattery.

For a long time C.C.P. asked Bonotto to find weaving looms that were properly 'mechanical' in order to allow for direct interaction with the process of making, rather than letting computerised systems perform operations that, once set in motion, cannot be intervened in or altered. These old machines with many heavy parts and slow, deliberate operations had always been used to develop a particularly dense and durable weave from organically dyed yarns – something that would become an important feature within the sustainable ecology of *la fabbrica lenta*. After much research, Bonotto acquired (in 2007) eight 'President' looms at an auction in Japan, which had been manufactured in 1956 in the Belgian factory of Charles Steverlynck. This factory had used designs by the Spanish engineer Jaime Picañol to pioneer multi-colour looms since 1952 in its production facility near Zandberg in Zillebeke. The Picañol company was famous as a manufacturer and worldwide exporter of automated shuttle looms, but had made its name in Japan, especially, by supplying experimental looms for rubber and metal to the tyre maker Bridgestone, which used them to compete with its rival Firestone. Giovanni Bonotto had lived in Nagoya for some time before taking over his father's company as creative director in 1996, and he knew the market in Japan quite well. He was impressed both by the industrial heritage of post-war Japanese weaving as well as by the promotion of artisanal expertise as part of national identity. Furthermore, the Japanese expertise in weaving and dyeing cotton yarns for very dense denim fabrics suggested to C.C.P. and Bonotto that appropriate looms could still be found there. Acquiring machines in Japan therefore felt like an informed choice, and the looms were duly disassembled and shipped to Molvena, where they now occupy a separate part of the weaving section, including cabinets for spares and tools.

Production on Picañol's 'President' looms has an expressively 'mechanical' character that makes their set-up and maintenance akin to that of an old car that needs constant servicing with wrenches, grease and oil. Their fuel is petrol-based and the smell, as well as the operating noise, underscores the old-style, direct and almost aggressive approach to the weaving operation when compared to today's smooth and much more silent Dobby power looms. The weave from the Picañols is very dense, since the warp yarns are tightly packed on spools that can measure only 75 cm in width. The shuttle drags the weft yarns up and under the warp with great thrust and noise. The reed battening down the weft into the fell (the part of the cloth that is not yet wound up on the take-up roll of the loom) is extremely hard and tough, so that the resulting cloth shares these features: it is strong yet eminently pliable, thick and solid yet organic, like the body of the wearer.

The selvage, the edges of both ends of the fabric that are woven to prevent the fabric from unravelling, appear very prominent on the 1950s Picañol, due to the narrowness of the beams and spools that can be employed. When looking down on to the narrow take-up roll on the loom during weaving, the red and off-white selvage seems almost like a wide pattern, framing the (mostly sombre) body of the cloth. Usually, selvage is cut from the fabric when it is used by a designer, since it is a now defunct reminder of the previous process that is superseded by cutting and tailoring the garment. An exception can be noted in the tradition of jeans manufacture, where the selvage became a feature inside the trouser leg to distinguish a particularly weave or a rarer form of denim; therefore it was sometimes revealed in the turn-up by the wearer to denote 'connaisseurship' or being member of a certain group or subculture.

C.C.P. explored the feature of selvage extensively for a collection of designs that used the denim-type weave of heavy cottons, which he commissioned from the newly installed Picañols at Bonotto's. The series of pieces, collectively entitled 'self-edge', began in 2009 after C.C.P. and Giovanni Bonotto had installed the machines, experimented with their working mechanism and were satisfied finally with the quality of the woven cloth. The self-edge pieces employed an extravagant production principle, for which each seam in the cut for jackets, trousers and so on had to follow – and feature – the selvage itself. This is not a problem for a straight trouser leg, but is much more difficult when calculating the back seam of a jacket, for instance. Given the classic forms of (male) tailoring, the 'self-edge' principle challenged the pattern cutters at C.C.P. to develop new blocks that omitted curves as much as possible – although some seams could be adapted by hot-ironing the selvage into bends. Featuring the selvage of the Picañol-woven cloth in even the smallest pattern piece also meant a large amount of textile residue. For the belt loop on trousers, this means just using a tiny part of the cloth (in fact, just the selvage on either side), while the remaining 70 cm or so cannot be used for the detail. In turn, this means that while a traditional pattern cut for a suit can be completed with 3–3.5 metres of cloth (based on the orthodox width of 1.5 metres), for a suit in self-edge fabric C.C.P. needs 6 or 7 metres. This increases the material costs of production, which is ameliorated somewhat by the long-lasting quality of the fabric and also by the fact that C.C.P. does not use any lining for jackets or coats. The latter feature is intended to demonstrate to the wearer the exact construction of the cut and the expert hand-finishing of seams. In the case of the 'self-edge' designs this meant that the body canvas of the jacket was adapted to the overarching principle, by weaving a similarly coloured 'selvage' into the horsehair that is used for inlays and then cutting these to the selvage line as well. Such attention to detail, which will only be noted by a devoted wearer rather than being visible as a stylistic feature to others,

13 Detail of a Picañol loom at the Bonotto textile factory in Molvena, October 2016

is born from respect for the material as primary matter and principal guideline for the design idea. It is not the look of the object that is brought to the fore, nor mainly its construction, but rather the production of its base material provides both form and features for the finished garment.

The other looms that Bonotto favours for his 'slow factory' were made by Vamatex, a family company that had been founded in 1974 and was run for many decades by Nello Pezzoli in Bergamo (in Lombardy, some 200 kilometres west of Molvena), before being incorporated into a larger conglomerate. The Vamatex air-jet looms at Bonotto all are at least twenty years old. The company no longer makes them, partly because of the change in ownership but mainly because of changed production lines. There is little or no demand for these looms since they are regarded as too slow and too cumbersome, with too many parts and higher maintenance requirements than modern computerised power looms. Bonotto is still acquiring old Vamatex looms for parts from local factories that have folded or retired the machines. The set-up and operation of the Vamatex looms from the 1980s and 1990s remains an individual affair: one worker is responsible for his or her machine and knows its quirks and ticks, so that these particular characteristics can be enhanced by altering parts or intervening in processes that are suggested by the specification sheet.

A principal rationale for *la fabbrica lenta* lies in pursuing an anti-cyclical movement and in matching increased labour costs with the added responsibility and agency of the worker in the production – a 'more "natural" rapport between man and machine', as Lorenzo Bonotto has made clear.[36] Across the textile industry in northern Italy, higher wages have steadily impacted on the time that each worker is allowed to spend on a piece and on the way in which she or he relates to the increasingly automated processes.[37] Factory owners and manufacturers invest in quicker and quicker looms to increase output, so that they can balance out the labour costs and maintain profits in the face of competition from the Far East. The key word for them is automisation rather than any amelioration of production. Simplifying and speeding up the spinning, weaving and finishing processes dramatically reduces the opportunities for workers to interact with the machines, while the computerised looms with their fewer parts and fully automated set-ups no longer present opportunities to adjust working parts so that one can creatively intervene in production or experiment with unorthodox specifications. In marked contrast,

14 Carol Christian Poell, Self-Edge tailored suit jacket (detail), 2010, Male Self-Edge Collection

the Vamatex looms of *la fabbrica lenta* are 'slow' indeed – literally, in terms of their working speed compared to contemporary machines, but also in having many (serviceable) parts that require and permit interaction and intervention during set-up and operation. Giovanni Bonotto talks of these looms having 'great sensibility' due to the many interacting components, a sensibility that he trains the worker operating the loom to share.[38] The set-up of the Vamatex is changed according to each piece – and there are 600 pieces each season, although only 10 per cent of these are 'experimental' and require substantially new and different approaches – yet each set-up on the Vamatex is still to some extent a creative act by the worker. Bonotto likened it to 'tuning a Ferrari Formula Uno' in the workshop with a team of engineers.[39] The aspiration for Bonotto is to engage and emancipate the worker through this process; words such as 'master craftsman' or 'artisan' are used by him and his brother, emphasising the effort to counter alienation in industrial manufacture, even if this seems to be contradicted by the mechanisation that governs production at Molvena and Schio. Yet there are clearly financial benefits in the attention and care that goes into the research and practice of the spinning, weaving and finishing processes. Bonotto has stated that many of his fabrics have become so research- and labour-intensive that they wholesale to clients at a price of 100, 200 or even 300 euros per metre – far in excess of what others, including Zegna, would be able to charge.[40]

Bonotto follows the guidelines that govern apprenticeship processes in Italy – *apprendistato professionale* or *formazione* – and there is movement between sectors of the factory, although there is not necessarily a strict hierarchy between workstations. Bonotto has expressed his surprise that the weavers at the noisy looms remain in their arduous positions for decades rather than wanting to move to other parts of the factory. Apparently, once a weaver-apprentice takes to the task, he or she gets hooked on the work after just a day or two. This might also have to do with the salary level, which is higher in weaving than in spinning or in the archive. It is noticeable that gender is pretty mixed across weaving, spinning, finishing and so on, which further suggests that there is parity in salary levels across the company and that low-skilled or low-paid jobs are not the exclusive domain of the female workforce (with the exception of the cleaning staff).

Conclusion

The experience at Bonotto corresponds very much with that at C.C.P. The economic limitations of the post-crash economy of northern Italy led both of them to explore new solutions that involved material production and the conditions of labour as the basis for innovative making. C.C.P. refused to produce new collections and proceeded slowly in research projects across seasons; Bonotto refused to update his machinery and instigated the slow factory.[41] Both have thus succeeded in an industry that is ostensibly built on novelty and constant renewal by their very refusal of such tenets.

In 2014 Lorenzo Bonotto, who is responsible for the finances of the company, gave an account of the material progress of *la fabbrica lenta*.

> According to the financial records of our company, in 2007 and in the two-year period of 2008–09 we experienced what was frankly an absurd drop, losing 50% of our turnover. We sat ourselves around a table and looked into each other's eyes in order to determine a new strategy. And now, since 2013, we have closed the gap completely, arriving back at the numbers of 2007. For 2014 we have recorded growth of more than 18% to date (of which 44% is achieved in Italy, with France and China as our 2nd and 3rd market).[42]

Like his brother, Lorenzo Bonotto measures material progress not simply in financial terms. He emphasised in the interview the deliberate tempo for creative innovation in his factory. 'The quality of textiles lies in the time that they take to be produced. *Just in time* does not interest us. Rather we are interested in a vision of modern labour and enterprise.'[43] In the context of restructured labour, the example of C.C.P. and Bonotto is significant not only for analysing material products but also how materiality reflects changing labour practices. Their collaboration in laboriously acquiring weaving looms and determining a new form of (old) production generates a whole new practice that includes training, set-up, operation and maintenance of facilities. In the present case it is ironic, but perhaps fitting for fashion, that these labour practices are determined by machinery from yesteryear. The Picañol and Vamatex looms suggest in their present usage – out of time and out of place – a fundamental alteration of working processes that allows for more input and more reflection by the worker: first, through the deliberately slowed down function, in combination with the increased materiality (more noise, more force, a much denser fabric); secondly, through the feedback loop with the designer who demonstrates the unusual weaving in the very structure of his garments – by literally making the visible trace of the labour, the selvage, the guiding line for his pattern cuts and designs. It therefore allows for radical reflexivity – literally gaining a 'self-edge' – that moves across all stages of the production, from cotton/wool fibres to finished suit.

Carrying over Negri's analogy between SME manufacturing and socio-cultural dynamics since the mid-1970s to Bonotto would imply mapping the father's ideal of the 'factory as total artwork' and the sons' vision of the 'slow factory' on to a changing landscape of labour in northern Italy, especially in the Veneto region. Is the creatively slow process of quasi-artisanal work at Bonotto reflected in the social composition of small towns and villages now? For example, are well-established centres of textile production such as Biela, which are now heavily populated by East Asian immigrants and where many companies now have Chinese owners and an exclusively Chinese workforce, indicative of the future of production? The Venetian economist Marco Bettiol recently suggested that the mapping of the social condition of labour in the Veneto might work through historical and contemporary narratives that are shared by the local community. He posits the notion of 'Made in Italy' as being at the centre of an understanding and self-reflection that is shared by Giovanni Bonotto.[44] Others have defined the area simply as 'the new post-industrial Veneto', as but one example of specialised production leaving traditional centres in Europe, where global service and digital industries are replacing small and medium-scale manufacturers.[45] Locality is not just a place, of course, but also a historical fact. The tradition of textile production around Vicenza certainly inspired and animated the 'return' to *la fabbrica lenta*, to a time in 1912 when the Bonotto company was founded by Giovanni's great-grandfather and when artisanal work dominated the local economy. Yet Bonotto's enterprise and the return to a sustained materialism, for which research and an in-depth understanding of materiality form the basis of production, is certainly a new phenomenon. Like C.C.P., the return to primary matter, to material that determines design, not simply as stuff but as the object of labour and as such in relation to the subject, is a recent antidote to the runaway excesses of fast fashion. The slow factory is the expression of an actualised and substantial materialism in fashion.

Notes

1. See the initial reactions of the Italian financial pages, for example 'La manifattura Bonotto passa al gruppo Zegna', *Il sole 24 ore*, 4 October 2016; 'Al gruppo Ermenegildo Zegna il controllo della manifattura tessile Bonotto di Vicenza', *Il sole 24 ore*, 6 October 2016; 'Zegna compra la fabbrica lenta di Bonotto', *Il Giornale di Vicenza*, 4 October 2016, p. 9; and Luisa Zargani, 'Ermenegildo Zegna Group Buys Majority Stake in Bonotto', *Womens Wear Daily*, 3 October 2016.
2. All quotes from Luigi and Giovanni Bonotto pertain to interviews conducted at Molvena, across three days between 3 and 5 October 2016.
3. Giovanni Bonotto in conversation with the author, 4 October 2016.
4. See, for instance, the toying with racial stereotypes in Diesel's (mock) lifestyle journal *The Daily African* during 2001.
5. See, for instance, Guilla Crivelli, 'Stilli (Otb): «Nel 2015 Marni e Margiela in forte crescita»', *Il sole 24 ore,* 1 May 2015.
6. Maria Cristina Tommasini, 'Slow Loom', *Domus*, 124 (April 2009), p. 87. Bonotto studied with Umberto Eco on the Università di Bologna course in General Semiotics and, from 1992 onwards, Media Studies [*Scienze della Comunicazione*]; he later worked as a teaching assistant for Eco.
7. Giuseppe Nardin, *La Benetton: Strategia e struttura di un'impresa di successo* (Rome: Edizioni Lavoro, 1987), p. 85.
8. See, for example, concerns in the local press: 'Popolare Vicenza e Veneto Banca, il crac spiegato in parole semplici', *Il Mattino di Padova*, 1 June 2016.
9. Marco Magalini, 'Bonotto: la fabbrica lenta dialoga con l'arte', *The Lifestyle Journal: Diary of Slow Living*, 6 July 2015, p. 30.
10. Verena Lenna, 'Un ecosistema per la cultura', *Tafterjournal 55* (January 2013).
11. Antonio Negri, 'Les PME italiennes, l'exemple Benetton et le nouveau chef d'entreprise en Europe' [1989], in Maurizio Lazzarato, Yann Moulier Boutang, Antonio Negri and Giorgio Santilli, *Des Entreprises pas comme les autres: Benetton en Italie, Le Sentier à Paris* (Paris: Publisud, 1993), pp. 25–134, here pp. 81–8. Negri completed his study on Benetton in 1988 for a French research project and while the Italian original was never published, the economist Yann Moulier Boutang later translated the extended essay for the above volume.
12. Conversation with the author, 3 October 2016.
13. Enrico Mannucci, 'Molvena: Tessere è un'arte che ci ha insegnato Duchamp', *Corriere della Sera*, 19 August 2016.
14. See Mannucci, 'Molvena: Tessere è un'arte che ci ha insegnato Duchamp'; Simone Sinico, 'Giovanni Bonotto: Con Fabbrica Lenta rendiamo sexy la nostra cultura', *Industria Vicentina*, 31 July 2013; and Lenna, 'Un ecosistema per la cultura'.
15. Peterlini in an interview with the author, 4 October 2016; see, for

example, the office machine performance by George Maciunas, *In Memoriam to Adriano Olivetti Versions 1–5* (1962) or the thrift shop installation by Robert Filliou and George Brecht entitled *La cédille qui ne finit pas* (1965) – all in the Bonotto collection.
16. Tommasini, 'Slow Loom', p. 87.
17. Filomena Greco, 'Bonotto punta sulla "fabbrica lenta" e cresce facendo rinascere antichi telai', *Il sole 24 ore*, 6 November 2015.
18. Gianluca Bolelli, 'Bonotto punta a diventare un brand e continua a crescere', *FashionNetwork.com*, 18 October 2014, http://it.fashionnetwork.com/news/Bonotto-punta-a-diventare-un-brand-e-continua-a-crescere,436731.html#.WNQ5sY61uXQ (last accessed 23 March 2017).
19. Conversation with the author, 3 October 2016.
20. Conversation with the author, 4 October 2016.
21. Negri (together with Michael Hardt) would later generalise this process within his Marxist/materialist analysis of imperialism. In capitalism the first phase of material expansion (investment in production) is inevitably followed by a second phase of financial expansion (speculation). See Antonio Negri and Michael Hardt, *Empire* (Cambridge, MA: Harvard University Press, 2000), p. 239.
22. In particular during the years of industrial growth in Italy (1983–87) when the – nominally socialist – government of Bettino Craxi abolished in its negotiations with labour unions the wage–price indexation (*scala mobile*) that had linked wage increases to inflation.
23. PMI stands for 'piccole e medie imprese'.
24. Lorenzo Bonotto, quoted in Emily Backus, 'Italian Mills Count on Innovation', *WomensWearDaily*, 23 September 2014, p. 9.
25. Negri, 'Les PME italiennes, l'exemple Benetton', p. 121.
26. Ibid., p. 122. Negri's focus on the worker has its origin in the method developed by him and other political scientists since the late 1960s that have been grouped by the term *operaismo*. This 'workerism' centred on the autonomy of the worker, labour process and its social conditions as means to develop an understanding of modern capitalist power structures. On the history of *operaismo*/workerism, see for example Giuseppe Trotta/Fabio Milana, *L'operaismo degli anni Sessanta: Da 'Quaderni Rossi' a 'Classe Operaia'* (Roma: DeriveApprodi, 2008) or Mario Tronti, 'Our Operaismo', *New Left Review*, 73 (January–February 2012), pp. 119–39.
27. See Negri's 'anthropology' of the new entrepreneurs from the 1960s generation, in 'Les PME italiennes, l'exemple Benetton', p. 121, and the political positioning of entrepreneurs such as Rolf Fehlbaum at the furniture manufacture Vitra, who had graduated in sociology and in 1977 defined his company as a 'cultural-economic project'; or Miuccia Prada, who graduated in 1978 with a degree in political science and who has spoken of her 'radical' past as a socialist.
28. Negri, 'Les PME italiennes, l'exemple Benetton', p. 130.

29. See Chapter 6 on negation in C.C.P.: 'materiality as primary object'.
30. Conversations with the author, 3 and 4 October 2016.
31. Guido Lorenzon, 'Quel fascino rinascimentale', *Milano Finanza*, 30 March 2015, p. 67.
32. Raffaele Ricciardi, 'La "Fabbrica Lenta" di Vicenza che ribalta il concetto di produttività', *La Repubblica*, 5 October 2013.
33. Bacrus, 'Italian Mills Count on Innovation', p. 9.
34. Tommasini, 'Slow Loom', p. 87.
35. Alessandra Carini, 'Bonotto, il tempo lento di una fabbrica a Km 0', *La Repubblica*, 15 June 2009, p. 15.
36. Bonelli, 'Bonotto punta a diventare un brand e continua a crescere'.
37. Interestingly, Nardin, who was born in Vicenza and drew his research principally from this area, observed that labour costs between 1980–84 in artisanal production were some 20–25 per cent lower than in industrial production. Yet in 1984 Benetton's labour costs were only at 7.5 per cent of overall expenditure, while Marzotto, the only other weaver still remaining near Molvena, had labour costs of 37.5 per cent. Nardin, *La Benetton*, pp. 91, 86.
38. Conversation with the author, 4 October 2016.
39. Ibid.
40. Giovanni Bonotto in the television programme by Duilio Giammaria, 'La sfida globale del made in Italy', broadcast on RAI Uno, 22 September 2014 (his statement comes at 3' 53").
41. Bonotto recalled in an interview of 2013 the time in 2007 when his competitors made fun of him for acquiring outdated looms at a Japanese auction: 'Look, he has no money to buy new machines.' Ricciardi, 'La "Fabbrica Lenta" di Vicenza che ribalta il concetto di produttività'.
42. Bonelli, 'Bonotto punta a diventare un brand e continua a crescere'. The most recent sales at Bonotto had grown to 30 million euros, just before its partial sale to Zegna; see Zargani, 'Ermenegildo Zegna Group Buys Majority Stake in Bonotto'. Bonotto's rise came at a time when the Italian texile industry as a whole had contracted in 2012 by –3.2 per cent, in 2013 by –2.8 per cent, and only returned to growth of 3.1 per cent in 2014. See Emily Backus, 'Mood Improves Heading to Milan Unica', *WomensWearDaily*, 2 September 2014, p. 1.
43. Bonelli, 'Bonotto punta a diventare un brand e continua a crescere'.
44. Marco Bettiol, *Raccontare il Made in Italy: Un nuovo legame tra cultura e manifattura* (Venice: Marsilio, 2015), pp. 31–2 on Bonotto. See also the economic data for the changing industry in the Veneto region in the article by Mattia Pertoldi, 'Tessuti, vini, bibite: vola il nordest che si reinventa', *La Tribuna di Treviso*, 19 January 2016, pp. 22–5.
45. Anon., 'Design, ricerca e tecnologie le tre chiavi della rinascita', *La Repubblica*, 5 May 2008.

Conclusion

This book is situated within the history of ideas, so it is the *idea of fashion* that becomes central. But that does not mean that the text has to move exclusively within a discursive realm or within a context of representation. On the contrary, *the idea of fashion is an idea of production*: the cultural context of making seen through economic, political and social prisms of making. In materialism, especially in its historical formation, concepts and ideas are not passive and subjective reflections of the material world but products of labour, and the contradictory nature of these concepts therefore has its origin in the contradictions within society and its social conditions of production. For Marx and Engels, the latter of whom had developed his understanding of materialism from the concrete experience of his family's textile mills in Manchester, dialectics were not something imposed from an abstract vantage point of pure reason but were a product of human labour changing society. Their form was determined and developed by people and could only be understood by the practical struggle to overcome contradictions and negations – not just in thought, but in practice. This also implies that women and men are thrown back on to themselves and are made responsible for their own actions, which must be seen as part of collective patterns. Lefebvre, in the quote with which I opened this book, spoke of contemporary technicities changing humanity's relation with the world but not with him- or herself. A lack of critical action prevents an understanding of fashion as a practice that is not simply transformative of corporeal appearances but that can transform socio-economic structures. The more technicity allows for productive structures and logistics that aid the imprinting of fashion not just on clothing or consumer goods but on the arts, the culture industry at large and even the representation of politics, the greater is the necessity to analyse fashion for its proper meaning, a meaning that emerges from its materiality but which goes far beyond materialising desires, objectifying sexuality or commodifying the body.

We are all complicit in the production of fashion, in designed commodities in general and in the rapid turnover of garments and accessories in particular. As demonstrated in the first chapter, the economic and structural relation between production and consumption makes us, as producers *and* consumers, complicit in the ever-narrowing cycles of fast fashion. Critics have pointed out for some time now that such cycles are not sustainable, either ecologically or economically. By how much can we reduce the retail price of a T-shirt before the exploitative system of fashion manufacture collapses around us (even when considering the T-shirt only as a promotional tool and not as an actual commodity that generates surplus value)? At what point do labour costs, even of a child sewing a garment in an unregulated sweatshop, fall out of line with profits? When is it no longer economically viable to ship containers full of trend-predicted commodities around the globe, and when does the landfill of discarded fashion products intrude all too noticeably on the environment of even the most elite member of a post-industrial society?

Once we stop regarding fashion as a supreme right of individual self-expression (through particular clothes, food, travel, etc.) and see it rather as part of a larger exchange system that exploits and alienates labour, we might begin to consider our behaviour. Fashion is not a representation of constantly changing styles or movements to titillate and entertain but a material reality with concrete economic and ecological repercussions for all of us. For instance, when we re-advertise fashionable looks through online photo-sharing, re-post modish expressions or resend memes, we provide free labour (in the form of content) for the owner of the means of production: the social media provider. Such providers do not produce anything material; they simply profit through advertising and, more significantly, through financial speculation with capital (which we collectively provide them with), often in the form of direct investment in companies that manufacture fashion commodities in the widest sense. Novelty and contemporaneity keep the manufacturers and media platforms in profit, even when the proclaimed innovation is purely self-referential and reflexive, rather than productive. Similarly, when we discard clothes after a few months in order to replace them with others that are so cheaply (and badly) produced that their designed obsolescence does not even last until the next seasonal changing point, we are complicit in a cycle that wastes an enormous amount of natural resources and non-renewable energy.

Yet the repeated warnings of theorists, researchers and critics have had very little impact on the fashion industry, let alone affected the wider fashion system of constantly renewed consumption of commodities. Consumption is posited as an inalienable right for people in industrialised and post-industrial societies, in the same way that financial speculation and protection from the redistribution of income and wealth is seen as a supreme right of global elites. As Marx clarified already in 1845, any work on social development and change always needs to refer back to materiality.[1] Recognising the dialectic of materialism and fashion means that we should start reading fashion as bound up in an intimate relationship with material production as well as the materialist critique thereof. This book has aimed therefore to present fashion as a combination of 1) a critical nexus for the history of ideas; 2) a temporal structure for looking at cultural production; 3) a form of cognition that realises immediacy and contemporaneity; and, finally, 4) a field for innovative crafts, design and industrial manufacture.

In post-industrial and post-democratic societies where speculative capital and the financialisation of political and social spheres have taken an absolute hold, understanding the impact of fashion as a system of thought that underpins capitalism is crucial. Yet more crucial is the simultaneous realisation that a critical understanding of fashion can serve to expose the capitalist system and its persuasive employment of the culture industry across constantly repeated historical patterns. From the viewpoint of theoretical discourse alone, my hope is that people involved in cultural studies (fashion, design, media, etc.) incorporate analyses from the history of ideas – from philosophy proper but also from its application to historical or cultural tendencies – into their research, as well as turning towards a critical perspective on economic and political orthodoxies. For instance, it is inappropriate simply to accept the transfer of trickle-down theory or capital formation to fashion history. As argued above, fashion is generated by people from all social classes and geographies, and not just by a Western social elite, so the celebration in fashion's past and present of the same actors (royalty, rich heiresses, stage and screen actresses) from an occidental, bourgeois cultural hegemony must be opposed. Similarly, the complicity of historians and theorists in the promotion of brands through merely rehashing myths about designers and accepting timelines about fashion innovations, without investigating the actual material production and labour processes involved in historic and contemporary trend-patterns, needs to be addressed. Fashion researchers must engage with production and distribution, alongside representation and consumption, to be able to put forward proper analyses of fashion's networks and systems. My hope is that some readers are or will be associated with fashion, in the most expansive sense of the word, and its production and industry. For those readers, especially, this book can serve as a starting point for a critical engagement with their fields and prompt an investigation and questioning of the fundamental structures in which they partake.

Note

1. See Marx and Engels, *The German Ideology*, pp. 67ff. This first part of the book developed a radical conception of history, following on from Hegel but in express opposition to the materialism espoused by left-Hegelians in the 1840s in Germany, such as Ludwig Feuerbach, Bruno Bauer and Max Stirner. From this opposition Marx and Engels demonstrated an understanding of history that is based on patterns of production and the social production of labour. The original manuscript of this passage contained references to the industrialised textile mills of Manchester, with their exploitation and alienation of labour, which would have shown Feuerbach a present that was quite distinct from the idealised work of yesteryear's spinning wheels and handlooms, had he only engaged with the real world; see Karl Marx and Friedrich Engels, *Die Deutsche Ideologie, Werke, Band 3* (Berlin: Dietz, 1978), pp. 43–4.

Select Bibliography

Adorno, Theodor W., *Aesthetic Theory* [1973], London: Routledge, 1984.
Althusser, Louis, *For Marx* [1965], London: Verso, 2005.
Althusser, Louis, with Étienne Balibar, *Reading Capital* [1968], London: Verso, 2009.
Armitage, John, and Joan Roberts (eds), *Critical Luxury Studies: Art, Design, Media*, Edinburgh: Edinburgh University Press, 2016.
Assouline, Pierre, *Grâces lui soient rendues: Paul Durand-Ruel, le marchand des impressionistes*, Paris: Gallimard, 2004.
Austin, James Lloyd, and Henri Mondor (eds), *Stéphane Mallarmé, Correspondance IV*, Paris: Gallimard, 1973.
Balzac, Honoré de, 'Des mots à la mode' [1830], in *Œuvres complètes*, vol. 39, Paris: Conard, 1938, pp. 33–5.
— 'Physiology of Attire' [1830], trans. R. G. Elliott, *Art in Translation*, 7.2 (2015), pp. 177–85.
Barbey d'Aurevilly, Jules Amadée, *Œuvres romanesques complètes*, vol. 2, Paris: Gallimard, 1966.
— *Premiers articles*, Paris: Les Belles lettres, 1973.
Barbon, Nicolas, *Discourse on Trade*, London: Milbourn, 1690.
Barthes, Roland, *Michelet*, Paris: Seuil, 1954.
— 'Histoire et sociologie du vêtement: Quelques observations méthodologiques', *Annales: Economie, Sociétés, Civilisations*, 12.3 (1957), pp. 430–41.
— *Essais critiques*, Paris: Seuil, 1964.
— *The Fashion System* [1967], London: Cape, 1985.
Baudelaire, Charles, *The Painter of Modern Life and Other Essays* [1863], trans. J. Mayne, London: Phaidon, 1993.
— *Œuvres completes*, vols. 1 and 2, Paris: Gallimard, 1975–76.
Baudrillard, Jean, *The System of Objects* [1968], London: Verso, 1996.
— *Symbolic Exchange and Death* [1976], trans. I. H. Grant, London: SAGE, 1993.
Bellers, John, *Essays About the Poor, Manufactures, Trade, Plantations & Immorality . . .*, London: Sowle, 1699.

Bellour, Raymond, *L'Analyse du film*, Paris: Albatros, 1979.
Benjamin, Walter, *The Origin of German Tragic Drama* [1924/25], trans. J. Osborne, London: New Left Books, 1977.
— *The Arcades Project* [1929–40], Cambridge, MA: Belknap Press of Harvard University Press, 1999.
— 'Centralpark' [1939/40], *New German Critique*, 34 (1985), pp. 32–58.
— 'On the Concept of History' [1939/40], in *Selected Writings*, vol. 4, Cambridge, MA: Belknap Press of Harvard University Press, 2006, pp. 389–400.
— *The Correspondence of Walter Benjamin 1910–1940*, trans. M. R. and E. M. Jacobson, Chicago: University of Chicago Press, 1994.
Bertin, Celia, *Haute Couture: terre inconnue*, Paris: Hachette, 1956.
Bettiol, Marco, *Raccontare il Made in Italy: Un nuovo legame tra cultura e manifattura*, Venice: Marsilio, 2015.
Blanc, Louis, *Organisation du travail*, Paris: Administration de librairie, 1841.
— *Histoire de la Révolution de 1848*, vol. 2, Paris: Marpon/Flammarion, 1880.
Blaszczyk, Regina Lee (ed.), *Producing Fashion: Commerce, Culture and Consumers*, Philadelphia: University of Pennsylvania Press, 2008.
Bloch, Ernst, *Subjekt-Objekt: Erläuterungen zu Hegel* [1949], Frankfurt a.M.: Suhrkamp, 1962.
Boime, Albert, 'The Salon des refusés and the Evolution of Modern Art', *The Art Quarterly*, 32 (winter 1969), pp. 411–26.
— 'Les hommes d'affaires et les arts en France au 19e siècle', *Actes de la Recherche en Sciences Sociales*, 28 (1979), pp. 65–8.
Brady, Patrick, *'L'Œuvre' de Émile Zola, roman sur les arts: manifeste, autobiographie, roman à clef*, Geneva: Droz, 1967.
Brewer, John, and Roy Porter (eds), *Consumption and the World of Goods*, London: Routledge, 1993.
Brill, Leslie, *The Hitchcock Romance: Love and Irony in Hitchcock's Films*, Princeton: Princeton University Press, 1988.
Butor, Michel, 'Fashion and the Modern' [1968], trans. R. G. Elliott, *Art in Translation*, 7.2 (2015), pp. 266–81.
Calvet, Louis-Jean, *Roland Barthes: A Biography* [1990], Cambridge: Polity, 1994.
Camus, Albert, *L'Homme révolté*, Paris: Gallimard, 1951.
Carter, Michael, *Fashion Classics from Carlyle to Barthes*, Oxford: Berg, 2003.
Change 4, Paris: Seuil, 1968.
Corber, Robert J., *In the Name of National Security: Hitchcock, Homophobia, and the Political Construction of Gender in Postwar America*, Durham, NC: Duke University Press, 1993.
Dior, Christian, *Je suis couturier*, Paris: Éditions du Conquistador, 1951.
— *Dior by Dior: The Autobiography of Christian Dior*, New York: Dutton, 1957.

Eagleton, Terry, *Marxism and Literary Criticism*, Berkeley: University of California Press, 1976.
Engels, Friedrich, 'Dialectics of Nature' [1873–83], in Karl Marx and Friedrich Engels, *Collected Works*, vol. 25, London: Lawrence & Wishart, 1987, pp. 313–588.
— 'Anti-Dühring' [1876–78], in Karl Marx and Friedrich Engels, *Collected Works*, vol. 25, London: Lawrence & Wishart, 1987, pp. 15–289.
— 'Socialism: Utopian and Scientific' [1880], in Karl Marx and Friedrich Engels, *Collected Works*, vol. 24, London: Lawrence & Wishart, 1989, pp. 281–324.
Ferry, Jean, 'The Fashionable Tiger' [1953], in *French Short Stories/ Nouvelles Françaises 1*, Harmondsworth: Penguin, 1966.
Figal, Günter, *Objectivity: The Hermeneutical and Philosophy* [2006], trans. Th. D. George, Albany, NY: State University of New York Press, 2010.
Flügel, John C., *The Psychology of Clothes*, London: Hogarth, 1930.
Fohlen, Claude, *L'Industrie textile au temps du second empire*, Paris: Plon, 1956.
Gautier, Théophile, 'Salon de 1852', *La Presse*, 16 (27 May 1852), pp. 1–3.
— *De la mode*, Paris: Poulet-Malassi & de Broise, 1858.
de Goncourt, Jules, and Edmond de Goncourt, *Journal. Mémoires de la vie littéraire. Vol. II. 1864–1874*, Paris: Fasquelle/Flammarion, 1956.
Green, Nicolas, 'Dealing in Temperaments: Economic Transformation of the Artistic Field in France During the Second Half of the Nineteenth Century', *Art History*, 10.1 (1987), pp. 59–78.
Grelé, Eugène, *Jules Barbey d'Aurevilly: sa vie et son oeuvre*, Caen: Jouan, 1902.
Grumbach, Didier, *Histoires de la Mode*, Paris: Seuil, 1993.
Guiral, Pierre, *La Vie quotidienne en France à l'âge d'or du capitalisme: 1852–1879*, Paris: Hachette, 1976.
Habermas, Jürgen, *The Aesthetic Discourse of Modernity* [1985], Cambridge: Polity, 1987.
Hegel, Georg Friedrich Wilhelm, *Phenomenology of Spirit* [1804], trans. A. V. Miller, Oxford: Oxford University Press, 1977.
— *Science of Logic I* [1812/13], London: Allen & Unwin, 1929.
— *Aesthetics: Lectures on Fine Art. Vols I and II* [1835/1842], Oxford: Clarendon Press, 1975.
Humilière, Jean-Michel, *Louis Blanc (1811–1882)*, Paris: Éditions ouvrières, 1982.
Jameson, Fredric, *The Prison-House of Language*, Princeton: Princeton University Press, 1972.
— 'Marxism and Historicism', *New Literary History*, IX.1 (1979), pp. 41–73.
— *The Political Unconscious* [1981], London: Routledge, 1996.
Jhering, Rudolf von, *Der Zweck im Recht* [1877/1883], Leipzig: Breitkopf & Härtel, 1905.

Kaern, Michael, Bernard S. Phillips and Robert S. Cohen (eds), *Georg Simmel and the Contemporary Sociology*, Dordrecht: Kluwer, 1990.
Kittsteiner, H. D., 'Walter Benjamin's Historicism', *New German Critique*, 39 (1986), pp. 179–215.
Koselleck, Reinhart, *Futures Past: On the Semantics of Historical Time* [1979], trans. K. Tribe, Cambridge, MA: MIT Press, 1985.
Krüger, Hans-Peter, *Heroismus und Arbeit in der Entstehung der Hegelschen Philosophie (1973–1806)* [1979], Berlin: Akademie/de Gruyter, 2014.
Lacan, Jacques, *The Four Fundamental Concepts of Psycho-Analysis* [1973], New York: Norton, 1978.
Lafont-Couturier, Helène, and Pierre-Lin Renié (eds), *Gérôme et Goupil: art et entreprise*, Paris: Éditions de la réunion des musées nationaux, 2000.
Lange, Friedrich Albert, *The History of Materialism and Criticism of Its Present Importance* [1866], trans. E. C. Thomas, Boston: Osgood, 1877.
Lazzarato, Maurizio, Yann Moulier Boutang, Antonio Negri and Giorgio Santilli, *Des Entreprises pas comme les autres: Benetton en Italie, Le Sentier à Paris*, Paris: Publisud, 1993.
Lefebvre, Henri, *Dialectical Materialism* [1939], Minneapolis: University of Minnesota Press, 2009.
— *Introduction to Modernity: Twelve Preludes, September 1959–May 1961* [1962], London: Verso, 1995.
Lehmann, Ulrich, *Tigersprung: Fashion in Modernity*, Cambridge, MA: MIT Press, 2000.
Lukács, Georg, *History and Class Consciousness* [1923], London: Merlin, 1971.
Mallarmé, Stéphane, *Œuvres completes*, Paris: Gallimard, 1945.
Marx, Karl, 'Economic and Philosophical Manuscripts of 1844' [1844], in Karl Marx and Friedrich Engels, *Collected Works*, vol. 3, London: Lawrence & Wishart, 1975, pp. 229–326.
— *The Eighteenth Brumaire of Louis Napoleon* [1851–52], in Karl Marx and Friedrich Engels, *Collected Works*, vol. 11, London: Lawrence & Wishart 1979, pp. 99–181.
— *Grundrisse: Foundations of the Critique of Political Economy (Rough Draft)* [1857–58], trans. M. Nicolaus, London: Allen Lane, 1973.
— *Capital*, vol. 1 [1867/1890], in Karl Marx and Friedrich Engels, *Collected Works*, vol. 35, London: Lawrence & Wishart, 1996.
Marx, Karl, and Friedrich Engels, *The German Ideology* [1845–46], in Karl Marx and Friedrich Engels, *Collected Works*, vol. 5, London: Lawrence & Wishart, 1973, pp. 19–451.
Matteucci, Giovanni, and Stefano Marino (eds), *Philosophical Perspectives on Fashion*, London: Bloomsbury, 2016.
Mehlmann, Jeffrey, *Revolution and Repetition: Marx/Hugo/Balzac*, Los Angeles: University of California Press, 1977.
Merleau-Ponty, Maurice, *The Visible and the Invisible* [1959/60], trans. A. Lingis, Evanston: Northwestern University Press, 1964.

Metternich, Princesse de, *Souvenirs de la Princesse Pauline de Metternich (1859–1871)*, Paris: Plon, 1922.
Michelet, Jules, *Cours au Collège de France II* [1846–50], Paris: Gallimard, 1995.
Moissonnier, Maurice, *Les Canuts: 'Vivre en travaillant ou mourir en combattant'* [1958], Paris: Messidor/Editions Sociales, 1988.
Mouclier, Jacques, *Haute Couture*, Paris: Laffont, 2004.
Nardin, Guiseppe, *La Benetton: Strategia e struttura di un'impresa di successo*, Rome: Edizioni Lavoro, 1987.
Papetti, Yolande, et al. (eds), *La Passion des étoffes chez un neuropsychiatre: G.G. de Clérambault, 1872–1934*, Paris: Solin, 1980.
Perrault, Charles, *Parallèle des anciens et des modernes en ce qui regarde les arts et les sciences* [1693], ed. Hans-Robert Jauß, Munich: Eidos, 1964.
Plekhanov, Georgi, *Selected Philosophical Works, vols 1–5*, Moscow: Progress, 1974–81.
Pouthas, Charles H., et al. (eds), *Démocratie, réaction, capitalisme, 1848–1860*, Paris: Presses Universitaires de France, 1984.
Ritter, Joachim, *Hegel and the French Revolution* [1957], Cambridge, MA: MIT Press, 1982.
Rose, Gillian, *Hegel Contra Sociology*, London: Athlone, 1981.
Rude, Fernand, *L'Insurrection lyonnaise de novembre 1831: le mouvement ouvrier à Lyon de 1827–1832*, Paris: Anthropos, 1969.
Saillard, Olivier (ed.), *Paris Haute Couture*, Paris: Flammarion, 2012.
Schmidt, Alfred, *History and Structure: An Essay on Hegelian-Marxist and Structuralist Theories of History* [1971], trans. J. Herf, Cambridge, MA: MIT Press, 1981.
Sebag, Lucien, *Marxisme et Structuralisme*, Paris: Payot, 1964.
Simmel, Georg, 'The Metropolis and Mental Life' [1903], in Kurt Wolff (ed.), *The Sociology of Georg Simmel*, New York: Free Press, 1950, pp. 409–26.
— 'Fashion' [1904], in *On Individuality and Social Forms*, Chicago: University of Chicago Press, 1971, pp. 294–323.
— *The Philosophy of Money* [1907], trans. T. Bottomore and D. Frisby, London: Routledge, 1990.
Smith, Gary (ed.), *Benjamin: Philosophy, History, Aesthetics*, Chicago: University of Chicago Press, 1989.
Strijenova, Tatiana, *La Mode en union soviétique 1917–1945*, Paris: Flammarion, 1991.
Spyer, Patricia (ed.), *Border Fetishisms: Material Objects in Unstable Spaces*, London: Routledge, 1998.
Tabarand, Alphonse, *La Vie artistique au temps de Baudelaire* [1942], Paris: Mercure de France, 1963.
Tarde, Gabriel, *The Laws of Imitation* [1890], trans. E. C. Parsons, New York: Holt, 1903.
Thoré, Théophile, *Les Salons de W. Bürger*, vol. 1, Paris: Renouard, 1870.

Timpanaro, Sebastiano, *On Materialism* [1970], London: New Left Books, 1973.
Truffaut, François, with Helen G. Scott, *Hitchcock by Truffaut: The Definitive Study* [1966], London: Paladin, 1978.
Vadé, Yves, *Ce que modernité veut dire*, vol. 1, Bordeaux: Presses universitaires de Bordeaux, 1998.
Wildenstein, Daniel, 'Le Salon de refusés de 1863', *Gazette des Beaux-Arts*, 66 (1965), pp. 125–52.
Worth/Paquin, 'Sketchbooks', London: The Victoria & Albert Museum, 1957.
Wood, Robin, *Hitchcock's Films Revisited*, London: Faber & Faber, 1991.
Žižek, Slavoj (ed.), *Everything You Always Wanted to Know about Lacan (But Were Afraid to Ask Hitchcock)*, London: Verso, 1992.
Zola, Émile, *The Kill* [1871], trans. A. Goldhammer, New York: The Modern Library, 2005.
— *The Masterpiece* [1886], New York: Oxford University Press, 2008.
— *Mes Haines, Mon Salon, Édouard Manet*, Paris: Charpentier/Fasquelle, 1893.
— *Écrits sur l'art*, Paris: Gallimard, 1991.

Index

abstraction, 12, 31, 35, 46, 50, 55, 86, 90–1, 166, 190, 192; *see also* objectification / reification
action (social, political), 1, 3, 24, 26, 43, 54, 59, 87, 135–6, 164, 166–7, 170, 186, 191, 216, 230
Adorno, Theodor W., 58–9
alienation, 26, 29, 58, 93, 135, 166–70, 174, 178, 216–17, 224
Althusser, Louis, 33n11, 91, 131, 155n8
art market / art production, 5, 104–5, 116–18, 121, 195–6n44, 204; *see also* gallery system / gallerist
artisan, 22, 26, 29, 38, 71, 165, 175, 177, 198, 209, 214, 217–19, 224, 226

Balzac, Honoré de, 25, 70–3, 78–84, 86, 88, 92–3, 99–100, 104
Barbey d'Aurevilly, Jules, 70–3, 84–8, 92–3, 99–100
Barbon, Nicolas, 20–1
Barthes, Roland, 77, 91, 93, 104, 130, 132–3, 136–7, 141, 143, 146, 154, 157n28
Baudelaire, Charles, 19, 25–6, 44, 56, 59, 63, 73, 78, 86, 89, 91–2, 105, 109–11, 115–17
Baudrillard, Jean, 5–6, 16–20, 32n3, 33n11, 48, 77, 91, 93, 129
Bellers, John, 21
Benetton, 199–200, 203, 214–15, 229n37
Benjamin, Walter, 5–8, 26, 36–7, 42, 44–5, 48–63, 66n29, 73, 103, 105, 111, 120, 132, 162, 165

Bloch, Ernst, 5, 163–5, 168, 170–1, 181, 191
body, 5, 9–12, 15, 20, 35, 45, 54, 62, 70, 75, 79, 86, 89–91, 120, 131, 137, 151, 160–1, 166–9, 171–4, 182–92, 209, 212, 219–20, 230
corporeality, 15, 57, 91, 137, 169, 230
see also embodiment
Bonotto, 9, 176, 187, 197–226
Boussac, Marcel, 46, 62, 68n49; *see also* Dior, Christian

capital, 1, 18, 21, 24–6, 57, 62, 104–5, 109, 113, 116, 118, 130, 155n3, 165, 197, 200, 215, 218, 231–2; *see also* labour / work; Marx: *Capital*
C.C.P. (Carol Christian Poell), 9, 12–13n6, 160, 172, 175–8, 180–4, 186–8, 190–2, 197–8, 203, 209–10, 212, 216, 217–20, 225–6
change (abstract / structural / principle of), 1–2, 10, 19, 21, 25, 31, 37, 48, 50, 54, 70, 72, 90–1, 115, 132, 165, 215–16, 232
in fashion, 32, 40, 47, 56, 77, 82, 89–90, 96, 153–4, 165, 172–3, 183; *see also* fashion: ephemerality / transitoriness / immediacy; fashion: rhythm / cycles of
in industry / production, 4, 26, 57, 165
social / political, 3, 26, 46, 54, 76–7, 161, 164; *see also* revolution

Index

class, 2, 4, 14, 18, 20, 26, 28, 38–43, 53–4, 75–6, 80, 115, 118, 131, 154, 164–5, 167, 171, 182, 232
commodification, 6, 15–16, 19, 31, 56–7, 86, 90–1, 98, 111, 120, 130, 134, 136, 154, 156n18, 166, 230
copy / reproduction, 19, 37, 57, 85, 110–12, 119–20, 164, 176, 218
costume (costume history), 3, 8–9, 30–1, 37–41, 46–7, 59, 61, 70, 86, 108, 129, 131, 137, 140, 143, 157n28
  on stage / in moving images, 53, 59, 78, 86, 134
couturière / couturier, 17, 37–42, 46, 61, 70, 83, 88–9, 94, 99, 106, 108–11, 117, 120–2, 124; *see also* seamstress / dressmaker; tailor
culture industry, 3–5, 8, 11, 30, 36, 45, 71, 89, 103, 105, 112, 114, 116, 118, 120, 122, 133, 154, 176, 198, 230, 232

Deineka, Aleksandr, 167–8, 193n12
department store, 29, 56, 116, 120–1, 128n34, 135
dialectic, 2, 4–6, 10–12, 18–19, 21, 31, 42, 45–9, 53, 59, 61, 69, 83, 91–2, 110–12, 141, 160, 162–72, 182, 186, 191, 192n1, 200, 212, 215, 230
  dialectical image, 50, 53–5, 58–60
  of fashion and materialism, 5–6, 8, 10, 15–16, 19, 22, 24, 37, 49, 57, 69–71, 118, 132, 226, 232
  of modernity, 83–7, 91, 114–16
  of production and consumption, 15, 18, 19, 24, 26–7, 31, 37, 130
  see also negation
Dior, Christian, 5, 8, 45–6, 59–63, 68n49–50, 129, 209; *see also* Boussac, Marcel
dress (code in clothing), 9, 17, 20–1, 30–1, 47, 53–4, 58–62, 69–70, 72–8, 82–6, 89–90, 94, 96, 98–9, 106–11, 129–31, 134, 136–7, 140, 142–3, 153, 167–8, 173–4, 181
Durand-Ruel, Paul (Naudet), 116–17, 119, 121, 122–4, 127n26
Durkheim, Émile, 33, 40

Eco, Umberto, 198, 200
economics
  system / structure, 3–4, 6, 10–11, 15–16, 21, 27, 30–2, 49–50, 63, 92–3, 96, 104–5, 155, 166, 180, 216; *see also* capital; social relations
  theory / history, 1, 6, 14, 20–2, 24, 28, 32n3–4, 33n11, 42, 64n14, 75–6, 85, 99, 103, 112–13, 116, 125n8, 127n28, 130–1, 133, 166, 169, 199, 214–15
embodiment, 10, 15, 38, 59, 98, 131, 140, 144, 160, 164, 167, 173, 215
Engels, Friedrich, 3, 22, 25, 42, 50, 55–6, 59, 169, 230
Entziehung (withdrawal / privation), 178, 181, 191
exchange (symbolic, system of), 11–12, 16, 18–19, 20, 75, 94, 160, 165–6, 173, 176, 198, 215, 231; *see also* value: exchange-

factory, 9, 22, 26, 29, 41, 165, 167, 197, 199–207, 209–22, 224–6; *see also* manufacture; workshop / studio
fashion
  and art, 8, 31, 37, 41, 44, 59–60, 77–8, 89–90, 93, 103, 107–24, 167, 190, 204–5
  ephemerality / transitoriness / immediacy, 25–6, 40, 62–3, 71, 98, 99, 174
  fashion studies / theory, 2–3, 5, 12, 28, 52, 60, 103, 130, 160, 169, 230–2
  fashion system, 5–6, 8, 30, 63, 69–70, 103, 129–30, 133, 137, 143, 180–1, 184, 232
  fashionable, 3, 8, 27, 35, 39, 50, 55, 57–9, 70–3, 76, 78, 80–5, 96, 98–9, 108, 112–13, 117, 120–1, 131–2, 165–7, 169, 174, 183, 231
  history of, 14, 16–17, 30, 37, 40–1, 45–9, 53–7, 59, 61–2, 130, 160, 162, 232; *see also* costume
  industry, 3, 9, 16–17, 79, 92, 105, 175–7, 180, 199–200, 208, 215, 231

fashion (*cont.*)
  journalism / fashion journal, 71–100, 100n2
  in literature, 69, 71, 73–4, 77–81, 85–8, 93, 96, 101–2n27, 103, 107, 132, 136, 146
  as object, 11, 166, 169, 172, 182, 186, 189–92
  rhythm / cycles of, 17, 19–21, 32, 40, 47, 49, 59–60, 117
  subjectivity of, 2, 29–30, 38, 109
  see dialectic: of fashion and materialism; novelty; temporality
feminism, 52, 167
fetish / fetishism, 10, 12, 52–4, 57, 83, 86–7, 105, 120–1, 124, 133, 162, 166, 168–9, 172, 182, 190; *see also* commodification
Figal, Günter, 183, 188, 195n35
Fluxus, 9, 204–5
Freud, Sigmund, 135, 145, 149–50

gallery system / gallerist, 8, 60–1, 103, 116–21, 124, 127n28
Gautier, Théophile, 26, 44, 72–3, 92, 115
Gegenstand (object), 161–4, 168, 170–1, 175, 182, 184, 190–2; *see also* fashion: as object
Gegenständlichkeit (objecthood), 160–2, 170–1, 182–3, 186
Gérôme, Jean-Léon, 119–20
Goupil, Adolphe, 116, 119, 122
Grant, Cary, 134, 137–42, 144, 146, 148, 153–4, 157–8n32

haute couture / 'high' fashion, 8, 17, 37–8, 42, 45–9, 59, 63–4n5–6, 70–1, 77, 88–9, 92–4, 97, 105, 110–11, 117–18, 122, 165, 177, 209
Hegel, Georg Wilhelm Friedrich, 2, 5, 15, 28, 42, 55, 59, 103–4, 162–6, 168–71, 181–2, 188, 190–1, 196n47
hermeneutics, 43, 47–8, 52, 134, 160–2, 170–1, 182, 188, 191
historicism / historism, 8, 35, 42–50, 52, 56, 60–1, 91, 96, 112–14, 131–2, 165

history (political, materialist), 3, 5, 8, 10, 12, 19, 35–6, 41, 44, 46–9, 52, 54, 56–8, 69, 73, 82, 92, 96, 130–1, 168–9
  cultural / art history, 8, 14, 44, 52, 103–5, 108, 119
  of ideas, 4, 10, 230–2
  patterns / repetition in, 36, 52–4, 112, 162, 183
  philosophy of, 3, 8, 43, 47–9, 52, 162–6, 168, 191
  progress in / linear / historical continuum, 3, 6, 46, 49, 53, 55–6, 62; *see also* teleology
  social / labour history, 6, 48
  see fashion: history of; fashion: rhythm / cycles of
Hitchcock, Alfred, 5, 134–8, 140, 142–3, 145, 149, 153–4, 157n23

interaction, 1, 15, 29, 40, 44, 80, 87, 120, 168, 180, 210, 218, 224–6

Jameson, Fredric, 44–8, 66n25, 156n16–17, 159n42
Jhering, Rudolf von, 40

Koselleck, Reinhart, 48

labour / work, 2, 5, 9, 11, 14–15, 19, 21–7, 30, 38–42, 61, 71, 91, 109, 130, 161, 164, 166, 169–70, 175, 177, 182, 197, 200, 202–4, 206, 212, 215–17, 222, 230–3
  division of, 28, 110, 165, 199
  see production: means / ownership of; production: system / structure / processes of
labourers / workers, 21, 28, 41, 169
Lacan, Jacques, 135, 152
Landau, Martin, 141, 158n35
language, 16, 18, 77, 80–1, 83, 91–2, 96, 100, 129, 130, 132, 135–8, 140–1, 143–6, 150–4, 178, 131, 181; *see also* sign / signifier / signified
leather (production, use in fashion), 175–8, 180, 188–9, 191, 198
Lefebvre, Henri, 1, 5, 16, 19, 90–1, 104, 129–33, 230

loom, 9, 26, 165, 193n12, 200, 202, 204–9, 217–25, 229n41, 233n1
Louis Napoléon III, 53–4, 89, 93, 103, 111–13, 115
Lukács, György, 55–6
Lyon (silk weaving), 3, 26, 30, 38, 216

Mallarmé, Stéphane, 70–3, 84, 88–100
manufacture, 2, 9, 11, 38–9, 41–2, 56, 62, 82, 160, 165, 168, 170, 173, 175–8, 197–206, 212, 214–15, 217–26, 231–2
Marx, Karl, 2–3, 15, 18, 21, 25, 42, 50, 53, 55–7, 59, 86, 91, 111, 120, 130, 133, 162, 164–9, 181, 215, 230, 232–3
　Capital, 15, 22, 169
　coat, 15, 49–50, 54, 66–7n31–3, 180
　Eighteenth Brumaire, 53–4
　and fashion / textiles / clothing, 6, 24, 28, 49–50, 54, 55, 87, 169–70, 171
　Grundrisse, 15, 21–2, 24–7, 169
　see also dialectic: of production and consumption; Engels, Friedrich; political economy
Marxism, 8, 16–17, 36, 45, 47–8, 54, 59, 103, 130–2, 135, 202–3, 215
materialism (epistemology), 1, 2, 5–6, 8–12, 14–16, 19–21, 29, 35, 38, 42, 48, 53, 69–73, 79, 88–91, 93, 96, 100, 110, 114, 129–34, 155, 160–2, 183, 206, 212, 215, 226, 230, 232
　dialectical-, 2–3, 66, 91, 161, 165, 183
　historical-, 2–3, 10, 15, 25, 30, 35, 42–9, 52, 54, 59, 91–2, 134, 161–2, 203, 216
　mechanistic- / mechanical-, 1–2, 15, 42, 161, 163, 165, 197
　see also dialectic: of fashion and materialism
materiality, 2, 11, 21–2, 27, 35, 62, 69–74, 88, 90–4, 104, 134, 136, 152, 154–5, 160–1, 168, 175, 177, 183, 186–7, 199, 206, 212, 225–6, 230, 232
matter (*materie prime* / primary matter), 1, 11, 172, 197, 199, 202, 212, 217–18, 222, 226

mechanisation / serialisation, 17, 38, 42, 78, 109–11, 119, 165, 205–8, 210, 218–19, 224; see also copy / reproduction; *Poncif*
Merleau-Ponty, Maurice, 162, 171
mistake / fault (in production), 172, 188, 200, 202–4, 206, 214
modernity / *modernité*, 6, 8, 15, 20, 24, 26, 28–30, 36–7, 44, 48–52, 54, 57–8, 67n43, 69, 72, 83, 85, 87–91, 98–9, 105, 108, 114–17, 122, 124, 130, 161, 168, 173–4
　fashion and / *mode et*, 19, 26, 32, 36, 56, 59, 73, 91, 96, 98, 100, 109–11, 113, 115, 125n4

Nardin, Guiseppe, 9, 199, 203, 213–14, 216
negation, 2, 4, 11, 19, 24, 27, 31–2, 49–50, 71, 115, 159n45, 164–5, 172, 178, 180–3, 186, 190–2, 192n1, 195n44, 200, 230
Negri, Antonio, 9, 203, 213–16, 218, 226, 228n26–7
novel / novelist, 29, 70, 78–9, 81, 83–4, 93, 100, 106–8, 112–13, 116, 118, 161, 178; see also fashion: and art; Zola, Émile
novelty, 11, 37, 39–41, 46–50, 52, 54–5, 57, 60, 62, 69, 75–9, 83, 86, 91–3, 96, 98–9, 105, 109, 116, 122, 129, 131, 165, 167, 225, 231

objectification / reification, 5, 10, 15, 22–30, 50, 87, 90–1, 111, 117, 129–31, 164, 166, 169–70, 173–5, 212, 230
objectivity, 28, 42, 131, 160–1, 183

pattern
　in history, 3–4, 6, 17, 32, 35–7, 42–3, 46, 49, 53, 57, 59–60, 62, 91, 96, 111–12, 131, 165–6, 203, 232
　pattern cutting, 16, 38–9, 46–7, 56, 89, 109–11, 126n11, 138, 167, 176, 180, 187–8, 209, 220, 226; see also mechanisation / serialisation

pattern (*cont.*)
  social (of consumption), 15, 21, 39, 42, 57, 130–1, 230
  in textiles, 45, 138, 150, 164, 167, 175, 202, 205–8, 219
performance, 16, 39, 76, 80. 84, 87, 92, 120, 160–1, 173–6, 190; *see also* body: corporeality; embodiment
phenomenology, 25, 45, 82, 162–4, 166, 168–9, 170–1, 175, 182–3, 190, 203; *see also* hermeneutics
Poiret, Paul, 41, 44, 60, 109,
political economy, 5, 6, 11, 18–21, 38, 40, 42, 69, 75, 86, 89, 91–4, 117, 132, 166, 169, 197
poncif, 87, 101n20, 109–11, 116–17, 120, 126n10, 174
positivism, 3–4, 10–11, 26, 43–4, 47, 49, 54, 56, 60, 87, 114, 164, 169; *see also* history: progress in / linear / historical continuum; teleology
practice
  creative- (art, fashion, design), 8–9, 12, 14, 36, 69, 160, 190, 204, 218, 224, 230
  labour-, 14, 36, 124, 169, 212, 224–5
  political- / *Praxis*, 1–3, 5, 9, 25, 18, 28, 43, 54, 56–7, 160, 164–5, 186, 200, 230
present, 36, 42–3, 46–7, 50, 52, 54–9, 73, 96, 98, 107, 113, 233n1
  contemporaneity, 10, 231–2
  Jetztzeit (now-time), 53–4, 59
production
  art- / cultural / literary, 5, 70–3, 79, 83–4, 100, 103–4, 109, 113, 115, 122, 134, 180, 199
  conditions of, 1–2, 11, 28, 104, 131, 133, 160–1, 165, 190, 198–200, 203–4, 214–16, 230
  fashion- / repeated, 5–6, 17, 27, 42, 77, 83, 96, 104, 111–12, 167, 198, 214, 232–3; *see also* novelty
  material-, 2, 8–9, 17, 19, 22–4, 38, 41–2, 62–3, 72, 83, 85, 107, 154, 172–3, 175, 180–4, 197–8, 202, 205–6, 209, 217, 231–2

  means / ownership of, 3, 29, 105, 109, 162, 167, 171, 199, 213, 215, 231
  system / structure / processes of, 11, 24, 26, 37, 44, 60, 92, 104–5, 108–9, 110, 115, 122, 129, 134, 162–5, 168–70, 175, 177–8, 181, 186–7, 212–13, 218, 226
  see copy / reproduction; dialectic: of production and consumption; social relations
Proust, Marcel, 36, 44, 52–3, 56, 63

quotation (sartorial), 47, 50, 55–7, 59, 98, 162

ready-to-wear / *confection* / *prêt-à-porter* / off-the-peg / mass-produced, 8, 17, 29, 37–9, 41, 44, 62, 108, 140, 204, 208
representation, 3, 6, 8, 15–16, 19–20, 30, 36, 44, 69, 72, 74, 78, 85, 90, 93, 104, 130, 134, 154, 160–2, 168–9, 171, 175, 182, 200, 230–2; *see also* materiality; simulacrum; simulation
revolution, 2, 18–19, 38, 43, 53–8, 60, 73, 75, 78, 80, 84, 87, 90, 96, 104–5, 112, 114–15, 118, 129, 162, 164–5, 167, 192–3n3, 216

Saint, Eva Marie, 135, 142, 145
Salon (art exhibition / drawing room), 5, 61, 72, 82, 87, 99, 106–9, 112–14, 116–17, 120–2, 125n4, 126n15–6
Sand, George (Amantine Lucile Aurore Dupin), 70, 78, 86
Schmidt, Alfred, 5, 56–7, 131
seamstress / dressmaker, 37–8, 74, 77, 84, 89, 94, 110, 121, 177, 184
Sebag, Lucien, 5, 135, 141
sexuality / sexual politics, 16, 70, 75, 80, 85–6, 99, 121, 135, 142, 149, 181, 230
sign / signifier / signified, 15, 17–20, 27, 77, 80, 87, 91, 93, 110, 130–2, 136–8, 140–5, 147–8, 150–1, 153, 170, 175, 181, 198, 200, 204; *see also* simulacrum; simulation

Simmel, Georg, 5, 24, 28–9, 34n28–33, 52, 63, 118, 127n29
simulacrum, 17, 19, 90, 93, 96, 130, 161; *see also* copy / reproduction
simulation, 18–22, 77, 88–9, 161, 166
social relations, 10, 29, 30, 83, 87, 91, 105, 130–1, 160–6, 169, 181, 190, 215
structuralism, 4, 6–9, 16, 47, 90–1, 101n25, 129–38, 152, 155, 170
subject-object relation, 2, 12, 15–16, 26, 28–9, 31, 70, 160–4, 166, 168–71, 183, 189, 190–1, 212
subjectification, 24, 28, 31, 36, 43, 111, 117
subjectivity, 2, 16, 25–30, 38, 90, 109–10, 117, 122, 172–4; *see also* fashion: subjectivity of

tailor, 22, 28–9, 38–9, 74, 107, 110, 140
Tarde, Gabriel, 40, 118, 127n29
teleology, 47, 122, 164, 173, 180, 183, 202
temporality, 5, 15, 24–5, 40, 43, 46–8, 55–6, 71, 73, 75, 77, 79, 82, 88, 93, 108, 174–5, 182, 186, 232
Thoré, Théophile (William Bürger), 114–15

Tigersprung (tiger's leap), 6, 36, 55–8, 63n3, 165
Timpanaro, Sebastiano, 5, 91, 131–3, 155n11, 156n14
Truffaut, François, 135, 142

value (material), 15, 18–20, 22, 24, 27, 37, 45, 50, 69–72, 75, 77–8, 87, 94, 120, 122, 124, 165, 174, 210, 216
  equivalent-, 24, 27, 50, 122, 124
  exchange-, 18–20, 27, 45, 87, 96, 117, 198
  of labour, 22, 27
  surplus-, 16, 20, 24, 26, 45, 50, 82, 87, 90, 96, 116, 124, 216, 231
  use-, 20, 22, 24, 38, 41, 45, 58, 94, 124
vertically integrated manufacture, 175, 198–9, 214

workshop / studio, 2, 9, 38, 109–12, 160, 165, 172, 174–8, 180–4, 187–8, 203–5, 218, 224
Worth, Charles Frederick, 38, 88–9, 92, 97, 108–10, 112, 117–18, 121

Zola, Émile, 29, 107–8, 110, 112–13, 115–16, 118–21, 125n7–8

EU representative:
Easy Access System Europe
Mustamäe tee 50, 10621 Tallinn, Estonia
Gpsr.requests@easproject.com